P9-BZA-906

THOMAS HARDY ANNUAL No. 3

Like its predecessors, *Thomas Hardy Annual No. 3* offers a collection of new essays by an international team of Hardy scholars and critics. The range of approaches represented is again wide: there is special emphasis upon some of the literary and artistic influences on and parallels to Hardy's prose and verse, but other subjects covered include such diverse topics as his humour, his use of dialect, and his presentation of death-scenes. There are also substantial reviews of some of the most recent works of Hardy scholarship and criticism, and a survey and bibliography of Hardy studies that update the information given in previous volumes.

There is now world-wide interest in Hardy's work both among general readers and among students of literature, social history, and the history of ideas. His unique status as a major novelist and a major poet who was both a Victorian and a modern writer is now generally acknowledged. The *Annual* continues to make available some of the most important research that is being done over a wide spectrum of topics and in many parts of the world.

The editor

Norman Page is Professor of English at the University of Alberta, Canada. A graduate of the Universities of Cambridge and Leeds, he is a Fellow of the Royal Society of Canada and has held a Guggenheim Fellowship and a Canada Council Leave Fellowship.

His recent books include *A. E. Housman: a Critical Biography*, *A Dickens Companion*, *A Kipling Companion* and *Henry James: Interviews and Recollections*.

In the same series

THOMAS HARDY ANNUAL Nos 1 and 2
Edited by Norman Page

O'CASEY ANNUAL Nos 1–4
Edited by Robert G. Lowery

YEATS ANNUAL Nos 1 and 2
Edited by Richard J. Finneran

YEATS ANNUAL Nos 3 and 4
Edited by Warwick Gould

Further titles in preparation

THOMAS HARDY ANNUAL No. 3

Edited by Norman Page

M

© Norman Page 1985

All rights reserved. No reproduction, copy or transmission
of this publication may be made without written permission.

No paragraph of this publication may be reproduced, copied
or transmitted save with written permission or in accordance
with the provisions of the Copyright Act 1956 (as amended).

Any person who does any unauthorised act in relation to
this publication may be liable to criminal prosecution and
civil claims for damages.

First published 1985

Published by
THE MACMILLAN PRESS LTD
Houndmills, Basingstoke, Hampshire RG21 2XS
and London
Companies and representatives
throughout the world

Typeset by
Wessex Typesetters
Frome, Somerset

British Library Cataloguing in Publication Data
Thomas Hardy Annual.—No. 3—(Macmillan
literary annuals)
1. Hardy, Thomas, *1840–1928*—Societies,
periodicals, etc.
823′.8   PR4754
ISBN 0–333–36459–7

Contents

List of Illustrations

Editor's Note

Contributions for future volumes of the *Annual* are welcome at any time. There is no limit on length, and illustrations may be included where appropriate. Contributions should be typewritten (double-space throughout, including quotations and footnotes). References to Hardy's novels should be identified by chapter-number, thus: (*The Woodlanders*, ch. 10). Footnotes should be kept to a minimum and brief references worked into the text wherever possible.

All contributions, correspondence and books for review should be sent to the editor at the Department of English, University of Alberta, Edmonton, Alberta, Canada T6G 2E5; or at 41 Trent Road, Oakham, Rutland LE15 6HE, UK.

The Contributors

Bryn Caless has taught in England and Japan and has published articles on Hardy.

Michael Collie is Professor of English at York University, Toronto. His most recent book is *George Borrow: Eccentric* (1982).

Samir Elbarbary is Lecturer in English Literature at Kuwait University.

Simon Gatrell teaches at the New University of Ulster. He has published widely on Hardy and was a contributor to *Thomas Hardy Annual No. 2*.

Joan Grundy was formerly Professor of English at Royal Holloway College, University of London. Her publications include *Hardy and the Sister Arts* (1979).

Timothy Hands is researching on Hardy at Oriel College, Oxford, and was a contributor to *Thomas Hardy Annual No. 2*.

J. T. Laird is Associate Professor of English Language and Literature in the University of New South Wales. His publications include *The Shaping of 'Tess of the d'Urbervilles'* (1975).

Robert Langbaum is James Branch Cabell Professor at the University of Virginia. His publications include *The Poetry of Experience* (1957) and *The Mysteries of Identity* (1977).

Michael Rabiger teaches in the Film Department at Columbia College, Chicago.

J. B. Smith is a lecturer in German at Bath University. His publications include articles on dialect and oral tradition.

Rosemary Sumner teaches at Goldsmiths' College, London, and was a contributor to *Thomas Hardy Annual No. 1*.

Richard H. Taylor is Director of Schiller International University (London campus). His *The Neglected Hardy* is reviewed in this volume.

George Wing is Professor of English at the University of Calgary. His books include the volume on Hardy in the 'Writers and Critics' series.

Editor's Introduction

Reviewing a mixed bag of Hardyana, including the first volume of the present series of annuals, in the *London Review of Books*, Donald Davie improved the occasion with some animadversions on 'the Hardy industry', an enterprise which publications such as the present one seek 'to batten on and to legitimise'. His review refers to Hardy scholars as 'the Trade Union' and as investors in a 'newly enhanced commodity', and further tells us that, 'the Joyce industry and the Pound industry' being both 'overmanned' and 'stony and difficult terrains', 'second-class minds' are attracted to Hardy. One would never guess from this riot of metaphor that Professor Davie is a distinguished poet with a reputation for a chaste and disciplined style, or, more importantly, that he has published a book on Hardy and done his own not inconsiderable bit to promote the 'industry' he deplores. But it is hard in any case to see why Hardy studies should be singled out for this snide and peevish attack. If Professor Davie wished to denounce the ills of the body academic, 'the Shakespeare industry' or 'the Dickens industry' might have furnished him with a better text.

The fact is – and it is a fact that his own *Thomas Hardy and British Poetry* has helped to corroborate and promulgate – that Hardy was for far too long underestimated, and it is only quite recently that recognition of his perhaps unique status as a major poet and a major novelist has become widespread. The neglect was not, of course, at the hands of the common reader, with whom his major novels at least have always been firm favourites, but by the professors and mandarins. The well-known disparagements of Eliot, Leavis and others inhibited serious critical and scholarly attention to Hardy's prose and verse until well after the time by which younger writers such as Lawrence, Joyce, Pound, and Eliot himself had become firmly (in some cases perhaps excessively firmly) established in the academic pantheon.

As I suggested in introducing the first volume in this series, Hardy has had a long wait for critical justice. What is striking about recent trends in Hardy criticism is that critics of the front rank on both sides of the Atlantic have taken Hardy, as poet and novelist, very seriously indeed; and higher claims are now being made for him than ever before. In the present volume, for instance, Robert Langbaum argues very cogently the case for seeing Hardy as occupying a very significant place in the development of the novel:

> . . . Hardy is the first English novelist to treat the unconscious analytically and to organize characterization and plot for the purpose of revealing the unconscious.

Some of the best living critics, including John Bayley, J. Hillis Miller, and Robert Langbaum himself, have felt themselves challenged by Hardy's teasing but unignorable greatness and by what Timothy Hands later in this volume calls his 'contentiously enigmatic quality'. Almost no writer is more different from Jane Austen than Hardy, yet he shares the quality that Virginia Woolf found in her, of being extraordinarily difficult to catch in the act of greatness.

The amount of attention that has lately been given to Hardy (not in itself, of course, a matter for rejoicing) is demonstrated by *Thomas Hardy: an Annotated Bibliography of Writings about Him – Volume II, 1970–1978, and Supplement for 1871–1969*, edited by W. Eugene Davis and Helmut E. Gerber (De Kalb, Illinois: Northern Illinois University Press, 1983). For the eight years 1962–69, 734 items are abstracted in this volume and its predecessor; for the next nine years, 1970–78, there are 'over 1316 items', or nearly double that number. No doubt many of them are trivial or useless; but many – including the seven from Professor Davie's pen – are nothing of the sort. Whether the figures are evidence of an 'industry' and a unionized workforce who are at the same time canny investors, or whether they represent a belated institutional recognition of Hardy's greatness, must remain a matter for argument. More impressive to my mind, in any case, is the evidence given of Hardy's impact on the largely non-academic world:

> The massive reviewing activity extended to nearly every

country in the world, not only America, England, and the major countries of Western Europe, but also Japan, the Scandinavian countries, and the Slavic countries. Further, his work was persistently reviewed in provincial cities and even quite small towns. Hardy surely was one of the most widely reviewed, and presumably read, major English writers of his time. (p. 11)

A large number of people 'in provincial cities and even quite small towns' are still reading and re-reading Hardy for better reasons than to improve their chances of gaining promotion or tenure; and it is by their continuing recognition of his vitality that, as Dr Johnson said, 'after all the refinement of subtilty and the dogmatism of learning, must be finally decided all claim to poetical honours'.

Like its predecessors, the present volume tries to present a wide range of responses to Hardy and his work. A particular feature of this collection is the exploration of Hardy's relationship to other novelists and poets: Joan Grundy shows his debt to Milton and draws attention to some striking Miltonic echoes (in, for instance, the closing paragraph of *Tess*); Robert Langbaum investigates Hardy's influence upon D. H. Lawrence; Samir Elbarbary suggests that Joyce may have been indebted to Hardy in his *Portrait*. The reviews section prompts the reflection that important and necessary work on Hardy is still being done and remains to be done: a critical edition of Hardy's finest novel, the first instalment of a major edition of his poems, a further volume in the collected edition of his letters, and the first full-length studies of his minor novels and his short stories is an impressive harvest. These are no mere doodlings in the margins of scholarship but important undertakings that implicitly recognize and celebrate Hardy's stature.

Versions of the essays by Joan Grundy, Robert Langbaum, Norman Page and Rosemary Sumner were given at the Thomas Hardy summer school organized by the Thomas Hardy Society and held at Weymouth in August 1982. Anyone who has attended one of these biennial gatherings will have been impressed and even moved by the sustained, in many cases lifelong, enthusiasm that brings together a large number of people who are certainly not all professional scholars but come from many walks of life and share an informed interest in Hardy. Anyone who is inclined to be depressed or cynical about the survival of literature in contemporary society and the current state of literary scholarship would find it heartening to attend the next gathering. I commend the experience to Professor Davie. Things may be bad in Nashville, Tennessee, but in Wessex there are still grounds for 'some blessed Hope'.

NOTE: Dr Simon Gatrell asks me to point out that his essay 'The Early Stages of Hardy's Fiction' in *Thomas Hardy Annual No. 2* should have included a reference to R. L. Purdy's 'A Source for Hardy's "A Committee-Man of 'The Terror'"', *Modern Language Notes*, LVIII (1943) pp. 554–5.

Throughout this collection, *Life* refers to the single-volume edition of Hardy's autobiography: F. E. Hardy *The Life of Thomas Hardy 1840–1928* (London: Macmillan, 1962).

ESSAYS

Hardy and Milton

Joan Grundy

Hardy was well read in Milton: this is clear from his frequent quotation from and allusion to him, as well as from the markings and annotations in his own copy of Milton, preserved in the Dorset County Museum. His allusions to him start early, and interestingly, in his first published novel, *Desperate Remedies* – interestingly, because they are allusions to 'Lycidas' (the 'Fame is the spur' passage, and the earlier one in which the ambitious young shepherd-poet scorning delights and living laborious days wonders whether he would not after all be better off sporting with Amaryllis in the shade along with his fellows) which, although applied to the novel's hero Edward Springrove, seem equally relevant to the novel's author, making his first bid for fame but worried also by problems of love and finance. Thereafter there are the apt quotations from time to time within the novels. But it is in Hardy's later works – in *Tess of the d'Urbevilles*, *Jude the Obscure*, and *The Dynasts* – that the presence of Milton is felt most strongly. If one speculates as to why this should be – why Hardy should become so markedly Miltonic at this particular stage of his career – I think the answer may be that as his plans for writing his epic-drama *The Dynasts* took definite shape (from the late 1880s onwards), he came to see himself as challenging the succession from Milton, and thus to make a careful re-reading of him. (Perhaps significantly, 'Milton' is the first name on his list of 'books read' in 1887.) In *Jude the Obscure*, of course, the Miltonic presence is that not of Milton's poetry but of his prose, namely the Divorce pamphlets, more especially the first, *The Doctrine and Discipline of Divorce*, from which Hardy quotes in *Jude* and also in his poem 'Lausanne: In Gibbon's Old Garden: 11–12 p.m.'. In this case it seems clear that Milton provided Hardy with a welcome piece of background reading, and agreeably confirmed, or even

3

perhaps suggested, many of his own positions. Hardy recognised their kinship, not only in their endeavours, but in the public odium that greeted them. 'Milton,' he commented, 'and many others of the illustrious, reaching all the way back to the days of Protagoras, had undergone the same sort of indignity at the hands of bigotry and intolerance' (*Life*, p. 277).

In any consideration of Hardy's relationship to Milton, however, it is *Tess of the d'Urbervilles* that is of central importance. It, rather than *The Dynasts*, is his *Paradise Lost*. If we miss in *The Dynasts* the deep and close affinities with Milton's epic we may have expected, that need not surprise us: they are there already in *Tess of the d'Urbervilles*. This is because, beyond and within its particular study of Tess as the victim of nineteenth-century morality, it shares the same themes – the loss of Paradise and of innocence – as *Paradise Lost*, in expressing which it alludes not only to their common source, *The Book of Genesis*, but also with varying degrees of explicitness to *Paradise Lost* itself.

The most explicit of these allusions is Alec d'Urberville's jesting recognition of his resemblance to Milton's Satan, whom he quotes. Less obviously, there is Hardy's statement, in his description of Tess and Angel's rapturous meeting on his return from Emminster to Talbothays: 'she regarded him as Eve at her second waking might have regarded Adam'. The apparent subtlety of that '*second* waking' is elucidated by a reference to *Paradise Lost*, where Eve's *first* waking (IV, 450) is from the sleep in which she was created. Hardy is not, as he may appear to be, discriminating, for the purpose of his comparison, between Eve's feelings on her first and second mornings as a bride: he is thinking of the first morning.

Other passages in which Hardy seems consciously or unconsciously to be echoing Milton have been noticed by Allan Brick in his essay 'Paradise and Consciousness in Hardy's *Tess*' (*Nineteenth Century Fiction*, XVII, 1962–63). One such is Tess's comparison of the stars to 'the apples on our stubbard-tree', which may have been suggested by Milton's likening of the 'other worlds' of the planets to 'those Hesperian gardens famed of old' (III, 568). I would add that, if this was in his mind, he may also, in having Tess describe Earth as one of the blighted stars, be remembering how, in *Paradise Lost*, after the Fall, the stars became 'blasted', 'and Planets, Planet-strook' (X, 411–12), to say nothing of the actual blighting of the Earth by Sin and Death.

Also quoted by Brick is that passage in *Paradise Lost* in which Satan tempts Eve in a dream several days before the actual Fall. In this dream Satan offers the fruit (the forbidden fruit) to Eve's mouth, just as Alec d'Urberville was to offer the strawberry to Tess's, on that first visit when she goes to 'claim kin', when, as Hardy tells us, she is so overwhelmed by Alec that 'she obeyed him like one in a dream'. A recognition of this parallel enables us to see that Alec is already assuming the role of Satan the tempter, and Tess's fall is being pre-enacted.

It is, however, in the *re*-enactment by Tess and Angel of episodes in the life of Milton's Adam and Eve that the impress of *Paradise Lost* upon the work is felt most strongly. It is most strongly and painfully present in those scenes at the Wellbridge farmhouse after Tess has made her confession to Angel. They are now husband and wife, and a husband and wife estranged, as Adam and Eve were estranged in Milton's poem after the Fall. The two women, Tess and Eve, since they are held responsible for the change, have each now to suffer blame, and the withdrawal on their husbands' part of an affection that had earlier seemed so complete and inalienable. The desolation of those days of estrangement in Hardy's novel is made as painfully actual as is the corresponding desolation in *Paradise Lost*, and the situation in Hardy gains in power, I think, from the shadowing in it of the primal, universal desolation of Milton's poem – the first ever domestic quarrel. That effect had been prepared for earlier by similarities in Hardy's handling of Tess's confession to Milton's handling of the Fall itself: in, for instance, his account of the change in the weather beginning that evening – wind, then rain – and then, after the confession, of the changes in 'external things' – the fire, the fender – which grin impishly, demoniacally (Hardy's own words); almost, we might say, as if they were Satan and his crew rejoicing at their own success. Again, in the days that follow we find Angel picturing to Tess the misery under these circumstances (of Tess's earlier liaison with Alec) of any children that might be born to them; to which Tess responds by offering to prevent this and all other unfortunate consequences by committing suicide. This episode too has its parallel in *Paradise Lost*, where Eve proposes to Adam this means of avoiding bringing 'into this cursed world a woeful race' (x, 979ff.). Thus Hardy's treatment of the whole of this disastrous series of events, from Tess and Angel's wedding to their parting, gains an added resonance from its association with the events of the Fall, as Milton presents them. For Tess the fruit of the forbidden tree has certainly brought death into the world and all her woe (though the death – her death – is deferred, as indeed it is in *Paradise Lost*. She must first experience the 'growing miseries' (Milton's phrase), as Adam and Eve had to do).

In the scenes at Wellbridge, Tess also resembles Eve in her meekness and abjectness, and her prayer for forgiveness:

> Creature so fair his reconcilement seeking,
> His counsel whom she had displeased, his aid.
>
> (x, 943–4)

Those are Milton's words, but how perfectly they fit Tess too. Hardy and Milton are here alike in the tender understanding they show for their heroines.

Tess's attitude to Angel is very much that of Eve to Adam. Hardy repeatedly tells us that she looks up to him as to a god, and quite probably he is consciously recalling the second half of Milton's notorious line, 'He for God only, she for God in him' (IV, 299). But Tess also resembles Eve in the way in which she looks to Angel for knowledge and education. And at times the 'she for God in him' aspect is intensified in Hardy to such an extent that Angel comes to resemble, not simply Milton's Adam, but Milton's God. Even at their first encounter in Talbothays' garden this development seems adumbrated, when, as Tess creeps away after overhearing Angel's harping, Angel calls out, 'What makes you draw off in that way, Tess? Are you afraid?', an episode which surely recalls the passage in *Genesis* in which Adam and Eve hear the voice of the Lord God walking in the garden in the cool of the day and hide themselves because they are naked. (*They* are afraid.) Later, after Tess's confession, Angel comes to resemble Milton's God (and I mean by Milton's God the forbidding figure he appears to William Empson in his celebrated book of that name, and to the many readers of *Paradise Lost* who share his view) in the rigorous, inflexible way in which he metes out punishment to Tess, a punishment which Tess contritely accepts, 'because', as she tells him, 'you know best what my punishment ought to be'. Moreover, as Angel hardens and becomes less sympathetic to the reader, Alec, for all his faults, comes to seem in some ways the more attractive of the two, so that we have, ironically, a further parallel with *Paradise Lost*, in which for many readers Satan seems more attractive than God. And I think on the whole we have to see Alec's role in the novel as that of Satan, the Tempter, the 'Enemy in the shape of a Friend'. His changing shapes – Methodist preacher, young buck, peasant, d'Urberville effigy – are a characteristic he shares with the Devil, certainly as Milton portrays him. As *Stoke* d'Urberville, he even comes, correctly, from the north; and 'Stoke' is as appropriate to the fires of Hell as to the blast furnaces of industry.

But of course in the earlier part of the story (Phases the Third and Fourth), Angel's role *is* that of Adam to Tess's Eve. Froom Valley becomes a kind of Garden of Eden, its fertility corresponding to what Milton calls the 'enormous bliss' of Paradise, and like Adam and Eve Angel and Tess are both workers and lovers there, and are pictured in the early morning, as Adam and Eve are, going out together to their tasks. Earlier still, the Vale of Blackmoor, the vale of Tess's birth, has also seemed a Garden of Eden in its seclusion and fertility; and Tess's seduction, although taking place outside the valley, is spoken of in terms of the Fall: Tess has learned that 'the serpent hisses where the sweet birds sing'. Thus the myth of the Fall hovers, so to speak, over the whole of the work – over Tess's relations with Alec as well as her relations with Angel – and the novel's theme, as I suggested earlier, could itself be said to be that of Paradise lost: the paradise of childhood and innocence in the earlier part, and in the later the paradise of love.

The change in Angel Clare from Milton's Adam to Milton's God, Tess's lover to Tess's judge, has a further significance. As Tess's sufferings and the pressure from Alec increase, she begins to question Angel's justice. 'The punishment you have measured out to me is deserved – I do know that – well deserved – and you are right and just to be angry with me', she writes to this human Jehovah. 'But, Angel, please, please, not to be just – only a little kind to me . . .'. And her last, passionate note, written as she and her family prepare to leave the old home, is accusatory:

You know that I did not intend to wrong you – why have you so wronged me? You are cruel, cruel indeed! I will try to forget you. It is all injustice I have received at your hands!

Tess of the d'Urbervilles is, among other things, a novel about justice, or its lack. In this respect it both compares and contrasts with *Paradise Lost*, the 'great argument' of which seeks 'to justify the ways of God to men', and does so by insisting on the combination of justice and mercy in God's scheme of grace and redemption:

> in mercy and justice both,
> Through heaven and earth, so shall my glory
>   excel,
> But mercy first and last shall brightest shine
>
> (III, 132–5)

Milton's argument asserts the external Providence which Hardy's novel explicitly denies. For Hardy's characters God is *not* in his Heaven, and all is wrong with the world. But in so far as man, living in a godless world, must seek to embody the divine virtues within himself, justice fails at this level also, both in that god-in-man (to Tess), Angel Clare, and in society itself, both of whom fail to exercise that loving-kindness or charity which is Hardy's equivalent for the divine mercy.

I may add that the final paragraph in Hardy's novel brings together, in its first sentence and its last, the likeness-with-a-difference to *Paradise Lost* I have been outlining here:

> 'Justice' was done, and the President of the Immortals, in Aeschylean phrase, had ended his sport with Tess

– that is the sorry conclusion of Hardy's 'great argument'. Then:

> As soon as they had strength they arose, joined hands again, and went on

– that is the banishment from Paradise, Hardy's version of Milton's

> They hand in hand with wandering steps and slow,
> Through Eden took their solitary way.

It would seem that Hardy wanted this Adam and Eve ending so badly that he even provides a Tess Rediviva, in the person of 'Liza-Lu her sister, to achieve it. And just as it is to the eastern side of Paradise that Adam and Eve look back and see it 'With dreadful faces thronged and fiery arms', so it is to the 'eastern horizon' that Angel and 'Liza-Lu look back to see something equally dreadful – the black flag signifying that Tess is dead.

Thus we may say that the similarity between *Tess of the d'Urbervilles* and *Paradise Lost* lies in their subject, and the dissimilarity in their argument. But for many readers of *Paradise Lost*, of whom I am one, the argument of the poem speaks less convincingly than does its action. This is not the place to argue the case for this view of *Paradise Lost*, but as a short cut it will be helpful to quote from one of the finest essays ever written on the poem, Frank Kermode's 'Adam Unparadised' (in *The Living Milton: Essays by Various Hands*, ed. Frank Kermode [London, 1960]). 'The poem is tragic', writes Professor Kermode, and he continues, 'The tragedy is a matter of *fact*, of life as we feel it', while 'the hope of restoration is a matter of faith' and cannot speak to our senses as does the experience of Paradise and its loss. (Notice the phrase 'life as we feel it'. Isn't this always Hardy's concern?) '*Paradise Lost* deals most directly with this basic theme', he says, 'the recognition of lost possibilities of joy, order, health, the contrast between what we can imagine as human and what is so here and now; the sensuous import of the myth of the lost Eden.' That is a statement, I would suggest, that could be equally well applied to *Tess of the d'Urbervilles* – and not only to *Tess*, but to much of Hardy's work in general, especially his lyric poetry: to, for example, 'Yell'ham-Wood's Story', with its sense of 'a thwarted purposing' ('Life offers – to deny!'), or to the beautiful and seminal 'Childhood among the Ferns', with its concluding cry against expulsion:

'Why should I have to grow to man's estate,
And this afar-noised World perambulate?'

Their 'profound and personal devotion' to that 'radical topic, potentially co-extensive with all human experience: the loss of Eden' (I am quoting Kermode again), seems to me to unite Hardy and Milton more strongly than their contrasting attitudes to Providence keep them apart.

Having said this, I am confronted by *The Dynasts*, the work of Hardy's which through its character as an epic-drama most obviously invites comparison with *Paradise Lost*, yet at the same time offers the starkest contrast to it through its total rejection of that 'local cult called Christianity' as the Spirit of the Years calls it; of Milton's celestial machinery; and of belief in a divine Providence. These matters have all been discussed by Harold Orel in his excellent article in the *South Atlantic Quarterly* (1953), and I do not propose to go over the ground again. Professor Orel concludes:

> Nihilism is at the core of Hardy's singularly strong-minded awareness of the impossibility of bringing intact Milton and the Miltonic dream to the modern world, a nihilism which negates three essential features of the Christian epic, God, Man ennobled with God's aid, and the possibility of Man's ascension to God.

This seems to me undeniable. Yet although Hardy may have rejected the philosophy of *Paradise Lost*, and have thereby created not a Christian but rather an anti-Christian epic, he has not rejected Milton's poem as poem. Considering it more purely as a literary creation, we may detect in *The Dynasts* a subtle but quite distinct Miltonic flavour. The Miltonic influence may have been thoroughly absorbed and assimilated, but it is there.

In the first place, *The Dynasts* resembles *Paradise Lost* in its scope and intention, the sheer reach of its vision. Both poems take as their subject all human woe: Hardy focuses on one particular action, the wars of Napoleon, while Milton, portraying the consequences of the Fall, takes in all human history from the beginning to the end of time. Yet Hardy, chiefly by means of the Spirits and their questionings, makes the smaller action symbolic of the larger, so that this difference is less than it seems. For although Hardy cannot share the Miltonic dream, Milton can and does share the Hardyan nightmare. True, he promises that we shall eventually awake from it, but not until Judgment day. Until then, for Milton as for Hardy, all Creation groans:

> so shall the world go on,
> To good malignant, to bad men benign,
> Under her own weight groaning till the day
> Appear of respiration to the just,
> And vengeance to the wicked

(XII, 537–41)

The spectacle of the future which Adam is set to watch from the Hill of Vision in Books XI and XII of *Paradise Lost* is as grim as that presented to the Phantom Intelligences in *The Dynasts*, and could almost be said to contain it; and Adam in his distress utters sentiments akin to those of the Pities. For although Milton's poem may be ultimately an expression of faith, it also incorporates all doubt, through the speeches of fallen man as well as those of the fallen angels, to say nothing of the way in which the action speaks for itself. No-one ever better fulfilled Hardy's principle, 'If way to the Better there be, it exacts a full look at the Worst.' *Paradise Lost* and *The Dynasts* are alike in being essentially *questioning* poems, and in asking the same fundamental questions concerning man's existence and his destiny:

What of the Immanent Will and Its designs?

That to the height of this great argument
I may assert eternal providence
And justify the ways of God to men.

Phrasing and form and ultimate intention may differ in these two statements, but it is still the same programme of investigation that is being announced.

And the investigation in each case takes the same form: that of an action or spectacle played out before watchers, usually at a distance. Hardy's play-shape makes this more explicit, but it is an implicit feature of Milton's narrative also. We have seen an example in Adam's observations from the Hill of Vision. Earlier, Adam himself had been the observed of all observers, his every action watched by God, by the angels, and by Satan: even our first idyllic view of Adam and Eve in the Garden comes to us through the eyes of Satan, perched like a cormorant on the Tree of Life. Hardy had already made much use of such watching techniques in his novels, so that the resemblance to Milton may indicate only a shared taste, or perhaps a shared artistic necessity. Yet the supernatural character of the observers in *The Dynasts*, the panoramic nature of their vision, and their constant intense concern with the actions and fate of the mannikins below, all suggest some more direct relationship to Milton. In his Preface to *The Dynasts* Hardy is careful to dissociate the Spirits of his Overworld from Milton's 'celestial machinery'. Yet despite the difference in character a resemblance in function still persists. And since even a Phantom tends to assume a personality when it speaks, there may even be a residual resemblance, not consciously intended, to Milton's divine personages: in the Ancient Spirit of the Years to God the Father, the embodiment of Reason and Justice, the Ancient of Days; in the Pities to God the Son, the embodiment of Mercy and Love; and in the Spirits Ironic and Sinister to twin aspects of Satan.

Finally, I would suggest that Professor Orel's pessimism exceeds Hardy's own, when he says of the work, 'The Sardonic rules here', and dismisses the 'food for final hope' offered by the Pities as of little relevance or validity. In terms simply of number of appearances, the Sardonic certainly does not rule: the Spirit Ironic continues to put in an appearance until the end, but the Spirit Sinister almost fades out completely in Part III, like Satan disappearing from view in the final books of *Paradise Lost*. He is allowed not one word in the 'After Scene', which is mainly a dialogue between the Years and the Pities. In giving the last word to the Pities:

> But – a stirring thrills the air
> Like to sounds of joyance there
> That the rages
> Of the ages
> Shall be cancelled, and deliverance offered from the
> darts that were,
> Consciousness the Will informing, till It fashion
> all things fair!,

Hardy is seeking, I think, to end on a note of catharsis, of reconciliation, as did that other drama not intended for the stage, Milton's *Samson Agonistes* – in 'calm of mind, all passion spent' – and also perhaps consciously to provide, even if only faintly, some equivalent to Milton's promise in *Paradise Lost* of a time when 'God shall be all in all'. The hope may be a forlorn one, more a desire than a hope. But as F. B. Pinion has said (*A Hardy Companion*, p. 108), the true hope lies in the existence of the Pities who have voiced it. They, 'our young Compassions', as the expression of that charity or loving-kindness in human beings which Hardy advocated as the one thing needful, are our true and only salvation. In *Paradise Lost*, Book III, God the Son, offering to die for man, is also seen as the embodiment of charity, of altruism in its highest form. *The Dynasts* is not so anti-Christian after all.

And this may lead me back to *Jude the Obscure*, for the need for loving-kindness is the message of that bitter book, as it is equally of Milton's Divorce pamphlets. Quoting Hardy's own phrase in his 1912 'postscript' to his 1895 Preface, C. A. Patrides, in the Introduction to his *John Milton, Selected Prose* (Penguin English Library edition, 1974) asserts that the pamphlets provide 'the tragic machinery of the tale'. This, though not impossible, seems to me difficult to prove; what can be shown is that almost every idea on marriage and divorce that Hardy expresses either through dialogue or through the action or narration has its counterpart in Milton – with the important exception that Milton never questions the institution of marriage itself, as Hardy does. Hardy is in this respect an even more radical thinker than Milton, though both were far too radical for their day. Even if Hardy's dependence on the Divorce pamphlets is not as complete as Patrides's statement suggests, he must at least have found them wonderful grist to his mill. Like Hardy, for instance, Milton sees the enforced continuation of a marriage that has failed as a cruelty, calling it 'a cruel and senseless bondage', and like Hardy he denounces the law's responsibility in this. Like Hardy, he appeals from man's arbitrary laws to the law of Nature. He insists, as Sue Bridehead does, that love cannot be compelled:

> to command love and sympathy, to forbid dislike against the guiltless instinct of nature, is not within the Province of any Law to reach,

and he cites as an example Henry VIII and his feelings about 'his Queen *Anne of Cleve*, whom he could not like after he had been wedded half a year'. One would not have thought of Sue as having anything in common with King Henry VIII, yet in her inability to 'stomach' Phillotson (Aunt Drusilla's word), perhaps she has.

Milton also suggests that unhappiness in marriage may drive a man to atheism, as happens with Jude; here indeed he may have provided the 'machinery of the tale'.

Even more striking than these agreements in argument, however, is the common passion, and compassion, that informs them. With a fervour born in part of their own unhappy experience, Hardy and Milton both insist on the priority of the individual's right to happiness, and in particular, where marriage is concerned, of their right to find this happiness in a true 'conjugal fellowship' (Milton's phrase), a union of souls. The single precept that Milton insists on, and with eloquence, throughout his *Doctrine and Discipline of Divorce* is that of *charity*; and he makes explicit reference to the passage in St. Paul which meant so much to Hardy, the passage Sue and Jude quote when they separate before Sue's remarriage. 'Its verses will stand fast when all the rest that you call religion has passed away' is Jude's comment. Charity is also the climax of the moral instruction St. Michael gives Adam in the last Book of *Paradise Lost*: to his newly acquired knowledge of God's scheme of salvation he should add

> Deeds to thy knowledge answerable, add faith,
> Add virtue, patience, temperance, and love,
> By name to come called Charity, the soul
> Of all the rest.

(XII, 582–5)

It is doubtful whether Milton's charity in practice extended as far as Hardy's. However much he would have endorsed, with regret, the truth of the description, we can never imagine Hardy writing so dismissively as does Milton in *Samson Agonistes* of 'the common rout' of men, of those who 'grow up and perish, as the summer fly,/Heads without name no more remembered'. Milton does not share Hardy's tender regard for 'Earth's humblest': for him it is the hero, even if only the 'one just man' in each generation, that matters. Hardy will in this respect always seem more human, or humane, than Milton. Nevertheless, as Hardy recognises in his recollections of Milton, conscious and unconscious, in the three works we have been considering, these two great writers had this fundamental affinity: they were both great humanists.

Hardy and Lawrence

Robert Langbaum

The best source of comparison between Thomas Hardy and D. H.
Lawrence is Lawrence's curious little book *Study of Thomas Hardy*
(the *Study* is curious in its mixture of literary criticism with
metaphysics, autobiography, cultural history and other things).
In the *Study*, Lawrence implicitly acknowledges Hardy as his
master. Hardy takes on new relevance and stature when we
realize that he is the principal influence on one of the two most
innovative, twentieth-century English-speaking novelists (the
other is Joyce); while we understand Lawrence better when we
realize that he differs only in degree from Hardy and when we can
trace the roots of Lawrence's art back through Hardy to George
Eliot and Wordsworth.

To some extent Lawrence's relation to Hardy illustrates
Harold Bloom's theory of influence, in that Lawrence in the *Study*
partly misreads and rewrites Hardy's novels as a way of arriving
at his own art. But the *Study* shows no sign of what Bloom calls 'the
anxiety of influence', in that Lawrence is not out to defeat Hardy
– he wants to complete him, to continue his direction, to fulfil the
implications of Hardy's art that Hardy as a Victorian could not
fulfil. It is true that Lawrence so assimilates Hardy that 'one can',
to borrow Bloom's words, 'believe, for startled moments' that
Lawrence is being 'imitated'[1] by Hardy. Such absorption is not,
however, necessarily aggressive; it can be a way of learning all one
can from the precursor before going on to take the inevitable next
step of finding one's own identity as a writer.

Although Lawrence criticizes Hardy for allowing his
metaphysic or moral judgment to outweigh his sympathy for his
convention-breaking characters, he writes about Hardy's novels
with such affectionate understanding that his admiration is what
we remember. 'Nothing in [Hardy's] work', says Lawrence, 'is so

15

pitiable as his clumsy efforts to push events into line with his theory of being, and to make calamity fall on those who represent the principle of Love. . . . His feeling, his instinct, his sensuous understanding is, however, apart from his metaphysic, very great and deep, deeper than that, perhaps of any other English novelist.'[2] The same criticism – that he is weak in metaphysic, strong in sensibility – is often made against Lawrence.

If we recall at what point in his career Lawrence wrote the *Study of Hardy*, we realize that Lawrence places himself in Hardy's line in order to understand himself as a novelist, to understand where he comes from and where he is going. It was on 15 July 1914, a moment of triumph, when he had married Frieda and sent off *The Rainbow* to Methuen, that Lawrence asked a friend to lend him Hardy's novels because he hoped 'to write a little book on Hardy's people'. August was a month of reverses. Methuen returned the manuscript and the war broke out. On 5 September Lawrence wrote to his agent: 'What a miserable world. What colossal idiocy, this war. Out of sheer rage I've begun my book about Thomas Hardy.'[3] The book on Hardy was conceived, however, in a moment of happiness; and there is no rage in it. The *Study of Hardy* is, like the final version of *The Rainbow* to which it provides the skeletal structure, optimistic about the possibility for the evolution of human consciousness through the right kind of marriage.

The apparent digressiveness of the *Study* has led most readers (and Lawrence himself at times) to conclude that Hardy is a mere pretext for Lawrence's expression of his own philosophy, and that the three chapters dealing directly with Hardy (chapters III, V, IX) have little to do with the other ten chapters. I want to argue, instead, that the *Study* does hang together, that the metaphysic no less than the criticism derives from Lawrence's understanding of Hardy's novels. 'Normally, the centre, the turning pivot, of a man's life', writes Lawrence in the *Study*, 'is his sex-life, the centre and swivel of his being is the sexual act.'[4] Hardy thought so too; he is the first Victorian novelist, perhaps the first English novelist, to have thought so. That is why he was always in trouble with the bowdlerizers and censors. Lawrence says that in the division of human life between the purpose of self-preservation and the sexual–creative purpose (the distinction corresponds to Freud's between the reality and pleasure principles), Hardy's people are mainly committed to the sexual–creative purpose. Thus Lawrence's metaphysic – which sees all life as sexual and equates sexuality with spirit – can be said to derive from his understanding of Hardy. Writers of course have always dealt with sex. The difference in Hardy and especially in Lawrence is the centrality of sex – the fact that sex is self-justifying, that it is not subject to judgment by other values but is indeed the source of other values. The ironic subtitle, *A Pure Woman*, to *Tess of the d'Urbervilles* challenges the quite opposite conventional judgment of Tess.

Far from being a digression, then, the chapters on the metaphysic – especially those that account for our cultural and psychic history by the necessary opposition of male and female principles – are necessary for an understanding of Lawrence's readings of Hardy's novels. Lawrence's valid insights outweigh his misreadings, making him Hardy's best critic, the first to understand Hardy's innovativeness and relevance to the twentieth century. We can never read Hardy in the same way once we have encountered Lawrence in the *Study* and the novels, and have come to realize that Lawrence took from Hardy the great new subjects of sex and the unconscious.

Lawrence's *Study of Thomas Hardy* influenced the final version of *The Rainbow*, as is amply demonstrated by Mark Kinkead-Weekes who shows that Lawrence needed to write the *Study* in order to find out what he had been up to in the vast draft, called *The Sisters*,[5] which by the time of the *Study* was separated into *The Rainbow* and what would be called *Women in Love*. Lawrence, according to Kinkead-Weekes, learned two main things from Hardy's example: he learned the necessity for and the danger of a metaphysic. Every great novel, Lawrence writes in the *Study*, 'must have the background or the structural skeleton of some theory of being, some metaphysic'. Hardy anticipated the modernists in being the first Victorian novelist and poet to feel the need of a system – a system he finally worked out in his mammoth, still-born epic poem *The Dynasts* (1903–8). It is because of Hardy's metaphysic that Lawrence places him on a level with Tolstoi; but their metaphysic, says Lawrence, damaged the art of both novelists when it overcame their 'living sense of being. . . . The metaphysic must always subserve the artistic purpose beyond the artist's conscious aim. Otherwise the novel becomes a treatise'. Lawrence seems to be thinking of the defeat by society of Hardy's Tess and Tolstoi's Anna Karenina when he goes on to say that

'Hardy's metaphysic is something like Tolstoi's. "There is no reconciliation between Love and the Law", says Hardy. "The spirit of Love must always succumb before the blind, stupid, but overwhelming power of the Law." '[6]

In determining that 'the metaphysic must always subserve the artistic purpose beyond the artist's conscious aim', Lawrence arrives at a theory of the proper subordination of conscious to unconscious intention. This connects with the other main thing that Lawrence probably learned from Hardy – a new sense of unconscious or impersonal identity. Lawrence found in Hardy, says Kinkead-Weekes, 'a language in which to conceive the impersonal forces he saw operating within and between human beings', and this helped him understand 'what the novel he had been trying to write was really *about*'.[7] It was about the new sense of identity, which is why Lawrence felt impelled, as a way of retracing his steps for the sake of understanding, to write about Hardy's *people*.

Hardy's new sense of identity is clearest, Lawrence implies, in the way he relates characters to landscape. In *The Return of the Native*, the people

> are one year's accidental crop. . . . The Heath persists. Its body is strong and fecund, it will bear many more crops beside this. . . . The contents of the small lives are spilled and wasted. There is savage satisfaction in it: for so much more remains to come, such a black, powerful fecundity is working there that what does it matter?[8]

The Heath is the external, impersonal identity of which the people are passing manifestations.

Out of this passage and the *Study*'s metaphysic of female and male principles emerge the great opening passages of *The Rainbow* (written after the *Study*),[9] where the Brangwens are portrayed as passing manifestations of the fecund landscape. The men are absorbed by organic connection with the female earth, by 'blood-intimacy': 'the pulse of the blood of the teats of the cows beat into the pulse of the hands of the men'; whereas the women look upward to the male church tower and aspire to a life of spirit.[10] The sexualization of landscape derives from Hardy – from the voluptuous landscapes in *Far From the Madding Crowd* and from passages in *Tess* like this one:

Amid the oozing fatness and warm ferments of the Froom Vale, at a season when the rush of juices could almost be heard below the hiss of fertilization, it was impossible that the most fanciful love should not grow passionate. The ready bosoms existing there were impregnated by their surroundings.[11]

Hardy and Lawrence sexualize Wordsworth's living landscapes.

That is because Hardy and Lawrence are Darwinians. 'Man has a purpose', says Lawrence in a statement describing his own novels while describing Hardy's, 'which he has divorced from the passionate purpose that issued him out of the earth into being.'[12] Human identity, in other words, is split between our conscious, individual purpose and the unconscious, biological purpose we also carry within us. Hence the importance of marriage in *The Rainbow* and in the *Study*'s theology of marriage as a way of reconciling our two purposes. Lawrence is more optimistic about marriage than Hardy, who mainly attacks the institution. The difference partly derives from their different experiences of marriage. But it may also derive from the fact that Hardy is still a social reformer, still out to free us from the bonds of established institutions, while Lawrence wants to restore values to a society disastrously free of them. The difference may be one reason why Hardy is ironic, while Lawrence is notably without irony.

Lawrence's optimism also derives from Hardy's post-Darwinian metaphysic about the inevitable evolution of human consciousness and even the consciousness of the Innate Will in nature. 'The sexual act', says Lawrence in the *Study*, 'is not for the depositing of the seed. It is for leaping off into the unknown',[13] for serving evolution. The sense of beyondness is the criterion of good sexual relations in *The Rainbow* and the novels that follow.

There emerges from Lawrence's analysis of Hardy's people a new diagram of identity as a small, well-lit area surrounded by an increasingly dark penumbra of unconsciousness opening out to external, impersonal forces. This leads to a system of judgment which condemns the attempt to shut out the darkness and live imprisoned in the well-lit ego. Thus Lawrence's analysis of the idealistic Clym in *The Return of the Native*:

Impotent to *be*, he must transform himself, and live in an abstraction, in a generalization, he must identify himself with the system. He must live as Man or Humanity, or as the Community, or as Society, or as Civilization. . . . He already showed that thought is a disease of the flesh, and indirectly bore evidence that ideal physical beauty is incompatible with emotional development and a full recognition of the coil of things.

Clym, who showed that highly conscious modern people cannot be beautiful, shut out the penumbra of unconsciousness connecting him with the Heath. The fenced-out darkness can seem as demonic as the fenced-in ego: 'Was it his blood, which rose dark and potent out of Egdon [Heath], which hampered and confined the deity [within him], or was it his mind, that house built of extraneous knowledge and guarded by his will, which formed the prison?'[14]

Ursula in *The Rainbow* arrives at a similar diagram of her identity:

This lighted area, lit up by man's completest consciousness, she thought was all the world: that here all was disclosed for ever. Yet all the time, within the darkness she had been aware of points of light, like the eyes of wild beasts, gleaming, penetrating, vanishing. And her soul had acknowledged in a great heave of terror only the outer darkness.[15]

She succumbs to the darkness because she has had only momentary, ego-centred intuitions of it as fenced-out; hence the wild beasts who are menacing when repressed. But Ursula advances beyond Clym because she learns to reconcile consciousness with unconsciousness.

In assimilating Clym to *The Rainbow*, Lawrence is not misreading. His analysis of Clym is brilliantly valid. The sign of this is that Clym, with his lofty intellectual ambitions, studies so hard that he becomes blind and his blindness leads him back to the Heath – he finds contentment as a furze cutter. Clym's salutary blindness, though Lawrence does not discuss it, may have given Lawrence the idea for his short story 'The Blind Man', in which Maurice Pervin's blindness restores 'the almost incomprehensible peace of immediate contact in darkness'.[16] Pervin's blindness improves his marriage; whereas Clym's destroys his marriage, because Clym alternates between consciousness and unconsciousness while his

wife Eustacia insists on his having both – his consciousness for
worldly prestige, his unconsciousness presumably for sex. Clym's
blindness seems to symbolize a decline in sexuality – a point
Lawrence surprisingly ignores.

According to Lawrence's analysis, the two human purposes –
individual and biological – determine the structure and imagery
of Hardy's novels as well as his characterizations. There exists in
Hardy's novels, writes Lawrence,

> a great background, vital and vivid, which matters more than
> the people who move upon it. . . . The vast unexplored morality
> of life itself, what we call the immorality of nature, surrounds us
> in its eternal incomprehensibility, and in its midst goes on the
> little human morality play, with its queer frame of morality and
> its mechanized movement; seriously, portentously, till some
> one of the protagonists chances to look out of the charmed
> circle, weary of the stage, to look into the wilderness raging
> round. Then he is lost, his little drama falls to pieces, or
> becomes mere repetition, but the stupendous theatre outside
> goes on enacting its own incomprehensible drama,
> untouched.[17]

The characters' two purposes parallel the two areas where the
action takes place – the small, well-lit circle of human morality
(and ego) versus the constantly encroaching amoral wilderness
around it. (In traditional literature, instead, the human moral
scheme pervades the universe.) Hardy's men – like Clym and
Angel Clare, on the side of goodness, and Alec d'Urberville on the
side of badness – alternate between the two areas. Hardy's tragic
figures – usually women, like Eustacia and Tess; Jude is the
exceptional male – inhabit both areas and are torn apart by the
conflict. A sign of the tragic conflict is *Tess*'s earliest manuscript
title: *The Body and Soul of Sue* (Tess's original name).[18]

Lawrence, I think, derives his metaphysic in the *Study* from the
conflict he discerned in Hardy between conscious and unconscious principles. Since Hardy's heroes are mainly weighted on
the side of consciousness and his heroines on the side of
unconsciousness, it follows that Lawrence in his metaphysic
(confirming in this contrast cultural prejudice) calls the conscious
principle *male* and the unconscious *female*, while acknowledging
that each person, and indeed each historical epoch, combines a

different mixture of male and female principles. The men in
Hardy who are in touch with unconscious forces of sexuality are
mainly villains – like Alec in *Tess* and Troy in *Far From the Madding
Crowd* (Arabella in *Jude the Obscure* is the exceptional woman in this
group) – because they are seducers: they exploit sexuality.
Lawrence, as we might expect, is more favourable to these
sexually charged characters than most readers up to his time have
been. But when Hardy ventures to say of Angel in *Tess*, who
displays the Victorian virtues of chastity and strict moral
judgment, that 'with more animalism [Angel] would have been
the nobler man',[19] when Hardy says this, he is on the way to
becoming Lawrence.

The great achievement of Lawrence's dialectical system in the
Study is the recognition of the female principle as a positive force,
equal if not superior in vitality to the male principle. When
women in traditional literature are strong, they tend to be evil –
like Lady Macbeth or Thackeray's Becky Sharp in *Vanity Fair*.
The intelligence and strength of will of Lawrence's mother, as
portrayed in *Sons and Lovers*, is on the whole damaging. Lawrence's
recognition of a healthy female vitality must have come from his
long tussle with his wife Frieda, a female powerhouse. But it
derived also from Hardy's women who – beginning with the
revolutionary character of the managerial Bathsheba in *Far From
the Madding Crowd* – are usually more intelligent and stronger-
willed than the men. The same can be said of the Brangwen
women in *The Rainbow* and *Women in Love* (only Birkin is a match
for them). The theme of many Hardy novels is the superior
woman's problem in finding a suitable mate – a theme Hardy took
from George Eliot, from Dorothea's problem in *Middlemarch*.
When Lawrence writes that the germ of his early draft, *The Sisters*,
was 'woman becoming individual, self-responsible, taking her
own initiative',[20] he is continuing the theme of George Eliot and
Hardy with additions to Hardy's increase of sexual ramifications.

The month before Lawrence announced his projected book on
Hardy's people, he wrote in the well-known 'carbon' identity
letter of 5 June 1914 a description of the new impersonal identity
to be found in *The Rainbow*. Although the 'carbon' identity letter
precedes the letter proposing the *Study*, we have to remember that
Lawrence when he wrote the 'carbon' identity letter was about to
*re*read Hardy and that what he had fundamentally learned had
been learned from earlier readings and was already mainly

incorporated in the novel he had just sent to Methuen. ('Have you ever read *Jude the Obscure*?' he asked Louie Burrows as early as 17 December 1910.)[21] The near coincidence of the "carbon" identity letter with the 15 July letter announcing his plan to write on Hardy's people suggests Lawrence's feeling that the new sense of identity in *The Rainbow* derived from Hardy and his consequent need to retrace his steps as a way of understanding what he had accomplished. The *Study of Hardy* confirms and systematizes the 'carbon' identity letter.

'You mustn't look in my novel', Lawrence writes in this letter, 'for the old stable *ego* – of the character. There is another *ego*, according to whose action the individual is unrecognizable.' This other ego is the unconscious, impersonal element, the 'carbon' identity. 'My theme is carbon', writes Lawrence. 'That which is physic – non-human, in humanity, is more interesting to me than the old-fashioned human element – which causes one to conceive a character in a certain moral scheme and make him consistent.'[22]

In the *Study*, Lawrence says much the same thing when he points out the inconsistency of Hardy's characters:

Nowhere, except perhaps in Jude, is there the slightest development of personal action in the characters: it is all explosive. . . . The rest explode out of the convention. They are people each with a real, vital, potential self, . . . and this self suddenly bursts the shell of manner and convention and commonplace opinion, and acts independently, absurdly, without mental knowledge or acquiescence. And from such an outburst the tragedy usually develops. For there does exist, after all, the great self-preservation scheme [society], and in it we must all live.[23]

In the 'carbon' identity letter and the *Study*, Lawrence is saying that he and Hardy treat their characters' social selves – the whole concern of the novel of manners – as the mere tip of the iceberg. The real action goes on underneath, rising to the surface sporadically in explosive or symbolic manifestations the logic and motives of which remain as mysterious to the characters as to the reader. In carrying the regression as far back as inanimate carbon, Lawrence goes a step farther than Hardy, who roots his characters in vegetated landscape. Behind them both stands Wordsworth, who was the first to root his characters in landscape and to intensify their being through regression as far back as inanimate objects: the quality of the old leech-gatherer's existence, in 'Resolution and Independence', is that of a huge stone that seems slightly, mysteriously animate. The innovation in Wordsworth, Hardy and Lawrence is the portrayal of characters as states of being rather than as defined by social class and moral choice – the criteria of traditional characterization. There remains, however, more social determination in Hardy than in Lawrence.

The paradigms of 'carbon' identity and explosive characterization are especially apparent in *Women in Love*, which proceeds through a series of discontinuous stills or set scenes each designed to manifest the characters' unconscious or 'carbon' identity. Gerald and Gudrun seal their sado-masochistic union in the scene on the island, where Gudrun defies the male principle by chasing away bullocks and finally by slapping Gerald across the face – a totally unexpected manifestation. Their relationship proceeds through arbitrary, unprepared for scenes in which Gudrun swoons with masochistic excitement while Gerald torments his mare and subdues a huge hare, whose savage energy in whirling round as Gerald holds him by the ears suggests phallic power. Lawrence's use of animals to reveal to his characters their unconscious desires may derive from Hardy – from a scene like the sheep-shearing in *Far From the Madding Crowd*, in which Gabriel and Bathsheba discover their desire for each other through Gabriel's sexually suggestive way of handling a ewe while Bathsheba watches. Gabriel, we are told, dragged

> a frightened ewe to his shear-station, flinging it over upon its back with a dexterous twist of the arm. He lopped off the tresses about its head, and opened up the neck and collar, his mistress quietly looking on. "She blushes at the insult," murmured Bathsheba, watching the pink flush which arose and overspread the neck and shoulders of the ewe where they were left by the clicking of the shears. . . . Poor Gabriel's soul was fed with a luxury of content by having her over him.[24]

Similarly, in *Sons and Lovers*, Paul's sexually suggestive cherrypelting of Miriam before their first intercourse may derive from Alec d'Urberville's sexually suggestive way of feeding Tess strawberries on their first meeting: 'Tess eating in a half-pleased, half-reluctant state what d'Urberville offered her. . . . She obeyed like one in a dream'[25] (this is the pattern of her later rape-seduction by Alec). *The Rainbow*'s spectacular dance under moonlight, which releases the erotic unconscious of Ursula and Skrebensky, echoes the scene in *Return of the Native* where Eustacia, temporarily fleeing her unhappy marriage to attend a village dance, meets there by Hardyan coincidence (as the fulfillment of her unconscious desire) her former lover Wildeve, who is also unhappily married. Their dance under moonlight provides erotic release: 'These two [were] riding upon the whirlwind. The dance had come like an irresistible attack upon whatever sense of social order there was in their minds.'[26]

The analysis of Hardy's explosive characterizations is Lawrence's most illuminating insight into Hardy's novels. It accounts for Bathsheba's sudden entanglement with Sergeant Troy, which runs counter to the sequence of events and Bathsheba's conscious intentions. Troy is a complete stranger to her when his spur becomes entangled in her dress one night in her garden. The crude bodily contact, which excites Bathsheba because of its outrageousness ("she blushes at the insult", she had said of the 'undressed' ewe), leads to the sealing of their union in the wildly explosive sword exercise scene, which with its phallic and sado-masochistic symbolism reveals to Bathsheba a stratum of sexual desire she knows nothing about. As Troy makes his sword cuts within a hair's breadth of her body, she feels penetrated: ' "Have you run me through?" ' The experience becomes psychologically a kind of intercourse: 'She felt powerless to withstand or deny him. . . . She felt like one who has sinned a great sin.' This last in response to what turns out to have been a mere kiss. Because of its sexual archetypes – the phallic performance takes place in a vaginal or womblike 'hollow amid the ferns'[27] – the sword exercise scene is the most Lawrencean scene in Hardy, though we probably have to have read Lawrence or Freud to appreciate the blatancy of its symbolism.

Bathsheba, the masterful woman who expresses her sexual interest in Gabriel Oak by tormenting him, gets a sexual thrill out of being brutally subdued by Sergeant Troy. Hardy's understanding of sado-masochism points toward Lawrence, whom Yeats wrongly credited with having discovered the cruelty in love. Tess's relation with Alec d'Urberville is also sado-masochistic. Alec subdues her at the outset by driving her at terrifying speed to the d'Urberville mansion where she will be a servant. Then he 'gave her the kiss of mastery'. The master–servant relation enhances sado-masochism. Gabriel is Bathsheba's servant; Troy is her servant's lover. When Alec in the end insists that Tess return to him, she (in a scene pointing toward the scene in which Lawrence's Gudrun strikes Gerald) slaps him across the mouth with her heavy glove, drawing blood.

> "Now, punish me!" she said, turning up her eyes to him with the hopeless defiance of the sparrow's gaze before its captor twists its neck. "Whip me, crush me. . . . I shall not cry out. Once victim, always victim – that's the law!"

Alec in replying fills the role required of him: '"I was your master once! I will be your master again."'[28] Tess returns to him.

Lawrence's analysis of Hardy's explosive characterizations accounts for the ambiguities of Tess's behaviour at crucial moments of her life. Why does Tess take the job at the d'Urbervilles when it is clear from the start that Alec will be a danger to her? Why, after all her determined resistance to him, does Tess, on that most crucial night of her life, suddenly leap behind him on his horse and allow herself to be carried into the dark wood where she falls asleep so willingly that it remains impossible to determine whether she is then raped or seduced? (Did Lawrence learn from this scene how to portray Gerald's rapelike way of taking Gudrun the first time when, with the mud from his father's grave on his boots, he steals like a criminal into her family's house and breaks into her bedroom determined to have her?) Why cannot Tess, despite her good intentions, bring herself to tell Angel before their marriage about her relations with Alec? Angel might not then have felt betrayed by the confession which came too late. When Tess learns that Angel never saw the confessional letter she slipped under his door because the letter slipped under a rug, she lets this accident make the decision for her not to confess. According to the Victorian reading, the accident is a typically contrived Hardy coincidence. If we take a deep psychological view of the incident, however, it exemplifies an advanced technique for making an external event confirm an unconscious desire – Tess's desire to let nothing impede her marriage to Angel.

Why does Tess go back to Alec? And why, after Angel's reappearance, does Tess murder Alec when all she has to do is leave him? And why, finally, does Tess show so little interest in escaping with Angel after the murder? Why in the end does she lay herself down, almost willingly, as a human sacrifice on the altar at Stonehenge to be captured and executed?

Hardy's explanations are in the deep psychological manner over-determined – which is to say that they are all partly valid, yet no one of them is the complete explanation. The reason Tess takes the job at the d'Urbervilles is to help her family financially; and that is one reason she goes back to Alec, though the reason is less satisfactory than before as a complete explanation. The night of the rape–seduction, she leaps onto Alec's horse in order to avoid a fight with his former mistress; but she also triumphs over the other girl by leaping onto the horse in front of her. Hardy suggests an even deeper reason when he says that Tess 'abandoned herself to her impulse . . . and scrambled into the saddle behind him'. Her unconscious acquiescence is confirmed by her falling asleep and by Hardy's further explanation that Tess was still a child with a woman's body. Another recurrent explanation is that Tess is the victim of a malignant fate – her mishaps are presented as ironies of fate.

Tess's problem throughout is her combination of strong conscience with strong sexual desire. She has one foot in what Lawrence calls Hardy's 'human morality play', and the other in the swirl of amoral biological force that joins our life to the cosmos. It is partly conscience, guilt over the ruin she feels she brought to her family's meagre fortune, that impels her toward Alec. Instead of feeling rage over Angel's abandonment of her, she takes the blame upon herself and goes to work on the brutal Flintcomb-Ash Farm, with its infernal landscape, as a kind of penance. Most of Tess's misery is created by her conscience; for she condemns herself more strongly than does anyone else.

Equally strong is Tess's unconscious desire for a biological fulfilment leading through sexuality to death. Like Gabriel Oak in *Far From the Madding Crowd*, Tess falls asleep at crucial moments that, with her unconscious acquiescence, advance her destiny. Here is Hardy's description of the conflict in Tess between conscience and biological destiny. She has just left Angel after promising to answer his proposal of marriage in a few days and at the same time tell him about her past.

Tess flung herself upon the rustling undergrowth of speargrass, as upon a bed, and remained crouching in palpitating misery broken by momentary shoots of joy, which her fears about the ending could not altogether suppress. In reality, she was drifting into acquiescence. Every see-saw of her breath, every wave of her blood, every pulse singing in her ears, was a voice that joined with nature in revolt against her unscrupulousness. . . . in almost a terror of ecstasy Tess divined that, despite her many months of lonely self-chastisement, wrestlings, communings, schemes to lead a future of austere isolation, love's counsel would prevail.[29]

Similarly Clym, while waiting for Eustacia, often flings himself down amid vegetation as if to draw erotic strength from nature. Lawrence's Birkin in *Women in Love* flings himself down so, after Hermione tried to kill him, as if to draw restorative strength from nature. Hardy's deep explanation as to why Tess finally consents to marry Angel without having confessed looks back to Wordsworth and forward to Lawrence: 'The "appetite for joy" [a Wordsworthian phrase] which pervades all creation, that tremendous force which sways humanity to its purpose, as the tide sways the helpless weed, was not to be controlled by vague lucubrations over the social rubric.'[30]

The same biological drive leads Tess to seek death as well. She expresses throughout her longing for death. Her murder of Alec is a way of bringing on her own death; but it is also a fulfilment of their murderous sexual relation, a relation like that of Gerald and Gudrun. Gudrun's words to Gerald after she has slapped him across the face would apply to Tess after she slaps Alec. '"You have struck the first blow"', says Gerald. '"And I shall strike the last"', Gudrun replies.[31] After the murder Tess tells Angel: '"I have killed him! . . . I feared long ago, when I struck him on the mouth with my glove, that I might do it some day."'[32]

There has emerged since Lawrence's time two ways of reading *Tess* and Hardy's other major novels – the Victorian or moralistic way and the Lawrencean or deep psychological way. According to the moralistic reading, Tess is entirely Alec's victim–she entertains no sexual feeling for him.[33] She goes to him only to help her family; their first intercourse is a rape; she murders him to avenge the harm he has done her. The novel is largely a reformist attack on the double standard of sexual morality. According to the moralistic reading a malignant fate is the prime mover of events, while in the *Study* fate is hardly mentioned. We need to combine both readings, but it is the deep psychological reading that reveals the full measure of Hardy's greatness and accounts for what have seemed flaws in his characterization and plotting. Through our reading of Lawrence, both in the *Study* and the novels, we have come to understand that Hardy is important in the history of the English novel because he is the first to elaborate the sphere of unconscious motivation. Sterne alludes to the unconscious; the Brontës show intuitive flashes into it; Dickens, we now realize as the Victorians did not, symbolizes the unconscious through projections of it in the world of objects. But Hardy is the first English novelist to treat the unconscious analytically and to organize characterization and plot for the purpose of revealing the unconscious.

In *Jude the Obscure*, Sue Bridehead is the best example of Hardy's explosive characterization. Sue's crucial decisions are never prepared for; it requires the deepest psychology to understand them, and many remain unfathomable. Why does she marry Phillotson, and even more puzzling why does she entirely on her own initiative return to him (repeating the pattern of Tess's return to Alec) when she is still in love with Jude, to whom she has borne children? The usual answer is that she wants to do penance for having lived in sin with Jude, but the return of her repressed Christian conscience masks deeper motives.

Why, in the chain of events leading to the children's deaths, does Sue tell the landlady that she and Jude are not married? Sue's unnecessary confession leads to the family's eviction from the only lodging they could find. The eviction and the refusal of other lodgings make a terrible impression on the oldest boy, who concludes: ' "It would be better to be out o' the world than in it, wouldn't it?" ' Instead of comforting him, Sue agrees:

> "It would almost, dear."
> "'Tis because of us children, too, isn't it, that you can't get a good lodging?"
> "Well – people do object to children sometimes."
> "Then if children make too much trouble, why do people have 'em?"
> "O – because it is a law of nature." . . .
> "I wish I hadn't been born!"
> "You couldn't help it, my dear."

"I think that whenever children be born that are not wanted they should be killed directly, before their souls come to 'em."

Instead of assuring the boy of their love, Sue 'did not reply'. And she unnecessarily volunteers the information that there will be another baby. The boy responds with such horror – '"O God, mother, you've never a-sent for another; and such trouble with what you've got!"' – as to indicate that this last piece of information makes him hang the other children and himself.

Hardy, in his usual way of offering an inadequate explanation in order to suggest others, begins this episode by saying that 'Sue had not the art of prevarication.' Would it have been a lie to tell the boy she loved him and to have withheld the information about the new baby? For all her beauty, intelligence and idealism, Sue emerges as a charming monster because she lacks instincts.

After the children's deaths, Sue realizes that 'her discourse with the boy had been the main cause of the tragedy'. She explains to Jude:

> "I talked to the child as one should only talk to people of mature age. . . . I wanted to be truthful. I couldn't bear deceiving him as to the facts of life. And yet I wasn't truthful, for with a false delicacy I told him too obscurely. . . . Why didn't I tell him pleasant untruths, instead of half-realities? . . . I could neither conceal things nor reveal them!"[34]

The things she concealed were the facts of sex, thus making her explanation even more terrifying to the boy. Sue's fear of sex is always the deeper motive beneath her apparent ones. Yet she subscribes – showing Hardy's analysis here and elsewhere of self-deceiving idealism – to an abstract ideal of free sex.

Lawrence brilliantly tells us that Jude and Sue do not feel that, in living together without marriage, they have sinned against Christianity or the community but that they have lied to themselves. 'They knew it was no marriage; they knew it was wrong, all along; they knew they were sinning against life, in forcing a physical marriage between themselves.' Their uneasiness makes them seem more illicit to others than do ordinary illicit lovers. Theirs was no marriage because Sue was no woman. It was wrong of Jude to have forced sex upon her, and wrong of her to have borne children in order to make a false show of being a woman. Because their marriage had no consummation in the interchange of male and female principles, 'they were', says Lawrence in a poetic passage showing his deep response to the novel, 'too unsubstantial, too thin and evanescent in substance, as if the other solid people might jostle right throught them, two wandering shades as they were': Dantesque shades.

Lawrence again reveals motives deeper than the ostensible Christian ones in explaining Sue's return to Phillotson after the children's deaths:

> Then Sue ceases to be. . . . The last act of her intellect was the utter renunciation of her mind and the embracing of utter orthodoxy, where every belief, every thought, every decision was made ready for her, so that she did not exist self-responsible. And then her loathed body, . . . that too should be scourged out of existence. She chose the bitterest penalty in going back to Phillotson. . . . All that remained of her was the will by which she annihilated herself. That remained fixed, a locked centre of self-hatred, life-hatred so utter that it had no hope of death.[35]

This sounds like a Lawrence novel. The last three sentences could be describing Gudrun, who chose the bitterest penalty in giving herself up to Loerke. Yet the analysis applies illuminatingly to Sue. Jude and Gerald, who have emotions, are granted the relief of death; Sue and Gudrun, who live entirely in the head, are not granted oblivion.

Lawrence's most important insight into *Jude the Obscure* is the statement that 'Jude is only Tess turned round about. . . . Arabella is Alec d'Urberville, Sue is Angel Clare.'[36] Since Lawrence says that both Tess and Jude contain within themselves the conflict between female sensuality and male intellect, one wonders why he goes on to speak of Jude as though he lived entirely in the head like Sue. Jude like Tess is strong in sexuality and conscience; that is why Jude succumbs to Arabella as Tess succumbs to Alec. The difference is that Jude is not on such friendly terms as Tess with his unconscious; he does not like Tess fall asleep at crucial moments.

Jude and Sue – Sue even more than Jude – are alienated from their unconscious. That is what makes them Hardy's first distinctively twentieth-century characters. Angel's repression of his unconscious is still Victorian in that it can be explained by lingering religiousness, as Jude's and Sue's cannot. Hardy's remark that Tess expresses 'the ache of modernism'[37] does not gibe with the rest of her character; but the phrase suits Jude and Sue, who appeared only four years later (*Tess*, 1891; *Jude*, 1895). It requires Lawrence's metaphysic – in which he traces the cultural evolution of the West from female communal Judaism to male individualistic Protestantism – to account for the astounding fact, finally stated in the *Study*'s penultimate chapter, that the male principle should have come to reside in a certain kind of modern woman. 'Sue', says Lawrence 'is scarcely a woman at all, though she is feminine enough. . . . One of the supremest products of our civilization is Sue, and a product that well frightens us.'[38]

Tess and *Jude* are the two Hardy novels Lawrence discusses in detail. We can see why since they are the two that treat sex most explicitly, making a bridge to Lawrence's own work. The chapter on *Jude* is the *Study*'s climax, and in this chapter the discussion of Sue makes the most important bridge to Lawrence's work. For it is in the character of Sue, as Lawrence analyses her, that Hardy makes the definitive break with the Victorian novel, in which the problem was to arrive at the point of sexuality by finding the right mate while staying within the laws of God and society. With Sue sexuality itself becomes the problem, even a problem in pathology. From Sue on, we encounter characters (especially in Lawrence) who do not want sex or want it perversely. The connection in Sue of idealism with sexual deficiency points toward Miriam in Lawrence's *Sons and Lovers*. Paul Morel's choice in that novel between Miriam and Clara resembles Jude's choice between Sue and Arabella, with the difference that Paul has his own problem in his Oedipal attachment to this mother. Lawrence reads more sexual problems into Jude (perhaps because he identifies himself with him) than most readers would find.

With Sue, as Lawrence points out, Hardy makes a first attack on the cult of virginity, on all those novelistic virgins who have been held up as eminently desirable for marriage. With Sue, Hardy shows how virginity can become a pathological state of mind. Sue remains psychologically a virgin (her name Bridehead means *maidenhead* or virginity) even after she has slept with Jude and Phillotson and given birth to Jude's children. We can read back from Hardy's explicit treatment of sexual deficiency in Sue to find hints that the idealism of earlier characters like Angel and

Clym may be linked with sexual deficiency. We can also read back from *Sons and Lovers* to find an Oedipal attachment between Clym and his mother, who sounds like Mrs Morel in opposing Clym's marriage.

So far Lawrence goes along with Hardy, explaining what he considers to be Hardy's conscious intentions. Lawrence breaks with Hardy over the issue of the sexually potent characters whom Lawrence calls 'aristocrats', and the issue of society's role in the novels. On these issues Lawrence apparently feels he is fulfilling Hardy's unconscious intentions.

Hardy, we are told, has the predilection of all artists for the aristocrat, because 'the aristocrat alone has occupied a position where he could afford to *be*, to be himself'. But Hardy also shares the bourgeois moral antagonism to the aristocrat, making his aristocrats die or making 'every exceptional person a villain'.[39] Lawrence seems to have derived from Hardy his romantic notion of aristocracy as signifying existential potency rather than social class. Hardy likes to give his existentially potent characters vaguely aristocratic or pseudo-aristocratic connections – Tess, Alec, Troy, Eustacia are the best known examples; Fitzpiers in *The Woodlanders* is another. Through the three versions of *Lady Chatterley's Lover*, Lawrence keeps refining the gamekeeper in order to show that he rather than Sir Clifford Chatterley is the true aristocrat.

Hardy's fault, says Lawrence, is that he always stands 'with the community in condemnation of the aristocrat', when 'his private sympathy is always with the individual against the community'. Hardy gives to his distinct individualities – characters like Troy, Clym, Tess and Jude (Lawrence should have added Sue) – 'a weak life-flow, so that they cannot break away from the old adhesion' to the communal morality. Tess, for example, 'sided with the community's condemnation of her'. Tess does, as I have suggested, internalize a social condemnation harsher than anything objectively apparent until her execution, which is itself curiously muted.

'Hardy is a bad artist', says Lawrence, 'because he must condemn Alec d'Urberville, according to his own personal creed.' But Alec is 'a rare man who seeks and seeks among women for one of such character and intrinsic female being as Tess'. Similarly Arabella's distinction is that she chooses 'a sensitive, deep-feeling man' like Jude, which no 'coarse, shallow woman' would do.

'Arabella was, under all her disguise of pig-fat and false hair, and vulgar speech, in character somewhat an aristocrat. She was, like Eustacia, amazingly lawless, even splendidly so. She believed in herself and she was not altered by any outside opinion of herself.' It is surprising to see Arabella labelled an aristocrat and Sue a bourgeois when Arabella is the conventional one who skilfully conceals her misdemeanors and manages to marry the two men she sleeps with.

Alec and Troy, we are told, 'could reach some of the real sources of the female in a woman, and draw from them. . . . And, as a woman instinctively knows, such men are rare. Therefore they have a power over a woman. They draw from the depth of her being. And what they draw, they betray'. The same applies to Arabella. These sensualists betray the depths they draw on because they are exploitative in love – they gratify themselves without giving back the male or female principles that would create an interchange. They dominate the relation because they are unwilling to submit to the development in themselves required for the male–female interchange that yields full consummation. 'Jude, like Tess, wanted full consummation. Arabella, like Alec . . . resisted full consummation.'[40] It is a sign of their inability to develop that both Arabella and Alec go through a period of evangelical conversion that leaves no final effect upon them. In *Women in Love*, Lawrence uses as a criterion of approval the capacity for development: Ursula and Birkin are the only characters with this capacity. Lawrence – whose aim is to reconcile the conflicts that Hardy leaves unreconciled – works out a way of achieving full consummation through what he calls 'star-equilibrium', a metaphor he may have taken from Hardy's description of Clym's and Eustacia's harmonious first months of marriage: 'They were like those double stars which revolve round and round each other, and from a distance appear to be one.'[41]

Lawrence criticizes Hardy for coming down, in the conflict between the individual and society, on the side of society when social judgments no longer express God's judgment but are merely relative. 'Eustacia, Tess or Sue', says Lawrence, 'were not at war with God, only with Society. Yet they were all cowed by the mere judgment of man upon them, and all the while by their own souls they were right. . . . Which is the weakness of modern tragedy, where transgression against the social code is made to bring destruction, as though the social code worked our irrevocable fate.'[42] Actually Hardy agrees, more than Lawrence realizes, about the relativity of social judgment. I have already quoted the passage in which he says that Tess's desire for Angel 'was not to be controlled by vague lucubrations over the social rubric'. Tess feels ashamed of having suffered over mere conscience, when she beholds nature's cruelty in the suffering of pheasants left wounded by hunters. Wringing the pheasants' necks to end their pain, 'she was ashamed of herself for her gloom of the night, based on nothing more tangible than a sense of condemnation under an arbitrary law of society which had no foundation in Nature'.[43] The injustice of society is attacked throughout *Jude*.

What surprises Lawrence is that Hardy portrays a world where society still sends out signals strong enough, even if of doubtful validity, to torment his characters. In Lawrence's novels, by the time of *Women in Love* (1920), such signals have ceased: social proprieties are no longer an obstacle to any one's desires. Lawrence portrays a world that has become increasingly apparent since World War I. In their treatment of society, the difference between Hardy and Lawrence is one of historical situation. Hardy's historical situation is better for the novel than Lawrence's, since the novel's original subject is the hero's exploration of and conflict with social reality. For such a subject the novelist requires a society complex enough to be worth exploring and powerful enough to be a worthy antagonist. Because such a society has largely disappeared by the time of *Women in Love* (1920), Lawrence evolves there and later a genre – the first signs of which are the ritualized scenes in *The Rainbow* (1915) – that substitutes for social notation the externalization of internal states of being: this genre exists on the borderline between myth and novel.

Already in Hardy's novels, where society still pretends to an authority it has lost, we find the beginnings of a transition to the mythical mode. The transition can be detected in Hardy's habit of presenting characters first as distantly perceived figures barely separable from the landscape before they approach and take on the lineaments of individuals. The transition can also be detected in Hardy's much criticized use of coincidences and other 'clumsy' narrative devices, all of which sacrifice verisimilitude to set up highly concentrated scenes that permit the explosive revelation of internal states of being. Hardy's coincidences point toward Lawrence's Freudian dictum that there are no accidents, for

Hardy's coincidences allow his characters to fulfill their desires and destinies. Hardy's irony derives first from the fact there still is a society worth attacking ironically, and second from the fact that what appears to be chance turns out to be design – that of fate and/or the characters' unconscious.

In the 'Moony' chapter of *Women in Love*, Lawrence uses a Hardyan coincidence and accounts for it psychologically. Ursula is walking by a lake in moonlight at a time when Birkin is abroad. 'She wished for something else out of the night.' Soon 'she saw a shadow moving by the water. It would be Birkin', she thinks before recognizing him. 'He had come back then, unawares.' That last word is ambiguous; it is the adverb Wordsworth uses with equal ambiguity when the narrator of 'Resolution and Independence' suddenly beholds the leech-gatherer standing by a pool: 'I saw a Man before me unawares.' In Lawrence 'unawares' seems to mean that Birkin has returned without telling her, also in response to her desire, also that he is unaware of being observed. Ursula justifies spying on him by thinking: 'How can there be any secrets, we are all the same organisms? How can there be any secrecy, when everything is known to all of us?'[44] Hardy's coincidences can be justified by the possibility that all the characters share one mind. The possibility dissolves the distinction between fate and the characters' individual unconsciousnesses.

In the *Study of Hardy*, Lawrence rewrites Hardy's novels and criticizes his deficiencies in such a way as to arrive at his own novels by an unbroken continuum. The *Study* is important as criticism just because it tells us as much about Lawrence as about Hardy, to the enlargement of both writers' stature. When we think of all Hardy managed to say under the restrictions laid down by readers and editors even more prudish than the ones who harassed Lawrence, we can only conclude from what Lawrence shows us in the *Study* that Hardy, with his sensitivity to historical change, would, had he been born a generation later, have become a novelist very much like D. H. Lawrence.

NOTES

1. Harold Bloom, *The Anxiety of Influence* (New York: Oxford University Press, 1968) p. 141. The fact that Lawrence in the *Study* says not a word about Hardy's poetry is only a minor influence on Lawrence's which owes far more to Walt Whitman.

2. D. H. Lawrence, *Study of Thomas Hardy*, first published in *Phoenix: The Posthumous Papers 1936*, ed. Edward D. McDonald (New York: Viking Press, 1968) p. 480. Lawrence also expressed his admiration for Hardy in many places other than the *Study*, for example: 'They are all – Turgenev, Tolstoi, Dostoevsky, Maupassant, Flaubert – so very *obvious* and coarse, beside the lovely, mature and sensitive art of . . . Hardy' (Letter of 27 November 1916, *The Collected Letters of D. H. Lawrence*, ed. Harry T. Moore, 2 vols [New York: Viking Press, 1962] I, 488.)

3. Lawrence, *Letters*, I, 287, 290. 'My book on Thomas Hardy . . . has turned out', he wrote Amy Lowell on 18 December 1914, 'as a sort of Story of My Heart' (I, 298).

4. *Phoenix*, p. 444.

5. In *The Sisters*, the name Templeman for Ella's (Ursula's) first lover (the original of Skrebensky in *The Rainbow*) may derive from Lucetta's adopted surname in Hardy's *The Mayor of Casterbridge*.

6. *Phoenix*, pp. 479–80.

7. Mark Kinkead-Weekes, 'The Marble and the Statue: the Exploratory Imagination of D. H. Lawrence', in *Imagined Worlds: Essays in Honour of John Butt*, ed. Maynard Mack and Ian Gregor (London: Methuen, 1968) p. 380.

8. *Phoenix*, p. 415.

9. See Charles L. Ross, *The Composition of The Rainbow and Women in Love* (Charlottesville: University Press of Virginia, 1979) pp. 28–31.

10. D. H. Lawrence, *The Rainbow* (New York: Viking Press, 1968) pp. 1–3.

11. Thomas Hardy, *Tess of the d'Urbervilles*, ch. 24.

12. *Phoenix*, p. 415.

13. *Phoenix*, p. 441.

14. *Phoenix*, pp. 416–17.

15. *Rainbow*, p. 437.

16. D. H. Lawrence, *The Complete Short Stories*, 3 vols (New York: Viking Press, 1967) II, 347.

17. *Phoenix*, p. 419.

18. See Michael Millgate, *Thomas Hardy: a Biography* (New York: Random House, 1982) p. 295.

19. *Tess*, ch. 36.

20. Lawrence, *Letters*, I, 273.

21. *The Letters of D. H. Lawrence*, ed. James T. Boulton (Cambridge: Cambridge University Press, 1979) I, 205.

22. Lawrence, *Letters*, I, 282, 281. My quotations are from Moore's edition of the *Letters*, except in n. 21 where I quote a letter not in Moore.

23. *Phoenix*, pp. 410–11.

24. Thomas Hardy, *Far From the Madding Crowd*, ch. 22.

25. *Tess*, ch. 5.

26. Thomas Hardy, *The Return of the Native*, Book Fourth, ch. 3.

27. *Madding Crowd*, ch. 28.

28. *Tess*, chs 8, 47. These quotations could also be read as signs of class oppression, but the examples are too extreme to support only that reading.

29. *Tess*, chs 10, 28.

30. *Tess*, ch. 30.

31. D. H. Lawrence, *Women in Love* (New York: Viking Press, 1966) ch. 14, p. 162.
32. *Tess*, ch. 57.
33. See, for example, Lascelles Abercrombie's *Thomas Hardy* (New York: Russell & Russell, 1912), the critical book Lawrence asked to borrow along with Hardy's novels when he was planning his book on Hardy. If we 'allegorize the story, then Tess will be the inmost purity of human life, the longing for purity which has its intensest instinct in virginity; and Alec d'Urberville is "the measureless grossness and the slag" which inevitably takes hold of life, however virginal its desires' (p. 149).
34. Thomas Hardy, *Jude the Obscure*, Part Sixth, ch. 6.
35. *Phoenix*, pp. 506, 508–9.
36. *Phoenix*, p. 488.
37. *Tess*, ch. 19.
38. *Phoenix*, pp. 496–7.
39. *Phoenix*, p. 436.
40. *Phoenix*, pp. 439–40, 488–90, 484, 490.
41. *Return of the Native*, Book Fourth, ch. 1.
42. *Phoenix*, p. 420.
43. *Tess*, chs 30, 41.
44. *Women in Love*, ch. 19, p. 238.

Some Surrealist Elements in Hardy's Prose and Verse

Rosemary Sumner

Surrealism has been defused, made harmless. In its debased form, it can be used to give a touch of the wittily bizarre to an advertisement. But surrealism itself was a challenge, an attempt to create a revolution in consciousness, to enlarge our concept of reality, to intensify our ability to see – both the visible and the invisible; the inner world and the unconscious are as 'real' as the known and the seen.

During the fifty years preceding the Surrealist movement, Hardy was making a similar challenge. His theories on art and on the nature of things resemble theirs, his hopes for the development of consciousness are like theirs, his visual images are so close to theirs that often they might almost seem to be a description of their pictures – though they had not yet been painted.

In the *Life*, Hardy said, 'Art is a disproportioning – (i.e. distorting, throwing out of proportion) – of realities, to show more clearly the features that matter in those realities, which if merely copied or reported, inventorially, might possibly be observed, but would more probably be overlooked. Hence, "realism" is not Art.' There is an example of such 'disproportioning' at the beginning of *The Return of the Native*, where the road across the heath is compared to a parting in a head of hair. If we imagine this, the heath becomes a scalp, beneath the scalp a head, beneath the head a vast body stretching down into the earth. The jolt to our normal sense of proportion is similar to the effect of Magritte's apple, filling a room (Plate 1a). Of course, we only get this jolt if we respond fully to the implications of Hardy's image.

Sometimes he spells it out for us, for example, in his treatment of the blood on the ceiling in *Tess*: 'The oblong white ceiling, with

39

the scarlet blot in the midst, had the appearance of a gigantic ace of hearts' (ch. 56). The emphasis on 'the oblong white ceiling' makes us visualize the huge playing card overhead. The 'disproportioning' is a bit unsettling; while there is nothing lurid or sensational about an outsize playing card, blood spreading on the ceiling certainly is sensational and horrifying. I think Hardy is here, as so often, making us respond in diverse, even contradictory ways simultaneously. On the one hand, there is the cool detachment of observing accurately that the ceiling is the shape of a playing card and that the red patch is the same shape and in the same position as the single red heart on a card; and on the other hand, there is the shock-horror of dripping blood and murder. I find that for many people the sensational image is so powerful that it swamps the invitation to detached observation. Perhaps such detachment seems incongruous at such a horrifying moment. However, it is characteristic of Hardy to want to pull us in opposite directions simultaneously, though it is perhaps questionable whether he succeeds on this occasion.

Such images create a sense of uncertainty, of being in a strange, inexplicable world. When Grace is sheltering in Giles' hut, she feels that a bough striking the roof is 'a gigantic hand smiting the mouth of an adversary . . . followed by a trickle of rain, as blood from a wound' (*The Woodlanders*, ch. 41). Here, Grace's disturbed mental state intensifies the effect of human forms grown monstrous or of trees turning into human creatures as in Max Ernst's 'Zoomorphic couple' (Plate 2). This disproportioning can be just as disturbing the other way round. In *Desperate Remedies* Cytherea's father is reduced to the size of a pigeon when she sees him through a window which frames and distances the scene of his fall from the scaffolding to his death. The effect of perspective accounts logically for the reduction in size, but at the same time there is the suggestion of a visual image of a man among the pigeons, in size like one of them. A similar image can enlarge rather than diminish: 'Marty stood encaged amid the mass of twigs like a great bird.' Magritte also fuses the opposites of enlargement and diminution in a single picture. In Magritte's 'Presence of Mind', it is uncertain whether we are looking at a miniature man or a giant bird and fish.

The examples I have given so far might seem to suggest that Hardy and the Surrealists were simply concerned with the bizarre, the unreal. This is not so. Both he and they were seeking a wider notion of what constitutes reality. One way of doing this is by looking with closeness and accuracy at the visible world. Clym furze-cutting is an example of this, and of the merging of the human and the natural which is central to Hardy's work and theirs. By focusing on the minute creeping and flying things Hardy shifts our normal angle of vision and makes us see with unusual vividness and minuteness: 'His familiars were creeping and winged things, and they seemed to enroll him in their band. Bees hummed around his ears with an intimate air . . . tribes of emerald green grasshoppers leaped over his feet, falling on their backs, heads or hips like unskilful acrobats' (*The Return of the Native*, IV, 2). André Masson's 'Summer Frolic' might almost have been painted to illustrate this passage.

Hardy insists that we look. He circumvents our tendency to explain away anything that conflicts with our concept of what is normal by giving us description first; explanation (rationalizing about the experience) may follow – or may not: 'the coffin with its twelve legs crawled across the isle . . . a fishing boat far out in the Channel being momentarily discernible under it' (*The Well-Beloved*, II, 3). This is a description of what is actually seen (rather than what is known to be there). This makes us see each thing afresh, individually, instead of as a known phenomenon; he prevents us from just seeing a coffin carried by six men. This is necessary because, as he said in the preface to *Wessex Tales*, 'our imperfect memories insensibly formalize the fresh originality of living fact – from whose shape they insensibly depart, as machine-made castings depart by degrees from the sharp hand-work of the mould'.

This insistence on accurate looking is highlighted by some of Hardy's own drawings for *Wessex Poems*. The drawing of the pair of spectacles superimposed on the landscape (Plate 3a) gives again the 'disproportioning' effect and also stresses the relationship of the act of seeing to the thing seen. I think Tom Paulin got this wrong in his otherwise interesting and illuminating *Poetry of Perception*: 'What we see are two physical objects – a landscape and a pair of spectacles – which have no apparent or necessary connection with each other and whose relationship is random and gratuitous, like objects in a surrealist picture. His looking at the scene, like his and our general experience of the outer world, has no relation to what he sees and is purely accidental. There is an eerie sense that no objects . . . have any relation to each other or to us . . . the illustration expresses the total lack of relation between object and perceiver.'[1]

There is some misunderstanding here, both about Hardy and about Surrealism. Surrealists do not suggest that 'no objects have any relation to each other', but precisely the opposite of this; they are centrally concerned with relationships between things, and show us things oddly juxtaposed in order to suggest that there are relationships between things which we usually fail to recognize. In 1926 de Chirico wrote: 'Have you ever noticed the singular effect of beds, wardrobes, armchairs, tables, when one suddenly sees them in the streets in the midst of unaccustomed surroundings as happens when one is moving? We then see the furniture grouped on the pavement in a new light, clothed in a strange solitude . . . we can imagine that if a man suddenly seized by panic were to seek asylum in this comity of objects, if he were to sink down in one of these chairs, he might feel immune there from the persecution of gods and men and wild crowds. . . . Furniture in empty spaces, in the midst of nature's infinity, can profoundly move us.'[2] He painted such scenes of furniture in empty landscapes – an interest which Hardy shared of course. His novels are full of carts laden with furniture creaking round the lanes – the Durbeyfields setting up house in the fourposter bed outside the church being perhaps the most striking episode. This is the Durbeyfields at their most insecure, yet the children settle down for the night in their fourposter contentedly enough. Again, contradictory states of mind – disorientation and reassurance – are suggested by the scene, as they are even more sharply in 'During Wind and Rain':

> Clocks and carpets and chairs
>   On the lawn all day,
> And brightest things that are theirs . . .
>   Ah, no; the years, the years;
> Down their carved names the raindrop ploughs.

Hardy usually gives some explanation for these odd juxtapositions, unlike the Surrealists who leave it to our intuition, but he emphasises their oddity; and this is crucial. De Chirico's use of a passage from Schopenhauer is relevant here, especially as he is an author Hardy also took some interest in: 'To have original, extraordinary and perhaps even immortal ideas one has to isolate oneself from the world for a few minutes so completely that the most commonplace happenings appear to be new and unfamiliar and in this way reveal their true essence.' This 'revelation of their true essence' is central to Hardy's conception of his art ('Art is a disproportioning of realities, to show more clearly the features that matter in those realities') and to the Surrealist's aim of achieving 'surrealism'.

So, far from suggesting, as Paulin says, 'an eerie sense that no objects have any relation to each other or to us', these scenes and images heighten and enlarge our sense of possible relationships. Much of Hardy's imagery intensifies our awareness of the relationship between human beings and the natural world. There are thousands of examples of this closeness, of the human and the natural world merging into one another: Giles is seen as 'Autumn's very brother', his face wheat-colour, his eyes cornflowers, his hands clammy with apples, his hat covered with apple pips, a portrait which is very similar to Penrose's 'Portrait of Valentine', with eyes made of butterflies and birds mingling with her hair.

Of course, such perceptions can be terrifying. Hardy said 'Apprehension is a great element in the imagination ... a semi-madness which sees enemies etc. in inanimate objects', and many of his descriptions are as macabre as Max Ernst's 'La Joie de Vivre' (Plate 1b) and his other woodland scenes, which seem almost designed to illustrate *The Woodlanders*:

> roots whose mossed rinds made them like hands wearing green gloves ... huge lobes of fungi grew like lungs ... the smooth surface of glossy plants came out like weak lidless eyes ... and peeps of sky between the trunks were like sheeted shapes and on the tips of boughs sat faint cloven tongues (chs 7, 40).

Ernst's painting even has the hands in green gloves and hints of leaves like weak lidless eyes, though he has nothing as macabre as 'rotting stumps rising from their setting like black teeth from green gums' (ch. 42). Like Hardy, Ernst recognized the part played by fear and 'semi-madness' in stimulating the imagination. In *Hardy and the Sister Arts*, Joan Grundy says that 'we seem to be in the surrealist world of Max Ernst. In fact, we are probably in the world of Max Ernst's ancestor, Grunewald'.[3] But there is no reason why we cannot place him in both worlds. Breton pointed out the close affinity of Surrealism with medieval art, an affinity lost through later over-dominance of the intellect; thus gargoyles and other early or primitive forms of art were of great interest to the Surrealists as they were to Hardy. Writing of the gargoyle in *Far From the Madding Crowd*, he says, 'there is no truer criterion of the vitality of any given art-period than the power of the master-spirits of that time in grotesque', and he goes on to speak of gargoyles 'of the most original design that a human brain could conceive' and of 'symmetry in their distortion' (ch. 46). His recognition of the value of the primitive in art is highlighted in the *Life* (p. 230), where he quotes Clodd: 'the persistence of the barbaric idea which confuses persons and things', and then punctures this by adding in parenthesis, 'this "barbaric idea" is, by the way, also common to the highest imaginative genius – the poet'. This view is the essence, too, of Ernst's art, which, says Nicolas Calas, 'gives life that powerful animistic interpretation where plans and human beings, insects, birds and fishes are found in everchanging appearances of existence as opposed to the death-like rigidity of pure abstraction'.[4]

This 'confusion of persons and things' is not restricted to things in nature, though this tends to predominate in Hardy, while the Surrealists focused as much on man-made objects and machinery. But Hardy, too, shows how things of this kind and people merge into one another; for instance, in *Far From the Madding Crowd*, where Gabriel 'stared at one lengthy and two round faces, which confronted him with the expressions of a fiddle and a couple of warming-pans' (ch. 46). Here there is the same kind of merger as Picasso made between human beings and musical instruments in his 'Three Musicians' or his 'Man with a Guitar'. Hardy says he almost always noticed 'such bizarre effects' as the view in Paris of the cemetery behind the heads of the can-can dancers, or a scene in church:

> The red plumes and ribbons of the two stylish girls' hats in the foreground match the red roses of the persons round Christ on the Cross in the east window. The pale crucified figure rises from a parterre of London bonnets and artificial hair-coils, as viewed from the back where I am . . . the congregation rises . . . every woman has a single thought – to the folds of her clothes. They pray the litany as if under enchantment. Their real life is

spinning on beneath this apparent one of calm, like the District
Railway trains underground just by – throbbing, rushing, hot
. . . (*Life*, p. 209)

I suppose can-can dancers seen in juxtaposition to a cemetery,
or even a fashionable congregation in juxtaposition with the
Crucifixion, could be said to have something intrinsically bizarre
about them. But, looked at with really open eyes, even the most
everyday occurrences take on this bizarre quality: 'The door
opened and three-quarters of the blooming young schoolmis-
tress's face and figure stood revealed before him: a slice on her
left-hand side being cut off by the edge of the door' (*Under The
Greenwood Tree*, I, 9). The language here is interesting. Though I
agree with Joan Grundy that there is an echo of contemporary
Victorian paintings of girls leaning flirtatiously round doorways,
I think the language points forward to a Surrealist way of looking
at the scene. The words 'slice' and 'cut off' suggest both a
mathematical exactitude and an actual slicing of the body. The
oddness of seeing people like this obviously made a deep
impression on Hardy; his curious sketch in *Wessex Poems* of the
coffin being carried downstairs, with the heads and feet of the
bearers cut off because of the angle from which the scene is
observed, has the same sort of disconcerting effect (Plate 3b).
Even more surpisingly, André Breton reacted to this kind of
experience in a similar way. In the First Surrealist Manifesto he
tells how the phrase 'There is a man cut in two by a window' kept
impinging on his consciousness and led to his recognition of the
importance of allowing elements from the unconscious to emerge
into art. And this can happen as a result of really looking, using
one's eyes.

This is why Hardy's books, like Surrealist art, are full of eyes.
Ernst's drawings of stones containing a single eye (Plate 4a) are
reminiscent of the trilobite in *A Pair of Blue Eyes* whose stone eyes
regard Knight as he hangs on the cliff; both suggest that the
human, the animal and the inanimate are not as differentiated as
we usually think. Also they both create the feeling of being
watched by inanimate objects. The two sovereigns left by the
hairdresser for Marty's hair are jaundiced eyes staring at her,
trees have inquisitive eyes, human glances can be like slaps to
Jude, and Tess feels even her back is 'endowed with sensitiveness
to ocular beams'. One would feel the same running the gauntlet of

Ernst's avenue of eyes (his Third Visible Poem, no. 2) (Plate 4b).

Conversely, the vulnerability of the eye figures conspicuously in these works. Perhaps the best-known Surrealist example is the eye-cutting scene in Bunuel's *Un Chien Andalou*. Magritte and Brauner painted portraits with damaged, bleeding eyes. This combination of blood and eyes fascinated Hardy too. In *The Mayor of Casterbridge* the setting sun is like a drop of blood on an eyelid, and in *Far From the Madding Crowd* the seal on the Valentine is a blot of blood on the retina of his eye to Boldwood. Elsewhere, the bonfires on Egdon Heath first look like wounds in a black hide and then like eyes. The precariousness of seeing is also suggested when Grace, lost in the woods, feels 'the darkness intense, seeming to touch her pupils like a substance'; a pool is like the white of an eye without its pupil; in *Far From the Madding Crowd*, in the fog, the air is 'an eye struck blind'. In these instances, there is almost a feeling that the thing observed is touching the pupil and that there is barely any distinction between the eye and the thing it looks at, as for instance, in Magritte's painting of an eye socket entirely filled with blue sky and clouds.

It is not surprising to find Hardy and the Surrealists obsessed with eyes since their whole emphasis is on seeing, but not, of course, merely on what is visible; 'an observative response to everything within the cycle of the suns' is essential, but this includes 'what cannot be discerned by eye and ear, what may be apprehended only by the mental tactility that comes from a sympathetic appreciativeness of life in all its manifestations'.[5] Though they are dealing with 'what cannot be discerned by eye and ear', the function of their art is to render such things in visual terms: 'My art is to intensify the expression of things, as is done by Crivelli, Bellini, etc., so that the heart and inner meaning is made vividly visible' (*Life*, p. 177). In spite of the reference to Crivelli and Bellini, the painter Hardy felt the greatest affinity with was 'the mad late-Turner', and a year after his statement, in 1887, he clarified his point: 'I don't want to see landscapes, *i.e.*, scenic paintings of them, because I don't want to see the original realities – as optical effects, that is. I want to see the deeper reality underlying the scenic. . . . The 'simply natural' is interesting no longer. The . . . mad, late-Turner rendering is now necessary to create my interest' (*Life*, p. 185). Hardy states this point again in an astonishing passage in *The Woodlanders* (which he was finishing at this time). It is a description of Mr Melbury in a state of acute anxiety: 'Could the real have been beheld instead of the corporeal merely, the corner of the room in which he sat would have been filled with a form typical of anxious suspense, large-eyed, tight-lipped, awaiting the issue' (*The Woodlanders*, ch. 23). The 'real . . . instead of the corporeal merely' is precisely what Surrealist art aims to show; as Herbert Read said, a better translation of the word would have been 'superrealism'. Nearly twenty years after this praise of 'the mad, late-Turner', Hardy compared him to Wagner, whose music gives a 'spectacle of the inside of a brain at work like the inside of a hive' (*Life*, p. 329). In the interval, his fiction had moved more and more away from the outer world towards exploring the inner subconscious and unconscious world, a world which is 'real' rather than 'merely corporeal'. The central issue for the Surrealists was the redefinition of reality so as to include both the conscious and the subconscious. Breton wrote: 'I believe in the future resolution of these two states which are dreams and reality, in a kind of absolute reality, surreality one might call it',[6] and Ernst, almost echoing Hardy's comment on Wagner, spoke of 'exploring uncharted depths of reality, tapping life's most secret sources . . . the painter gives form to what is visible inside him'.[7]

Breton suggests that Surrealism involves the whole sensibility – dreams, erotic experiences, the shiver felt in front of some mysterious types of beauty, moments when normality is shaken by something 'other', as in the loss of control in panic. The surrealists used the word 'convulsive' for this kind of experience. Hardy uses the same word for what happens to Carline in 'The Fiddler of the Reels'; the combination of the aesthetic (her response to the music), the erotic (her attraction to Mop), and her loss of control (in the compulsive dancing) corresponds precisely to what Breton meant by 'convulsive'. Anything which defies the established order is likely to be fruitful for the artist. The Surrealists collected newspaper cuttings about criminals, just as Hardy did. They felt that these defiers of the established order might be as significant for the artists as the erotic or madness because they create a disturbance which overwhelms reason. Like Hardy, they felt that the mind could be open to all possibilities, however strange, and it was this enlargement that they sought, not just as an aesthetic experience for themselves, but as something possible and valuable for all humanity. Magritte said: 'I make a point as far as possible of painting only pictures that evoke the mystery of all existence . . . images of everyday objects combined and transformed in such a way that their agreement with our preconceived ideas, simple or sophisticated, is obliterated.'[8] Similarly, Duchamp's ready-mades were meant to disturb the sense of reality and give a glimpse of the marvellous. Again, Hardy sees this quality in Turner: '[Turner] said in his maddest and greatest days: "What pictorial drug can I dose man with, which shall affect his eyes somewhat in the manner of this reality which I cannot carry to him?"' (*Life*, p. 216). Always the stress is simultaneously on the reality of what the artist perceives and on its difference from what is commonly regarded as normal.

The Surrealists saw chance as lying behind these moments when normality is shaken by something 'other'. As Hardy put it: 'A perception of the FAILURE of THINGS to be what they are meant to be, lends them, in place of the intended interest, a new and greater interest of an unintended kind' (*Life*, p. 124). Similarly, he explains the value of the 'unforeseen' in 'metre that infringes all the rules'. Perhaps this throws some light on the much discussed subject of his use of chance and coincidence in the novels. It has in the past been a common criticism that he overuses chance as a plot device and as a way of closing down all options for his characters, though this charge has been less frequently made since Roy Morrell's *Thomas Hardy: the Will and the Way* (1965). In fact, the chance occurrence is frequently used to highlight the possibilities open to the characters. Tess's 'too ready acquiescence in chance' when the letter slips under the mat and Troy's giving up because 'Providence is jeering at him' when the rain ruins the flowers on Fanny's grave are examples of characters using chance as an excuse for closing their minds to possible options. They are often balanced between alternatives 'so finely a feather would turn them', like Angel on the point of departure for Brazil. They have the opportuniy to rethink their concept of reality, just as the surrealist image with its 'delicate hesitation between opposites' (Breton) enlarges our perception of possibilities. The chance meeting with the cosmopolitan traveller is Hardy's way of making the external world, with its multiplicity of attitudes and cultures, eventually impinge on Angel.

Chance was used by the Surrealists as a way of gaining access to the unconscious. Found objects, ready-mades and 'frottage' are used to 'irritate' the vision and so allow chance to provoke inspiration. Ernst found that what seemed to come from outside

corresponded to his inner self. Hardy gives a perfect example of
this in his poem 'The Abbey Mason', where the mediaeval mason
is struggling to invent the Perpendicular style; he needs new forms
to solve the technical problem of making the transition from the
columns to the new, high, pointed arch, but is unable to think how
to do it. For weeks he struggles, until one day the board on which
has been despairingly drawing diagrams is left out in the
freezing rain. He is just about to clean it when

> He closelier looked; then looked again;
> The chalk-scratched draught-board faced the rain,
>
> Whose icicled drops deformed the lines
> Innumerous of his lame designs,
>
> So that they streamed in small white threads
> From the upper segments to the heads
>
> Of arcs below, uniting them
> Each by a stalactitic stem.
>
> – At once, with eyes that struck out sparks,
> He adds accessory cusping-marks,
>
> Then laughs aloud. The thing was done
> So long assayed from sun to sun . . .

The mason has used the patterns created by nature in exactly the
same way as Ernst did when he made frottages, taking a rubbing
of a rough surface and then 'venturing to acclimate the phantom'
(Aragon) by adding a pencil line or a little colour. But the mason's
troubles are not over, for the abbot saw his moment of inspiration
and its source, and watches him suspiciously as his fame grows,
till the mason begins to feel guilty and decides to make public the
way he got his idea. Then ensues the kind of debate which
followed the exhibition of Duchamp's ready-mades and, in our
own time, the Carl André bricks at the Tate Gallery. Hardy shows
the townspeople accepting his method –

> "'Tis your own doing, even with that!'

but they defer to the abbot's view that

> '. . . the devices seemed so great
> You copied, and did not create.'

Only after sixty years does a later abbot recognize that

> 'He did but what all artists do,
> Wait upon Nature for his cue.'

Though such methods are often regarded as a freakish modern development, the 'mad, late-Turner' Hardy so much admired used a similar method: he 'began by pouring wet paint on to paper till it was saturated. Then he tore, he scratched, he scrubbed at it in a kind of frenzy, and the whole thing was chaos – but gradually and as if by magic the lovely ship with all its exquisite minutiae came into being'.[9] Writers, too, from Dada onwards have used similar devices to give access to the unconscious. Schwitters used scraps of old newspapers from dustbins as starting-points, others use cut-up techniques or words picked out at random from a text and then edit their fragmentary raw material. This sounds utterly remote from Hardy's kind of writing, yet Millgate describes how he

> worked through a passage from the Old Testament or the Book of Common Prayer, picking up particular words and using them in modified grammatical forms and totally different contexts, evidently with the objective of developing and exercising a literary vocabulary of his own, generating new expressive phrases from the impulsion of great models of the past or even evolving the outline of a possible poem. Years later Hardy was to tell his second wife that the best way to find a starting point for a piece of writing was to go to some work by a major writer – Carlyle, for instance – and read at random until one came across an image or idea that stimulated one's own inventiveness.[10]

I think Millgate is right to emphasize that it was inspiration that Hardy was seeking, rather than self-education through imitation. The use of extracted phrases in different contexts and especially the 'reading at random' as a stimulus to 'one's own inventiveness' indicate that Hardy was interested in the possibilities of 'writing by chance', in much the same way that Ernst in painting and Schwitters in writing worked to let chance into their art. The random element allows unforeseen connections, not perceived by the logical mind, but emerging from the unconscious, to play a part in the shaping of a work of art.

Herbert Read tells a story similar to that of 'The Abbey Mason':

> Salvador Dali relates how a splash of paint on his palette had assumed *unknown to his conscious mind* the shape of a distorted skull which he had consciously and vainly been trying to discover.[11]

Read sees this as evidence of 'the superreality, the something-more-than-conscious naturalism, which encompasses all our actions'. Hardy puts it in different terms but, I think, implies a similar view: 'My own interest lies largely in non-rationalistic subjects, since non-rationality seems . . . to be the principle of the Universe' (*Life*, p. 309). However, a non-rationalistic universe does not imply chaos. For the Surrealists the interrelationship of all things was central, underlying the images they produced. Breton felt that man has difficulty in perceiving his relationship to the sensory world and especially to 'other creatures whose desires and sufferings he is less and less capable of appreciating the further down he goes on the scale he has constructed . . . the most effective means he has of doing this is the poetic intuition'.[12] The connection with Hardy is obvious. This poetic institution is one of the most distinctive qualities of his imagination. It is shown in his concern about animals and plants and in his ability to see, for instance, the Battle of Waterloo from the point of view of a worm. He not only connects but identifies the natural world with the human: 'In spite of myself I cannot help noticing countenances and tempers in objects of scenery, *e.g.* trees, hills, houses' (*Life*, p. 285). As Eluard said: 'It is not far – through the bird – from the cloud to the man; it is not far – through the images – from the man to his vision . . . everything is transmutable into something else.'[13] Hardy said the same in more abstract terms: '. . . all things merge in one another – good into evil, generosity into justice, religion into politics, the year into the ages, the world into the universe' (*Life*, p. 111).

To compare Hardy to the Surrealists is not to make very special or extraordinary claims for him, but merely to draw attention to one of the many ways in which his outlook and methods are modern. All writers of any significance are bound to be indebted both to their predecessors and to be exploring new possibilities, some of which may be developed, knowingly or not, by their successors. To call Hardy's 'idiosyncratic mode of regard' surrealist puts some of his ways of seeing and techniques of writing in a new light, and emphasizes his position among the innovators of the last hundred years. Norman Page has suggested that Hardy's 'pictorialism' as a method of telling a story 'shows marked originality and individuality';[14] recognition of the surrealist element in this 'pictorialism' adds an extra dimension of modernity. Hardy's acceptance of chance as a stimulus to the imagination extends the implications of his phrase 'a series of seemings'. When he said that 'Unadjusted impressions have their value, and the road to a true philosophy of life seems to lie in humbly recording diverse readings of its phenomena as they are forced upon us by chance and change',[15] he was repeating his point that his work does not express a coherent philosophy, in a way which reinforces the sense of his openness to experience, of his willingness to see things in a new light, to accept impressions without 'adjusting' them to some preconceived norm. An accident gives Knight a glimpse of a 'white border to a black sea' which in other circumstances would have been 'a deep neutral blue'. Alertness to the unforeseen, to the thing not seen before, enables Hardy to see tree stumps as black teeth in green gums and Christian's 'painfully circular eyes' as 'surrounded by concentric lines like targets'. Joan Grundy says, 'No one's eyes ever *really* looked like that.'[16] It depends what you mean by 'really'. By associating this kind of image with caricature she highlights one aspect of it. but I think it also has another kind of reality. If you insist on adjusting your impression to a standard, preconceived eye, then you will probably reject as 'unreal' anything that deviates too far from this norm. Intense looking can bring out things unobserved before, and the artist's 'disproportioning' enables others to see this too.

The similarity of the visual element in Hardy's writing to surrealist painting is an indication of the innovations he made in order to express 'ideas and emotions which run counter to the inert crystallised opinion – hard as a rock – which the vast body of men have vested interests in supporting' (*Life*, p. 284). He was fully aware that innovation in ideas and emotions required innovations in treatment, for 'treatment depends on the mental attitude of the novelist, thus entering into the very substance of the narrative . . . a writer who is not a mere imitator looks upon the world with his personal eyes and in his peculiar moods'.[17] It is entirely appropriate that his claim to be an innovator is based on his way of looking.

NOTES

1. Tom Paulin, *The Poetry of Perception* (London: Macmillan, 1976) p. 24.
2. Quoted by R. H. Wilenski, *Modern French Painters* (London: Faber & Faber, 1945) p. 274.
3. Joan Grundy, *Hardy and the Sister Arts* (London: Macmillan, 1979) p. 57.
4. In Max Ernst, *Beyond Painting and Other Writings by the Artist and his Friends* (New York: Wittenborn, Shultz, 1948) p. 193.
5. 'The Science of Fiction', reprinted in *Thomas Hardy's Personal Writings*, ed. Harold Orel (London: Macmillan, 1967) p. 136.
6. André Breton, 'First Surrealist Manifesto', in *Manifestoes of Surrealism*, trans. Seaver and Lane (Ann Arbor: University of Michigan Press, 1972).
7. Ernst, op. cit., p. 20.
8. Quoted in P. Waldberg, *Surrealism*, trans. Stuart Gilbert (New York: Skira, 1962).
9. Alan Burns, 'Writing by Chance' *Times Higher Educational Supplement*, 29 January 1982.
10. Michael Millgate, *Thomas Hardy: A Biography* (London: OUP, 1982) p. 188.
11. Herbert Read, *The Philosophy of Modern Art* (London: Faber & Faber, 1964) p. 137.
12. Breton, 'On Surrealism in its Living Works', op. cit., p. 304.
13. Ernst, op. cit., p. 191.
14. Norman Page, *Thomas Hardy* (London: Routledge & Kegan Paul, 1977) p. 64.
15. Preface to *Poems of the Past and the Present* (1901).
16. Grundy, op. cit., p. 49.
17. 'The Profitable Reading of Fiction', in Orel, op. cit., p. 122.

Tess and Saint Tryphena: Two Pure Women Faithfully Presented

Michael Rabiger

Thomas Hardy grew up in the busy, practical atmosphere of the country builder's business his father had inherited. All around him, his relatives worked in wood, brick, stone, mortar and plaster. Sometimes they were commissioned to put up new buildings, but more often they adapted and renovated the fabric of an old one to serve contemporary needs. The Hardys were also a family of story-tellers and musicians, father and son playing their fiddles side by side at country dances and local festivals, sometimes for hours on end. Not surprisingly, Hardy later found it natural to improvise, to adapt, and to generate variations in his own work, both as an architect's assistant and afterwards as a writer. In both prose and poetry, Hardy was drawn to refashioning established materials, and found a particular satisfaction in forging links between the present and an imaginatively heightened past. Some of Hardy's novels appear to have in their genesis two elements which seem to have been indispensable to fire his imagination. One was an artwork from earlier times, and this could be a work of literature, a genre of painting, or a theatrical model. The other element was a cast of actors drawn from Hardy's private emotional life who could energize the roles in a personally significant way. The preference in both cases reflects not only a willingness to extend established forms with the aid of 'real' people, but also the same uncertainty of confidence which led him to rely so heavily on notes, quotations and newspaper stories in his fiction.

Composing from these seminal materials – a 'text' and actors – he evolved re-enactments of the original work on paper in progressively modifying forms. The process, so far as it can be reconstructed, is akin to that of some modern theatre and film directors. Nowhere is this more apparent than in *Tess of the d'Urbervilles*, the heroine of which proves to have a twin sister in a Celtic folk-play. A comparison between the two seems to shed new light on Hardy's mood, intentions and creative process during the composition of this novel.

Hardy's special interest in traditional theatre, and theatrical heroines in particular, lasted throughout his very long life. He had made Eustacia Vye the only female performer in *The Play of Saint George*, the play for mummers used in *The Return of the Native*. In his only stage-play, written forty-five years later, *The Famous Tragedy of the Queen of Cornwall*, he reversed the Tristram and Iseult legend to focus the tragedy upon Iseult instead of Tristram. Theatrical form is deeply embedded in Hardy's dramatic vision, and Michael Millgate has pointed out how readily Hardy's works adapt to the stage, so influenced were they by Shakespeare, the Jacobeans, the Greeks and Ibsen: 'It is to the drama that one must often look for the models and techiques, even the terminology, most appropriate to the discussion of particular aspects of Hardy's fiction, and he himself repeatedly defines his aims and achievements in images from the theatre.'[1]

Sometimes the different and distinctive forms that Hardy employed for each new novel came directly from theatrical models. *The Return of the Native* adapts the structure and tone of Greek tragedy to humble Dorset life, while *The Trumpet-Major*, Hardy's foray into historical fiction, has been shown to follow the old theatrical form of the harlequinade, itself derived from the Italian Comedy of Masks.[2] In addition to direct theatrical models (to which I shall return later in reference to *Tess*), Hardy also brought his theatrical sensibility to art and literary genres, which are sometimes identifiable as particular works. *Desperate Remedies* shows the influence of both Wilkie Collins' *Woman in White*[3] and Harrison Ainsworth's *Old Saint Paul's*.[4] *Under the Greenwood Tree*, which Hardy subtitled 'A Rural Painting of the Dutch School', was probably conceived as a series of narrative word-paintings or tableaux to memorialize the vanishing world of Hardy's childhood.

Four other novels can be divided into two pairs, each pair showing the influence of a particular literary work. The first is *A Pair of Blue Eyes* and *Far From the Madding Crowd*, the second *Tess of the d'Urbervilles* and *Jude the Obscure*. The latter pair is also thematically linked to Hardy's play *The Queen of Cornwall*, although separated, unlike the composing of the two pairs of novels, by many intervening years. A brief examination of the early pair, and of the circumstances in which they were composed, is, I believe, a necessary guide to Hardy's writing processes.

A Pair of Blue Eyes (1873) was written while Hardy was courting Emma Lavinia Gifford, and draws heavily upon the scenery and events encountered while visiting her in Cornwall. Desmond Hawkins has noticed the novel's indebtedness to Jane Austen's *Emma*,[5] and it seems that in affectionate tribute to the far-off woman preoccupying his thoughts, Hardy took some of the names, characters and central relationships from *Emma* already paralleled in his own life, and refashioned them, assigning their roles to the friends and family who made up his constellation of close personal influences. In modern drama compositon, this is like a stage or theatre director taking a work, or themes from a work, and casting influential actors in the main roles. By encouraging the initiative of his players, by shaping and editing improvisatory extensions, he merges the actors' personalities and life experience into the thematic framework of the original text. It is an actor-centred process which Bergman, Fellini and Godard have all drawn upon during their careers. To some degree, all stage or screen drama evolves like this, as a collaborative whole greater than the sum of its parts. Of course, Hardy predates these developments in the theatre and cinema, but he must have been well aware that all works of folk-tale, folk-drama and folk-music owe their evolution to the informal workings of a similar process.

For *A Pair of Blue Eyes* Hardy took as quarry only four of Austen's six main characters: Emma, Mr Woodhouse, Mr Knightley, and Harriet Smith. In *Blue Eyes* they appear as Elfride, her father, Henry Knight and Stephen Smith. Elfride, the new Emma Woodhouse, has Emma Gifford's horse-riding skill, her romantic Cornish setting and her aspirations to be a writer. Parson Swancourt, the new Mr Woodhouse, is a composite of Emma's own father and her parson brother-in-law. Henry Knight, the new Mr Knightley, is endowed with many of the characteristics of Hardy's friend and mentor, the reviewer Horace Moule. The socially ambitious and naïve Harriet Smith of Austen's novel is transposed into a lowly born young architect, Stephen Smith, suggesting Hardy himself. Written in as the architect's parents are a stonemason father and a house-servant mother who unmistakably reflect Hardy's own parents. There is nothing unusual about a novelist deriving characters from life models, but a compositional procedure using familiar figures to re-animate existing literary roles is less common. Understandably, many of Hardy's personal preoccupations and anxieties seem reflected in the novel: about writing and a lack of originality, about a rival for Emma Gifford's affections arising in his absence, and about his sense of intellctual and social inferiority among those he most admired. Indeed, the book reads at times like a fictionalized confession, and was perhaps written partly with this intention, so that Emma Gifford, separated by a hundred miles during most of their courtship, should more thoroughly know him.

Significantly, I think, all the main characters in *Blue Eyes* struggle with different forms of inferiority, one aspect of which is the knowledge of their own lack of originality. Hardy's characterization of Stephen Smith must, I believe, be taken autobiographically:

His brain had extraordinary receptive powers, and no great creativeness. Quickly acquiring any kind of knowledge he saw around him, and having a plastic adaptability more common in woman than in man, he changed colour like a chameleon as the society he found himself in assumed a higher and more artifical tone. He had not many original ideas, and yet there was scarcely an idea to which, under proper training, he could not have added a respectable co-ordinate. (ch. 10)

If Hardy did indeed see himself more as an adapter than as an innovator while writing *Blue Eyes*, it seems not to have deterred him from using the same method and even the same quarry in the development of his next and much more successful novel, *Far From the Madding Crowd*. Here he incorporates characters and situations from *Emma* overlooked in *Blue Eyes*; specifically, Frank Churchill and his concealed liaison with Jane Fairfax (Frank Troy and Fanny Robin), their relationship toward Emma Woodhouse (Troy's and Fanny's toward Bathsheba), and Farmer Martin's patient and ultimately rewarded love for the socially aspiring Harriet Smith (Farmer Oak's for Bathsheba). Hardy's earlier triangle of fickle woman courted by *déclassé* younger man and a socially assured but sexually repressed older man is again present, though with the intrusion of a sexually adept and aggressive third contender, Sergeant Troy. Relationships alone are a fragile argument for an indebtedness, but Hardy appears to tacitly acknowledge Austen's influence in his choice of names: Weatherbury (Highbury), Norcombe (Enscombe) and Francis Troy, called Frank (Frank Churchill).

The characters in *Far From the Madding Crowd* have transcended the literalness of any models drawn from life or literature, as in all Hardy's more successful work. Nevertheless there are glimpses of the originals to be found in Puddletown records. Gabriel Meech, a woodman and later gamekeeper, suggests Gabriel Oak; Harriet Robins, who gave birth to an illegitimate daughter when Hardy was at the impressionable age of fifteen,[6] suggests Fanny Robin. For Bathsheba there is Hardy's energetic and attractive Puddletown cousin, Tryphena Sparks, who maintained a long friendship with a bailiff and his wife employed by Catharine Hawkins of Waddon Vale. Mrs Hawkins was an enterprising widow who took over her husband's farm and managed it herself, like Bathsheba Everdene.[7] Bathsheba's father's career matches that of Tryphena's grandfather Sparks, a venturesome Dorchester outfitter.[8]

This emerging pattern, in which Hardy develops the cross-fertilizing potential of a text, a chosen cast, and reinterpretive aims, is again visible in the second pair of novels, *Tess* and *Jude*. Thematically the emphasis is now upon marriage, and upon the stresses suffered by the individual in a society with inflexible moral attitudes towards liaisons contracted unwisely or involuntarily. Where *Blue Eyes* and *Madding Crowd* deal with sexual selection and courtship, *Tess* and *Jude* lament the unfulfillability of marriage itself. Again an autobiographical backdrop is suggested; during the composition of the first pair Hardy was approaching his own marriage, and by the later pair he and Emma had weathered two decades of less than satisfactory marriage. Influential upon both *Tess* and *Jude* is the classic tale of unhappy marriage and unfulfillable adulterous love, the legend of Tristram and Iseult. Eventually Hardy openly made Iseult the central figure in his play *The Queen of Cornwall* (1923), but the lovers' insoluble plight was fuelling his imagination while he wrote *Tess* in the late 1880s. S. L. Clark and Julian N. Wasserman in their essay 'Tess and Iseult'[9] point out the large number of medieval references in the novel, and show that Angel wavering between Izz Huett and Tess as he leaves for Brazil resembles Tristram wavering between his two Iseults – the one he loves, and the one to whom he is married – as he prepares to leave for foreign shores. The authors also show the obvious relatedness of Hardy's 'Izz Huett' to the name Iseult. Hardy's choice of names almost always signifies special qualities or derivation, so one may go a step further than Clark and Wasserman to wonder if Angel's 'Tessy' is but an inverted form of the Iseult variants (Isolde/Iseult/Isot . . . Ysset). Thus Izz and Tess represent the two Iseults. One may notice too that Tess and her three dairymaid friends are reminiscent of Malory's La Beule Iseult and her 'three damosels'.[10]

The essay further shows that Tess's baby Sorrow is named after Tristram himself, whose mother died at birth leaving him sorrowful (*triste*/Tristram). Hardy, the authors argue, has inverted this situation by making Sorrow die and his mother live on. They also show that Angel and Tess's flight together, and their days of shared bliss at Bramhurst Manor-House, are paralleled in Gottfried Von Strassburg's *Tristan*. King Mark finding the sleeping lovers, the ray of light falling on their faces, and other details make it unlikely that Hardy was not following Gottfried's episode closely. Also true to the tradition of Tristan as a 'harper' is Hardy's use of Angel's harp-playing to sway Tess's heart in the garden at Talbothays. There are further similarities not noticed in the essay; Tristan's foster parents have the same reputation for faith and generosity as Angel's (Rual le Foitenant, *foi-tenant* or holder of faith), and Tristan has Angel's contradictory feelings towards them. Angel and Tess's walks toegether in the dewy mornings are suggested by Gottfried's chapter 'The Cave of Lovers' when Tristan and Iseult are alone together for the first time.[11]

Turning now to *Jude*, we see a similar pattern in which the influence of *Tristan* is still alive in the way that of *Emma* was in *Madding Crowd*. The constant journeying of Tristan, his position as an orphan, his adulterous love of Iseult, her marriage to Tristan's patron, Tristan's own impulsive and doomed marriage, the corrosive guilt and pity the young couple feel towards the blameless King Mark, and the slow ruin the situation brings to the unhappy participants are all mirrored in *Jude*. Phillotson's pained recognition of Jude and Sue's unique love, his acceptance that it qualifies them to belong together, and his magnanimous release of Sue are strikingly similar to that of King Mark's action in Gottfried's *Tristan*:

> since I can read it in the pair of you that, in defiance of my will, you love and have loved each other more than me, then be with one another as you please – do not hold back from any fear of me! Since your love is so great, from this hour I shall not vex or molest you in any of your concerns. Take each other by the hand and leave my court and country.[12]

This situation, viewed from the displaced husband's point of view, is also to be found in Hardy's poem 'The Burghers' which may have been a way-station in the development of *Jude*. In the novel Phillotson writes to Sue, '"You may go – with whom you will. I absolutely and unconditionally agree."' Later he confides to Gillingham: '"I would have died for her; but I wouldn't be cruel to her in the name of the law. She is, as I understand, gone to join her lover. What they are going to do I cannot say. Whatever it may be she has my full consent to"' (IV, 4).

Twenty years after the publication of *Jude*, Hardy returned to the Tristan and Iseult theme and began *The Queen of Cornwall*, which he finished after some delays in 1923. The title page says that it is 'arranged as a play for mummers in one act requiring no theatre or scenery'. Of this play and of *Tess*, Clark and Wasserman say, 'especially striking is the similarity in the treatment and the sameness of situation of the tragic heroines of the respective works, for, in a radical departure from tradition, Hardy sees the story of the medieval lovers as the tragedy of Iseult, just as he sees the events of his novel as the tragedy of Tess and not the tragedy of Tess *and* Angel'.

However, a tradition does exist in which the tragic heroine is foremost, exhibiting the same fortitude and suffering as Hardy's Tess, and as his Iseult later. An obscure mystery play, on the fringes of Arthurian tradition, tells the story of a beautiful and moral young married woman called Queen Tryphena. Her marriage and good name are slowly destroyed by innuendo, and she ends up estranged from her good but credulous husband, imprisoned by him for adultery and infanticide, and facing execution on the gallows. It, too, is a piece of drama designed for production without 'theatre or scenery', and like *The Play of St*

George was kept alive by country people for their own entertainment and moral instruction. The play was available to Hardy and was, in my opinion, especially attractive to him for both thematic and personal reasons.

The mystery play is the life story of the Breton Saint Tryphena. It was pieced together and translated from Breton into modern French by the scholar François-Marie Luzel at a time of resurgent interest in Breton culture and published in 1863 as *Sainte Tryphine et le roi Arthur*.[13] Apparently of Arthurian derivation, it too sets out to define 'a pure woman' like Hardy's *Tess*. As one compares the novel to this folk-play about a beautiful woman's journey through martyrdom to sainthood, some fascinating compositional patterns emerge. For one thing it is clear that Hardy is also writing a morality play and stays close to *St. Tryphena*'s tradititional form. More interesting than similarities, though, is the consistency with which he departs from or even subverts the tradition's purpose. To fully appreciate this, it is necessary to examine the mystery play's content.

In essence, the play concentrates on the victimization of a beautiful and devout Irish princess, Tryphena, who marries the Breton King Arthur. Her brother Kervoura, secretly jealous that she has a crown and he does not, finds that he may be able to get the crown of England if he can cure the English king's leprosy. In what is only the first of a series of meetings with witches and demons, he enters into a pact with the powers of darkness. He receives a spell to cure the king which requires the roasted flesh of a first-born baby prince. Kervoura decoys Arthur abroad so that in the meantime he can take his pregnant and fearful sister to a specially prepared 'palace' recently built for him by two co-opted builders. Here, while she is in the delirium of labour, he abducts her firstborn, telling her afterwards that it was a false pregnancy and that no baby was born. The baby prince and his accompanying nurse are subsequently caught in a storm at sea and vanish. Hearing that his plans have misfired, Kervoura is furious, and this heightens the concealed malignancy he harbours for his sister. On King Arthur's return, the unsuspecting Tryphena is slandered by her brother, who confidentially persuades the King that she killed her baby because she does not love her husband. Forewarned of Arthur's anger, Queen Tryphena disguises herself as a servant and sets off into the night. During her flight she prays at a wayside cross, falling beside it in fatigue. Waking, she travels onward until she arrives at a church, where she falls asleep insensible with weariness.

The next day she is discovered and awakened by a duchess, who offers her work as a domestic. In her new job, however, Tryphena is persecuted for her ineptness with a broom by the housekeeper, who naturally is unaware that the new servant is really a queen. Tryphena is turned out of doors to mind turkeys and pigs, and the pigman, equally unaware of her nobility and married state, declares his attraction to her and tries to kiss her. For several years she uncomplainingly endures the toil of farmwork, eventually rising to the position of companion to the duchess. At this point she is discovered by one of her husband's courtiers who is travelling through, and is persuaded to relinquish her fears and rejoin her bereft husband. They spend a joyous year of reunion during which a daughter is born. But Kervoura, away from court at this time, sends a letter which reiterates Tryphena's immorality, and to prove it, he soon sets a trap for her in an orchard, where she is seen in a surprise encounter with two amorous soldiers by the King. Convinced that Kervoura's insinuations were all along true, the King is mortified and has her imprisoned. As much as anything, he wants to give himself time to think. Caught between loving her and loving his position, he delays bringing her to trial, and then delegates a court instead of judging her himself, During his indecision, Tryphena spends a long, lonely time of incarceration, feeling reviled and abandoned. Always devout, she looks increasingly to her religious faith and away from worldly concerns. Like Christ doubting upon the cross, she eventually abandons hope in her husband's justice. At the height of her anguish, an angel visits her and promises that the Holy Family are watching and will reward her in the afterlife. Meanwhile the evil Kervoura further stacks the evidence against her, and the Queen is sentenced to public humiliation followed by execution. After she has calmly forgiven her husband and her executioners, and is waiting for the compassion-stricken axeman to swing his axe, her long-lost son, guided by Providence, rides in and stops the proceedings. He denounces Kervoura and, in a divinely assisted duel, stabs him to death. The Queen is vindicated, and her forbearing saintliness revealed to her husband and the world. Good has triumphed over evil, and King Arthur and Queen Tryphena will live happily ever after with their children.

St Tryphena and *Tess* begin very differently and do not show any resemblance until their heroines become pregnant. The play invokes a complicated and sensational train of events to set up its trio of main characters, namely, a woman, her husband, and a persecuting male relative. Hardy goes a different route but arrives at the same situation. Twenty-four of *Tess*'s fifty-nine chapters are spent defining the combination of relentlessly augmenting pressures – social, hereditary, internal and external – which conspire with chance to deliver Tess into the fateful embrace of her 'cousin' and seducer Alec. It is at the onset of their sexual lives that the two women's careers begin to look similar. Tryphena's is exclusively with her husband in spite of the allegations by her brother, while Tess's has two parts, each dominated by a different man and a different principle. The first is with Alec, who is the embodiment of hedonism and physicality, and it yields Tess's only child, Sorrow. The second is with Angel, who is all spirit and ideals, and whose inability to perceive the real Tess does her even worse damage. Like Tess, Queen Tryphena's undoing is her beauty, her innocent trust, and the very fact that she is a woman at the mercy of men and their dreams. A detailed comparison between the two works shows a series of resemblances and, in some cases, significant inversions.

Tryphena like Tess is ruined by two men, one her deceiving brother Kervoura (like Tess's false cousin Alec), and the other her adoring, dilatory husband Arthur (Angel), whose rank and pride inhibit him from searching out underlying truths, and who acts upon appearances and innuendo (Angel again). Tryphena is tricked into giving birth in Kervoura's specially built, remote 'palace' (as Tess is tricked into living in the cottage Alec prepared on his estate). Tryphena gives birth unknown to Arthur (as Alec is unaware of Sorrow's birth), and she complains of the loneliness of being far from her family, who remain in Ireland (something like this is implied for Tess – it is certainly hard to believe that Joan and Jack Durbeyfield are only a bedroom away while Sorrow is dying). Tryphena is accused of hating her child's father and of infanticide (Tess hates Alec and her child dies), and when Arthur hears of this, she takes flight disguised as a servant (as Tess, after her confession, flees Marlott dressed meanly and with her beauty defaced so she can escape attention). Tryphena prays by a wayside shrine (Tess by Cross-in-Hand) and falls insensible during her nocturnal journey (Tess's night in the woods), then finds refuge in a church (Tess and her family at Kingsbere church). She is awakened by the duchess (Tess is offered the poultry-keeping job by 'Mrs d'Urberville'; in Kingsbere church she is offered salvation by Alec after he has 'awoken' from being a stone effigy). Tryphena begins earning her own living, first as a house-servant but fails to use a broom knowledgeably (as Tess fails at drawing reeds, a similar-sounding occupation) and invokes the anger of the housekeeper (as Tess's inexperience angers Farmer Groby). She is banished out of doors to look after pigs and turkeys (Tess works with hens and later cows), and is courted by the pig-keeper who tries to kiss her (as do Alec and later Angel). But the Queen won't accept his advances and cannot tell him of her rank or marital status (as Tess cannot tell Angel of her noble descent or prior relationship with Alec). After Tryphena is discovered she is reunited with her remorseful husband, time and contemplation having inclined him to over-look the past since he truly loves her (Angel's return, their brief time of happiness) and she bears Arthur a daughter (Tess bequeathing Angel her sister Liza-Lu). Kervoura renews his covert assault and sends King Arthur the warning of infidelity to come (Izz and Marion's warning note to Angel), and he rigs an encounter between Tryphena and some lascivious soldiers which is witnessed by Arthur (Angel finding Tess with Alec in Sand-bourne). Arthur is affronted by his wife's apparent adultery (Angel's shock at the wedding-night confession); and, torn between love for his wife and love for his rank, the king imprisons her but vacillates (Angel unable to terminate his marriage to Tess, leaving her to go abroad). He resorts to delaying tactics to avoid executing the woman he loves (Angel numbed by his consciousness of impending societal and family condemnation). The Queen remains imprisoned while Arthur tries to make up his mind (Tess imprisoned by labour contract to Farmer Groby while Angel is turning the question over in his mind in Brazil). He interrogates the Queen in an effort to establish the truth (Tess harassed at Flintcomb-Ash by Alec), but she will neither explain nor defend herself (Tess's silent resistance). Gradually she relinquishes hope in her husband's justice (as Tess in Angel's), but at the height of her anguish is visited by an angel who tells her the Holy Family will reward her in the afterlife (Alec, the devil-figure, appears to tempt Tess during her long, despairing wait for Angel; Angel searches out Tess in Sandbourne, partly because his 'holy family' could now accept her). Tryphena's martyrdom is proved by her willingness to die for her faith (Tess is willing to die for hers, which is love of Angel), and is prepared to sacrifice her earthly reputation for salvation in heaven (as Tess sacrifices her self-respect and good name in exchange for her family's economic salvation). Tryphena is publicly humiliated (as Tess is by resuming as Alec's mistress) and taken to the scaffold (Tess at Wintoncester), but the 'King of the Universe'[14] intercedes to avert the gross injustice (as Hardy's famous 'President of the Immortals' fails to do). Queen Tryphena is saved by her son's timely arrival and denunciation (Tess's child is dead) and afterwards he slays Kervoura with his sword (as Tess kills Alec with the kitchen knife). After this, family life can resume in tranquillity, and the Queen will be revered as a saint (Angel begins again with Tess's unsullied surrogate, Liza-Lu; Hardy canonizes Tess as the 'pure woman').

The similarities between the two works are mainly in their focus upon the victimization of a 'pure' woman, in the events, and in the pattern and development of relationships. There are strong resemblances in the triangular situations, in the identity of the protagonists, their social standing, the kinds of culpability for each, the hellfire affiliations of the villains, and in the pattern of flight, refuge, reprieve, detention, torment, loss of faith, martyrdom, trial and sentence of death upon the heroines. Though each work defines a 'pure woman' and indeed pure womanliness, *Tess*'s framing is in some particulars symmetrically opposed, as though Hardy was striving to create a modern obverse through a determined and systematic inversion of particular values in the morality play tradition.

Enough formal and thematic aspects of *Tess* are echoed in the Breton mystery play for us to ask whether Hardy read it and used a plot summary as a starting point in the way he seems to have done with *Emma* and *Tristan*. There is no record to show he knew of the play's existence, but this is inconclusive since if he had used it he would have concealed the fact to avoid further embarrassing charges of plagiarism.[15] But there is reason to suspect that he may have annexed the play, as Simon Stoke annexed the d'Urberville name, after research in the British Museum library. J. T. Laird's study of the manuscript of *Tess*[16] shows that all of the materials which might have come from *St Tryphena* were in place from the outset. The majority of Hardy's developmental work is concentrated in strengthening the portion of the novel which leads up to Tess's impregnation, the point at which we have said resemblances begin. The theme of heredity, the red-and-white imagery, the decline of agriculture and the peasantry, and the indifference of the cosmos are all aspects of the finished novel which emerged during successive layers of composition, deepening and strengthening the connection between what I have identified as the mystery play superstructure and the fabric of Hardy's own time. Tess's arrival at the d'Urberville church originally paralleled Queen Tryphena's church visit, and came before her arrival at Talbothays.

If we now return to the idea that Hardy habitually used a text and a cast of players to initiate his writing, it is evident that we have both a text and a reinterpretive pattern. The missing link is the cast from Hardy's emotional circle by whose influence the text evolved in his writer's imagination. The Reverend Clare and his wife seem based upon the Reverend Henry Moule and his wife, the parents of Horace Moule. The Moule family, and Horace in particular, were Hardy's stepping stone to intellectual life and middle class aspirations when he was in his teens and twenties. Hardy himself said that Angel was in part drawn from Horace's younger brother Charles.[17] But Angel's uncertainty of faith is much nearer that of Horace. Alec d'Urberville, who already seems to be the complementary half of Angel, also shows signs of derivation from Horace; his mother is blind, as Mrs Moule was in later years, and Alec makes the same chaotic transitions between hedonism and piety that increasingly plagued Horace Moule. His disintegration, through depression and drinking, probably originated from his inability to reconcile his family's high principles and his own unresolved sexual identity.[18] Like Alec, Horace died under a domestic blade, though wielded by his own hand.

This leaves Tess's inspiration to be identified. The play would be a stronger candidate text if there was a figure from Hardy's background as persuasively obvious as Emma Gifford filling the title role in *Emma*. Of course, such a figure exists in Tryphena Sparks, the cousin Hardy described in his poem 'Thoughts of Phena' as his 'lost prize'. She is not a new candidate[19] and most Hardy scholars are sceptical over her importance. According to Tryphena Sparks' daughter, Hardy and Tryphena were once engaged. For reasons that are unclear, the affair petered out or was broken off some time between 1870 and 1872. Hardy married

Emma Gifford in 1874 and three years later Tryphena married Charles Gale, who had been courting her in Devon where she was a headmistress. Hardy and Tryphena seem not to have communicated after Hardy married, and she died prematurely in 1890 while still less than forty years old.

In a recently discovered letter of 1888, Tryphena asks her Puddletown relatives if 'Aunt Hardy and Uncle [are] alive and well – ? I never have any news from you [her Aunt Mary, Hardy's mother's sister] – The Hardys never write – in fact they do not know anything about us as a family I think . . .'.[20] Even though she was out of contact and married in Devon, traces of Tryphena Sparks's career turn up in many of Hardy's heroines. An obvious example which reveals how Hardy employed factual detail to prime his imaginative process is that of Ella Marchmill in the short story 'An Imaginative Woman' (1893). She and her family lodge at Coburg House, 13 New Parade in Solentsea. Tryphena taught at Coburg Street School and later lived at 13 Fore Street, Topsham. Ella Marchmill's name is significant too; Tryphena was born in March next to a mill in Puddletown, and her look-alike daughter whom Hardy met only after Tryphena's death was named Eleanor. Ella Marchmill's four children are called Nelly, Frank and Tiny and her fourth child was a boy born in May. Tryphena's children were Nelly (Eleanor), Frank, Charles and a boy born in May.

Evidently, three years after her death, Hardy's cousin was very much in his mind. But why should he be thinking about her two years *before* her death, co-opt the only known theatrical work bearing her name, and start writing *Tess*? The answer seems to be that he knew she was going to die soon. Her letter quoted above also shows that her premature death was foreshadowed by the kind of ominous cough which accompanied consumption. Three women had died in her household recently, one being her favourite sister. The family was worried and undoubtedly Hardy was hearing about it during his regular visits to his mother, in spite of Tryphena's belief otherwise. One must take cautiously what he says in *The Life* about the composition of 'Thoughts of Phena', which he claims was 'a curious instance of sympathetic telepathy'. He goes on, 'the woman whom I was thinking of – a cousin – was dying at the time, and I quite in ignorance of it. She died six days later' (*Life*, p. 224). Elsewhere in *The Life* he claims the same kind of coincidental knowledge of another woman's approaching death, also one he had courted in youth.²¹ The incident led to the poem 'At Mayfair Lodgings' which memorializes another lost prize, Cassie Pole. New evidence indicates that Hardy kept himself informed of Cassie's advancing cancer, and, as the end drew near, slipped away to London on a publishing pretext and stationed himself within sight of her window while she died in the night.²²

Tess was begun while Tryphena Sparks was in decline, and finished in the year or so that followed her death. As in other periods of Hardy's life, a major work followed the death of a major figure from his emotional life. Moule's death was followed by Hardy's first artistic and commercial success, *Far From the Madding Crowd*, and Emma Hardy's death unquestionably sparked the extraordinary poems of 1912–13. Of the period during which he was writing *Tess*, Michael Millgate says: 'At no period in [his] career was Hardy more numerously, variously, or richly productive than during the three years which intervened between commencement of work on *Tess* in the autumn of 1888 and book publication of the novel in November 1891.'²³ During this span, the manuscript underwent some profound changes: 'The development of the character of Tess during the later manuscript layers could best be described as a process of refining, ennobling, and idealizing on the part of the author', says J. T. Laird.²⁴ Also appearing at this time is the tone of intense personal commitment to his heroine, and the touches which make her seem derived from a real-life model. Tess's voice, says Hardy in the novel 'will never be forgotten by those who knew her' (ch. 14). In October 1891 he wrote to an acquaintance, 'I am glad you like Tess – though I have not been able to put on paper all that she is, or was, to me.'²⁵

Both inside and outside the pages of the novel, Hardy hints at an actual woman now dead as the model for Tess. Of course, Tess is a fictional composite, but there is more than a little to suggest that his cousin was uppermost in the creation of this idealized woman. Tryphena Sparks was a country girl with Tess's attractiveness and unusual aptitude for learning. Of all Hardy's romantic interests, she alone made a social and intellectual leap analogous to Hardy's own. After her marriage she was abused by her husband, like Tess, for doing housework for which there was a servant.²⁶ Her initials, T. S., make Tess's name. Tess is given birds to care for, creatures that Tryphena particularly loved,²⁷ and one of these is a chicken called Phena. Oddly, if one takes the other chicken's name, Strut, one has a near-perfect anagram of 'St Tryphena'.

Did Hardy, then, seek the play out? And if so, how would he have found such an obscure publication? The play was in the British Museum library from 1869 onwards, and Hardy could have found it in a number of ways. Matthew Arnold, whom Hardy had met and whose own 'Tristram and Iseult' Hardy knew, was enthusiastic about Celtic literature and had written *On the Study of Celtic Literature* in 1883. Hardy was in the Reading Room in early 1888 (*Life*, p. 206) and could have stumbled upon the play's title while searching for either Celtic or Arthurian material. He later claimed to have been interested in King Arthur ever since 1870, when he had visited King Arthur's supposed castle at Tintagel with Emma, whom he described as 'an Iseult of my own'.[28] The interest was probably alive in 1887 when he read Malory, and his copy of *Morte D'Arthur* was at some time heavily annotated.[29] But the simplest and most likely way for Hardy to have found the play was the way by which I found it myself. Assuming I was Hardy idly searching the B. M. index for a favourite name, I found two of his interests in one title, *Sainte Tryphine et le roi Arthur*. My first thought was that it might prove to have been influential upon *The Queen of Cornwall*. When I studied the play (Hardy also read French) I realized that its resemblance was instead to *Tess*, a discovery with further-reaching implications.

It is impossible to say precisely why Tryphena Sparks meant so much to Hardy, but for some reason her decline seems to have initiated *Tess*. There are additional and independent reasons to suspect her presence behind Tess Durbeyfield. Tryphena had friends in Waddon Vale,[30] and may have taught at Coryates school.[31] This is near Langston Herring, an estate owned by her cousin William Sparks,[32] to whom her family were poor relations. Nearby is the monument to the illustrious Admiral Hardy, towards whom Thomas Hardy was, in his turn, an obscure and impoverished relation in the late 1860s. Within sight of the monument is the Hell Stone, the only cromlech in Dorset, a large flat stone resting on nine pillars which was believed to have been either a sacrificial altar or the resting place for chieftains of antiquity before they were buried in the nearby Valley of Stones.[33] The Hell Stone and its association with Tryphena may have set in motion ideas for *Tess* which were enventually played out in the more grandiose setting of Stonehenge. The Hell Stone also appears in the poem 'My Cicely', in which the narrator imaginatively traverses old haunts and associations to be at Cicely's funeral. His journey takes him through Blandford, Puddletown and Dorchester, until

> The Nine-Pillared cromlech, the Bride-streams,
>   The Axe, and the Otter
> I passed, to the gate of the city
>   Where Exe scents the sea.

The journey is to the area of Topsham, where a Mrs Gale had died on 8 March 1888. The news was misleading, for it was not Tryphena Sparks Gale who had died, but her mother-in-law. The poem describes an emotion-laden journey based on just such a misunderstanding.[34] Hardy was in the British Museum around this time, and left London some time between the 9 March and the 28 March. How long he was gone, or where he went, is not known, but his diary note written on his return hints at his having suffered a profound shock:

> March 28. On returning to London after an absence I find the people of my acquaintance abraded, their hair disappearing, also their flesh, by degrees. (*Life*, p. 206)

He may have actually journeyed to Topsham, as he later did with his brother Henry to visit Tryphena's grave, and as he appears to have done to be near Cassie Pole at her death. If he did, he would have found Tryphena alive though in poor health, perhaps even serving in her husband's hotel, like the Cicely of the poem. In fact, 'My Cicely' links Tryphena to both Tess and Sue Bridehead. The Hell Stone is not far from the source of the River Bride, or Bridehead as it is called. One of the names Hardy considered before settling on the name Tess was Sue. Another was Cis, which is short for the Cicely of the poem's title.

Quite obviously *Tess* is not a simple concealed biography of Hardy's cousin, any more than *A Pair of Blue Eyes* is a straightforward record of Hardy's courtship of Emma. Given Hardy's fascination with 'old flames', and the cathartic release in his creativity at momentous deaths, it sems quite consistent that he should exploit a work bearing his cousin's highly unusual name. Later in his life he told Florence Hardy that 'the best way to find a starting point for a piece of writing was to go to some work by a major writer – Carlyle, for instance – and read at random until one came across an image or idea that stimulated one's own inventiveness'.[35] The mystery play could scarcely be better devised to engage Hardy's creative energies. It had an attractively magnificent woman as its central figure, two stirring kinds of male culpability, and its action set in a universe overseen by the kind of benevolent deity which Hardy believed was tragically missing. The play also offered ideas for showing the kind of sexual victimization that Hardy had seen even in his own family[36] and which he could use to highlight the double standards of the time.

Tryphena Sparks' death helped direct Hardy's search for material. But what he found – the text, as I have called it – absorbed and metamorphosed its main actress into the theatrical personage of Tess, as well as the other feminine influences who went into her making. Tess's transcendence on Hardy's stage of Wessex is the product of his genius in its fullest intensity. While Tess's story is that of a saint in a morality play, she has been secularized and aimed like a Trojan horse at many of the values represented in the morality play convention.

Not all readers will accept that Hardy was influenced by the play or that his cousin was a considerable factor in the genesis of *Tess*. But the undeniable existence of *St Tryphena* and its many similarities to *Tess* provide even the most sceptical with an authentic folk-drama against which to reassess the novel's form and objectives.

NOTES

1. Michael Millgate, *Thomas Hardy: his Career as a Novelist* (London: Bodley Head, 1971) pp. 308–16.
2. Robert Gittings, *The Older Hardy* (London: Heinemann, 1978) p. 18.
3. W. R. Rutland, *Thomas Hardy: A Study of his Writings and their Background* (New York: Russell & Russell, 1962; orig. pub. 1938) pp. 141–6.
4. Robert Gittings, *Young Thomas Hardy* (London: Heinemann, 1975) p. 139.
5. Desmond Hawkins, *Hardy: Novelist and Poet* (Newton Abbot: David & Charles, 1976) pp. 47–8.
6. Puddletown Records, Dorset County Records Office.
7. Gittings, *Young Thomas Hardy* pp. 108–9.
8. Information from Celia Barclay.

9. *Thomas Hardy Society Review* (1979) pp. 160–3.
10. At the Castle of Lonazep, when Sir Tristram meets Sir Gawain.
11. Gottfried Von Strassburg, *Tristan*, trans. A. T. Hatto (Harmondsworth: Penguin Books, 1960) pp. 261–9.
12. Ibid., p. 259.
13. François-Marie Luzel, *Sainte Tryphine et le roi Arthur* (Quimperlé, 1863).
14. A literal translation with a striking resemblance to Hardy's famous 'President of the Immortals'.
15. Hardy lifted a drill scene in *The Trumpet-Major* from a military history, the author of which had, unknown to Hardy, plagiarized it from an earlier work of fiction. See Carl J. Weber, *Hardy of Wessex* (London: Routledge & Kegan Paul, 1965) pp. 116–22. Hardy also suffered the embarrassment of having two hundred words of *A Laodicean* traced to a Jesuit aphorist: see Irving Howe, *Thomas Hardy* (London: Weidenfeld & Nicolson, 1968) p. 69; Lennart A. Björk, *The Literary Notes of Thomas Hardy* (Gothenburg: Acta Universitatis Gothoburgensis, 1974), I (Notes) pp. 327–9.
16. J. T. Laird, *The Shaping of 'Tess of the d'Urbervilles'* (Oxford: Clarendon Press, 1975).
17. F. B. Pinion, *A Hardy Companion* (London: Macmillan, 1968), p. 281. Michael Millgate, *Thomas Hardy: A Biography* (New York: Random House, 1982) pp. 294–5, gives further reasons for believing that Angel Clare was drawn more from Horace Moule than from his brother Charles.
18. Michael Rabiger, 'The Hoffman Papers', *The Thomas Hardy Year Book*, no. 10, ed. J. & G. Stevens Cox (St Peter Port, Guernsey: Toucan Press, 1981) pp. 6–50.
19. Lois Deacon & Terry Coleman, *Providence and Mr Hardy* (London: Hutchinson, 1966) pp. 176–80; Robert Gittings, *The Older Hardy*, pp. 63–78; F. R. Southerington, *Hardy's Vision of Man* (London: Chatto & Windus, 1971) pp. 134–5; J. T. Laird, *The Shaping of 'Tess of the d'Urbervilles'*, pp. 120–1.
20. See Appendix to Michael Rabiger, 'The Hoffman Papers'.
21. Ibid., pp. 20–1.
22. Ibid.
23. Michael Millgate, *Thomas Hardy: His Career as a Novelist*, p. 263.
24. J. T. Laird, *The Shaping of 'Tess of the d'Urbervilles'*, p. 125.
25. Hardy to Thomas Macquoid, 29 October 1891, in Richard Little Purdy & Michael Millgate, *The Collected Letters of Thomas Hardy*, vol. I (1840–92) (Oxford: Clarendon Press, 1978) pp. 245–6.
26. Lois Deacon & Terry Coleman, *Providence and Mr Hardy*, p. 55.
27. Ibid., pp. 47, 56.
28. Hardy to Sydney Cockerell, 20 September 1916, quoted in Richard Little Purdy, *Thomas Hardy: A Bibliographical Study* (Oxford: Clarendon Press, 1954) p. 229.
29. Ibid., p. 229n.
30. Miss Samson of Upwey, mentioned in Tryphena's letter of 7 August 1875 (*Dorset*, no. 23, Spring 1972), also visited her during her Plymouth teaching days (Coburg Street School log). Mrs Spiller, mentioned in the letter, is probably the wife of Robert Spiller, bailiff to Catherine Hawkins, the Waddon Vale widow listed as 'farmer of 525 acres' in the 1871 census.
31. Robert Gittings, *Young Thomas Hardy*, pp. 108–9.

32. John Hutchins, *History and Antiquities of the County of Dorset*, 3rd edition, vol. II (London: J. B. Nichols, 1867) p. 746.
32. Frederick Treves, *Highways and Byways in Dorset* (1906) p. 247.
34. For more detailed interpretation, see Lois Deacon & Terry Coleman, *Providence and Mr Hardy*, pp. 122–3.
35. Michael Millgate, *Thomas Hardy: a Biography*, p. 88.
36. Robert Gittings, *The Older Hardy*, pp. 50–78.

Tess and Joyce's *Portrait*: a Possible Parallel

Samir Elbarbary

A scene at the end of Stephen Dedalus' experience on the beach (ch. 4, section 3) in Joyce's *A Portrait of the Artist as a Young Man* (1916) bears comparison with another in *Tess* (1891). The episode in Hardy's novel occurs at a point in the Third Phase, 'The Rally', where the attraction (mainly idealized) between Tess and Angel Clare is just beginning to develop. Aware of the defilement of her body (her 'corporeal blight', ch. 19) when she was entrapped by Alec in the Chase, the anxiety-ridden Tess is eager to dismiss the past. She longs to renounce physical emotion and to attain spiritual liberation where the soul is disentangled from the body. This disembodiment, she tells the Dairyman at Talbothays, involves lying 'on the grass at night and look[ing] straight up at some big bright star; and, by fixing your mind upon it, you will soon find that you are hundreds and hundreds o' miles away from your body, which you don't seem to want at all' (ch. 18). In this trancelike and transcendent state of being, Tess rises into higher realms and partakes of the infinite. She is held in a dreamlike mystic moment of visionary ecstasy and relaxation, which momentarily stills her fear of the actual. She is 'refining herself out of existence' – to borrow a phrase from *A Portrait*. Matter is changed into spirit.

Stephen enjoys an 'instant of ecstasy' – a similar mood of sublime serenity and 'static' calm – when he stretches out on the sand of the beach immediately after his revelatory vision of the girl he finds wading. We are told that he

> found a sandy nook amid a ring of tufted sandknolls and lay down there that the peace and silence of the evening might still the riot of his blood.

74

He felt above him the vast indifferent dome and the calm processes of the heavenly bodies; and the earth beneath him, the earth that had borne him, had taken him to her breast.

He closed his eyes in the langour of sleep. His eyelids trembled as if they felt . . . the strange light of some new world. His soul was swooning into some new world, fantastic, dim, uncertain as under sea, traversed by cloudy shapes and beings.

Here, Stephen's soul soars skyward in 'an ecstasy of flight' – from the nets laid out to him to the wide vistas of art. The soul seeks that which nourishes it. He lies with his back to the earth, which perhaps represents the narrow everyday actuality from which he wants to flee, or simply the 'elemental life' as Jane H. Jack observes.[1] His attitude to the beauty of the bird-girl shows a contemplative, aesthetic temperament (her thighs for instance, are seen as 'soft-hued as ivory', which suggests the Tower of Ivory, symbol of the Virgin). This contrasts with the sensual, earthly feelings excited in him and which led him to 'narrow and dirty streets', where he surrenders himself to the prostitute[2] at the end of chapter 2. (The chapters of the novel, as Hugh Kenner rightly observes,[3] repeat one another in an 'analogical structure' with thematic reversals.) Like Tess, he has allowed his passion to run wild like the 'rank weeds'. Stephen's posture, however, does not constitute a denial of the real (life is the material for art), but a freeing of his spirit – to be most freely himself. Three pages earlier, we read that he is transfigured: 'his soul was soaring in an air beyond the world and the body he knew was purified in a breath and delivered of incertitude and made radiant and commingled with the element of the spirit'. And this, we read on, 'was the call of life to his soul not the dull gross voice of the world of duties and despair'. It is significant that the upward surge of his spirit releases his artistic endowment and kindles it to poetic composition (ch. 5, section 2).

Following Tess's reference to her star-gazing, there is the famous garden scene, which, if read with Joyce's scene in mind, takes the parallel a step further. The scene describes Tess as she wanders through the unweeded garden one summer evening, and listens to Angel playing his harp. Her heart is touched and she moves closer and closer to the source of her attraction. Like star-gazing, Angel's music is ecstatic, it makes her 'conscious of neither time nor space'. 'The exaltation,' explains the narrator, 'which she had described as being producible at will by gazing at a star, came now without any determination of hers.' The sense of freedom from the limits of time and space transcends her ordinary awareness of life. In contemplating the beautiful, she is absorbed in the intensity of the moment. The result of the aesthetic experience is a revelation: she discovers the extent of her feelings for Angel: 'But *you*, sir, can raise up dreams with your music, and drive all such horrid fancies away!'. What is also noticeable is that some words and phrases in Joyce's scene are consonant with – if not in echo of – Hardy's phraseology:

a – a typical summer evening	a – Evening had fallen
b – soundlessness/the still air	b – peace and silence
c – The soundlessness . . . was broken	c – The first faint noise . . . broke the silence
d – Dim [notes]	d – dim waves
e – Tess, like a fascinated bird	e – a hawk-like man flying sunward/she seemed like . . . a strange and beautiful seabird.
f – blooming weeds/weed-flowers glowed	f – emerald trail of seaweed/endless drift of seaweed
g – made madder stains on her skin	g – seaweed had fashioned itself as a sign upon the flesh
h – [her] exaltation	h – joy/his ecstasy
i – harmonies passed like breezes through her	i – Her image had passed into his soul
j – her cheeks on fire	j – He felt his cheeks aflame/a faint flame trembled on her cheek/ His cheeks were aflame
k – Tess . . . moved away furtively	k – He turned away from her suddenly
l – Angel, however, saw her light summer gown	l – when she felt his presence

The esssential material of the two scenes – at large – renders them close indeed: a moment of vision which transcends sordid reality and the effect is one of enchantment, together with the basically spiritualized sensibility of the characters involved. Like Stephen, Tess is sensitive and visionary. She, we are told, is 'a sort of celestial person, who owed her being to poetry – one of those classical divinities Clare was accustomed to talk to her about when they took their walks together' (ch. 33); no wonder then that 'there was hardly a touch of earth in her love for Clare' (ch. 31). Angel, too, is spiritual, and his harp, taken as a symbol, would seem to bear this out. He is described as 'more spiritual than animal, . . . singularly free from grossness. Though not cold-natured, he was rather bright than hot – less Byronic than Shelleyan; could love desperately, but with a love more especially inclined to the imaginative and ethereal' (ch. 31). One may observe further that the two scenes are exquisitely pictured and phrased; the language is raised to an aureate pitch.

This parallel (or near-parallel) is perhaps not entirely coincidental. Stanislaus Joyce recounts how his brother was an avid reader of Hardy's novels.[4] There are further parallels to Hardy in Joyce – a subject which has not yet received its due. One such analogy: Stephen's fantasies of idealized women and their merging in an 'unsubstantial image which his soul so constantly beheld' (ch. II, section 1) are reminiscent of Pierston's well-beloveds. Indeed, *A Portrait* is steeped in the *fin-de-siècle* tradition that includes Hardy's late fiction.

NOTES

1. 'Art and the *Portrait of the Artist*', *Essays in Criticism*, 5 (October 1955) pp. 354–64.
2. Cf. the hero of Théophile Gautier's *Mademoiselle de Maupin*, who says:
    I should not be astonished if, after offering up so many sighs to the moon, staring so often at the stars, and composing so many elegies and sentimental apostrophes, I were to fall in love with some vulgar prostitute or some ugly old woman. That would be a fine downfall! Reality will perhaps revenge herself in this way for the carelessness with which I have courted her. (Trans. Burton Roscoe, New York, 1929, p. 92.) Quoted in R. V. Johnson, *Aestheticism* (London: Methuen, 1969) p. 49.
3. 'The Portrait in Perspective', collected in William M. Schutte (ed.), *Twentieth-Century Interpretations of 'A Portrait of the Artist as a Young Man'* (Englewood Cliffs, N.J.: Prentice-Hall, 1968) pp. 26–37.

4. See Stanislaus Joyce, *My Brother's Keeper* (London: Faber & Faber, 1958) pp. 68, 89–90. The enthusiasm is for *Tess of the d'Urbervilles* and *Jude the Obscure* in particular. See also Richard Ellmann, *James Joyce* (London: OUP, 1976) pp. 54, 365.

Dialect in Hardy's Short Stories

J. B. Smith

While a good deal has been written about Hardy's use of dialect, most discussions of the subject have centred on the novels.[1] In fact, dialect also plays an important part in many of the short stories, and we do not have to look far in these for explicit references to the question of standard and non-standard English. Thus, at the beginning of 'The Son's Veto', Sophy is upbraided by her son for using *have* instead of *has*. 'That question of grammar bore upon her history', Hardy remarks (ii, 34),[2] and, indeed, it also bears upon her future, it gradually becomes clear. In 'On the Western Circuit' we are told that Anna is taught by her mistress to talk correctly (ii, 95), an accomplishment that stands her in good stead in the initial stages of her relationship with Raye, since if she had been rough-spoken he would hardly have been deluded into believing that she had penned the letters he received from her. Comparable versatility, though with similar consequences, is shown in 'Dame the Tenth' by the hotel page-boy, who picks up the polite accent of the summer guests, but in winter reverts to the local dialect 'in all its purity' (i, 351f).

In such examples, not surprisingly in view of Hardy's preoccupation with class, the emphasis is on dialect in the vertical, social, dimension. Even when he refers to geographical differences, they too can take on social significance. Thus, in 'The Fiddler of the Reels' the distinct London accent which Car'line has acquired after two or three years in the metropolis is one of the attributes which seem to mark her off from her past, and which will perhaps act as a kind of talisman when she returns to Wessex (ii, 133). After this Car'line remains silent, so that we can have no idea of how, or if, Hardy would have represented a West Country accent overlaid with Cockney. However, it is perhaps significant that Car'line's husband Ned, who has lived in London four years longer than she, seems at the end to have made no concessions to its accent, thus bearing out Orton's remark that 'in this country men speak vernacular more frequently, more consistently and more genuinely than women".[3] Shadrach and Joanna Jolliffe in 'To Please his Wife' are another pair who seem to corroborate this.

Elsewhere Hardy will render a non-Wessex dialect by using clipped forms and colloquialisms. Thus in 'Enter a Dragoon' Sergeant-Major Clark, who, 'not being of local extraction, despised the venerable local language', is characterized by 'Sakes alive!', 'ain't', and sentences such as: 'There's a nine-gallon cask o' "Phoenix" beer outside . . ., for I thought you might be short o' forage in a lonely place like this' (ii, 306–9). Here 'forage' also gives a whiff of military usage.

But even within Wessex there is a geographical variation, we gather. Does not Shepherdess Fennel in 'The Three Strangers' detect in the speech of the first stranger the accent of her home (i, 19), which is apparently in the neighbourhood of Blandford Forum? However, the subtle differences which her ear makes out seem not to be rendered in the text, and it will be appropriate to ask at this point to what extent Wessex dialects are actually differentiated in Hardy's short stories.

In these stories characters who speak dialect come from all parts of Wessex, from Reading in the east to the Isles of Scilly in the west, from Dorchester in the south to the Mendips in the north. Over such a wide area there is bound to be much dialectal variation. But before we ask how Hardy comes to terms with it, we must consider his general approach to the question of rendering dialect. In discussing a passage from *Under the Greenwood Tree*, Page remarks that 'there are, strictly speaking, no dialect words, and the indications of non-standard grammar and pronunciation are not very numerous. What gives this dialogue its distinctive quality is the command of colloquial idiom'. Other factors which Page lists as contributing to the impression of dialect are the colloquial sentence patterns and the generally rather formal character of the narrative, which, with its learned vocabulary and elaborate syntax, provides a foil for the dialect speeches.[4] The latter point probably applies less to the shorter stories, but the point about colloquial sentence patterns and formulaic expression certainly holds. Take the following speech from 'What the Shepherd Saw':

'Blame thy young eyes and limbs, Bill Mills – now you have let the fire out, and you know I want it kept in! I thought something would go wrong with 'ee up here, and I couldn't bide in bed no more than thistledown on the wind, that I could not! Well, what's happened, fie upon 'ee?'   (ii, 332)

There is nothing in this that marks it out as peculiar to Wiltshire. Syntax and phraseology give it a dialectal ring, and there is a scattering of non-standard lexical items (e.g. *bide*) and 'phonetic' spellings (e.g. *hollerday* a little later on). The use of dialect grammar is sporadic, *thou* etc. alternating with *you* etc., for instance. This latter type of variation is entirely characteristic of Hardy. Whether or not it accurately reflects the usage of the time, it certainly helps the reader.

Hardy's approach seems to be similar when he moves even farther afield. Take 'The Romantic Adventures of a Milkmaid', which was originally set in Dorset,[5] but then transferred to Devon. Hardy not only changed the locale, but also adjusted the dialect, though for a variety of reasons. For instance, when 'the night-jar sounding his rattle' become 'the night-hawk sounding his croud' (ii, 417), or the 'cruel conspiracy' suspected by Margery becomes a 'footy plot' (ii, 465), it is primarily for reasons of style or characterization, one imagines. But when *you*, *do*, *two* etc. become *yew*, *dew*, *tew* etc., as they fairly regularly do, the aim is obviously to represent the front, close, rounded vowel which is a well-known feature of Devonshire pronunciation. This, however, seems to be Hardy's only positive attempt to represent Devonshire dialect. Elsewhere his changes are negative, in the sense that he will replace by a less dialectal expression one which probably seemed to him to be too closely associated with Dorset. Thus 'hontish' becomes 'haughty' (ii, 451), and 'vlankers' is transformed into 'sparks' (ii, 466). Moreover, 'keakhorn' becomes 'wyndpipe' (ii, 417), although *cacorne* is no stranger to Devon according to Wright's *English Dialect Dictionary* (= *EDD*).[6]

'A Mere Interlude' is set still farther to the west, mainly in Penzance and the Scilly Isles, and the most striking regionalism in the renderings of dialect is, apart from the adjective *wisht*, Mr Heddegan's frequent use of *mee deer* as a form of address. Otherwise, even in a longish speech such as that by the hotel maid (ii, 398), the impression of dialect is sustained without the inclusion of any feature that could be identified as peculiar to Cornwall.

If we now return to Hardy's native Dorset, we shall find that his strategies for representing its dialect do not differ materially from those outlined above. As Quirk points out in discussing varieties of English, regional variation seems to be rendered predominantly in phonology,[7] and it is precisely in representing phonology that Hardy makes the greatest concessions to those of his readers who are unfamilar with Wessex dialects, since non-standard spellings are not very frequent, and, of those he does use, a good number, such as *o'* for *of* and *'twas* for *it was*, are not exclusive to dialect, let alone peculiar to Dorset. Dialect grammar and lexis are of course represented, if sporadically, but since examples of these seldom remain obediently within the boundaries of any one shire, there is not a great deal in Hardy's Dorset stories to identify the dialect in itself as belonging specifically to that county. Thus, if we consult *EDD* for the distribution of the forty-three dialect words listed in the glossary to volume 1 of the stories in the New Wessex Edition, we find that, of the thirty-seven listed by Wright, only two, *a-scram* and *ewe-lease*, are not recorded as occurring beyond the confines of Dorset, though this in itself is of course not proof that they are localisms. Moreover, although a sentence such as 'Andrew knew no more of music than the Giant o' Cernel' (ii, 171) might be cited to the contrary, idiom, phraseology and sentence patterns are on the whole even less easy to identify as belonging to a particular area, and it is these that make a major contribution to the dialectal flavouring of the dialogue, as Page has pointed out.

If we pick out at random a couple of lines by William Barnes, we shall find that his approach to the representation of dialect is quite different from Hardy's. Take:

'Well run, an' ax vor woone. Fling up your heels,
An' mind: a speäde to dig out theäsem wheels,
An' hook to cut a little lock o' widdicks.'[8]

Here we have an attempt to represent specifically Dorset dialect at all levels, but at the expense of comprehensibility, at least for the desultory reader. For obvious reasons, Hardy could not afford to pay such a price, and in any case, as a writer of stories he had at his disposal a most effective device for suggesting local dialect: he could in his narrative give detailed information about the locale, the provenance of speakers, and even peculiarities of their pronunciation.

In the lines quoted above, over a third of the forms are non-standard, and this is by no means unusual for Barnes. By comparison, in Hardy's vernacular tale 'A Tradition of Eighteen Hundred and Four' the incidence of dialectal forms is less than 3 per cent, while in 'The Grave by the Handpost' it reaches the unusually high proportion of nearly 13 per cent. To be more precise, this last figure applies only to speeches by the Chalk-Newton choir. If we take Luke Holway's speeches, only 1.5 per cent of forms are non-standard, and most of these are not exclusively dialectal. Here, then, we return to the question of language as a social indicator, since it is clear that Hardy is making use of dialect to distinguish between the returning soldier who has risen above his peasant origins, and the humble countrymen who stayed at home.

However, we must not assume that dialect is reserved by Hardy for the lower classes. There is a certain type of rusticated squire who is as broad as any shepherd. Take Squire Everard in 'The Waiting Supper', whose voice is 'strongly toned with the local accent, so that he said "draïns" and "geäts" like the rustics on his estate' (ii, 215). His Doric is only matched by that of his colleague, the Squire of Athelhall.

Are we, then, to assume that those in the middle of the social scale are the only ones to be relatively free of dialect? Certainly Nicholas Long, the yeoman farmer in 'The Waiting Supper', starts off with far fewer non-standard features than Squire Everard, and returns from his travels after fifteen years with none at all. However, it is the urban middle classes of Wessex who approach nearest to the standard: Barnet and Downes in 'Fellow Townsmen', the Harnhams in 'On the Western Circuit', the Franklands in 'For Conscience' Sake'. When we come to look at those whose position is somewhere between the social extremes in rural, rather than urban, communities, the picture is a more complex one.

In 'Interlopers at the Knap', for instance, Helena is the 'daughter of a deceased naval officer, who had been brought up by her uncle a solicitor' (i, 143). She shows no sign of dialect. Her husband Philip, though of more modest background, has received an education, and has travelled overseas. His speech is not at all dialectal, unless we count the occasional *'twas*, but it is less formal ("'Don't let me ruin you by being seen in these togs, for Heaven's sake.'" "'I am confoundedly thirsty with my long tramp'''. (i, 134)) Next comes Charles Darton, 'a gentleman-farmer – quite a wealthy man' (i, 134), whose speech is on the whole marked by colloquialisms rather than dialect proper (0.7 per cent). Sally Hall, the woman he hopes to marry, and her mother, 'a substantial dairyman's widow' who has been brought up 'not without refinement' (i, 135), are considered, at least by themselves, to be slightly below Darton on the social scale. They use the occasional colloquialism or dialect expression (1 per cent). Japheth Johns, a dairyman and friend of Charles Darton, speaks quite a broad dialect. The incidence of dialect forms is 5 per cent, but this figure does not take into account his idiosyncratic manner of expressing himself ("'I have faced tantalization these twenty years with a temper as mild as milk!'" (i, 130)), 'his well-known style' (i, 140), as Hardy calls it. This reinforces the impression of broad dialect without inconveniencing the reader. Here, then, we have an attempt to represent not just dialect, but idiolect, even down to peculiarities of pronunciation (*natyves, contrairy*). Finally we have the boy Ezra, who speaks broad dialect (10.5 per cent).

In general, the evidence is that characters express their social status purely through the *incidence* of non-standard forms they use. At a given point they will choose between the two forms that are available, the standard and the non-standard. There seem to be few clear instances of a subtler gradation, such as that hinted at by Mrs Dewy, which enables a character to place himself on a scale descending from *potatoes* at the top, through *pertatoes* and *taters*, down to the *taties* used by the common workfolk (*UGT*, pt 1, ch. 8). It may, however, be that *am not*, *'m not*, *ain't* and *bain't* etc. represent a similarly complex system. The first two are standard, *'m not* being less formal, while *bain't* etc. was, until quite recently at least, the form used by the agricultural classes in Dorset, although *ain't* is gradually spreading westwards from the London area.[9] In Hardy's works there are fifty-one occurrences of the endemic forms *bain't* (= 'am not', 'are not'), *idden* (= 'is not') etc., and only eight of *ain't*.[10] Of the five Dorset characters who use this form, none belongs unambiguously to the rural working classes. Take 'Melia in the poem 'The Ruined Maid', whose talking now fits her for high company (*PPP*). And take Shadrach Jolliffe, whose 'Ay, sure; I ain't particular' near the beginning of 'To Please his Wife' (ii, 107) unobtrusively helps build up a picture of the taciturn seafarer whose speech and attitudes have been moulded by Dorset, but modified by his wider experience.

So far the indications are that dialect varies considerably according to the kind of person who is speaking. But what evidence is there that it varies in accordance with the situation? We have seen that a person will change his dialect in accordance with his circumstances and return to his native haunts a changed man, speaking a different kind of English. Bill Mills in 'What the Shepherd Saw' provides a striking example of this. But what of the transient changes that occur in response to a momentary situation and/or the company one is keeping at a given time? Changes of this kind would appear to be not very numerous.

Patricia Ingham has shown that in the novels, although major characters with a dialectal background do switch codes, they are made to do so by Hardy not necessarily as in real life, to suit their hearer, but in accordance with the broader requirements of the particular novel in question, to underline social contrasts. Thus in his revision of *Far From the Madding Crowd* Hardy actually strengthened Gabriel Oak's dialect in precisely those speeches where one would expect an approximation to the standard.[11] In the shorter stories there is of course less scope for such variation, and where it occurs it often seems to be handled in a different way. For instance, in 'The Withered Arm' Rhoda Brook starts off, in her conversations with her son, with some traces of dialect, but these rapidly fade away, and by the time she has met Gertrude Lodge all vestiges are gone. Even when talking to herself she is now capable of a sentence such as: '"O, can it be . . . that I exercise a malignant power over people against my own will?"' (i, 64) It is as if Hardy allows Rhoda Brook to grow out of her dialect as her stature increases in his eyes. But even where dialect recedes, forms of address remain as an important social indicator: Gertrude calls Rhoda by her christian name, but is addressed by her as *ma'am*, except at the very end. One is reminded of the explicit reference to the use of *madam* in 'An Indiscretion in the Life of an Heiress', where Geraldine tacitly forbids Egbert, although he is her lover, to use a more intimate form of address. *Madam* is symbolic of the barrier between them, 'and she may have caught at it as the only straw within reach of that dignity or pride of birth which was drowning in her impetuous affection'. (iii, 80).

Forms of address can also on occasion match subtle variations in a person's tone of voice. 'The Distracted Preacher' provides us with an interesting example. Here the type of variation we observe seems to reflect fluctuations in human relationships rather than the status of particular characters; Stockdale has previously addressed Lizzy Newberry by her christian name, but as their relationship comes under strain he reverts to a more formal title:

> 'You are going indoors, Mrs Newberry?' he said.
> She knew from the words 'Mrs Newberry' that the division between them had widened yet another degree.
> 'I am not going home,' she said. 'I have a little thing to do before I go in. Martha Sarah will get your tea.'   (i, 194)

Here Lizzy responds by herself adopting an almost frozen style. Her non-dialectal pronunciation of 'Martha Sarah' is for instance indicative of this. Compare her normal pronunciation in '"Perhaps you would like Marther Sarer to bring it up?"' (i, 158) Further evidence of the responsiveness of Lizzy Newberry's style to her state of mind is to be found in the scene where she becomes engrossed in telling Stockdale about the technicalities of smuggling:

> 'Then we shan't try anywhere else all this dark . . . and perhaps they'll string the tubs to a stray-line, and sink 'em a little-ways from shore, and take the bearings; and then when they have a chance they'll go to creep for 'em.'   (i, 179)

Here parataxis, colloquialisms such as *'em*, and dialect expressions such as *a little-ways* combine to suggest involvement, but the effect is of course heightened by the use of occupational dialect (*dark*, *stray-line*, *creep* etc.).

Occupational dialect, like other forms of dialect, is used by Hardy for a variety of purposes. Like local dialect, it can be embedded in the narrative to provide colour and authenticity, as when Hardy tells us about that part of the Hussars' uniform 'which was called the pelisse, though it was known among the troopers themselves as a "sling-jacket"' (ii, 198). Or it can be used in dialogue, as an aid to characterization, as when Sergeant-Major Clark refers to 'forage' (ii, 306), the seaman Shadrach Jolliffe says 'Not that I care a rope's end . . .' (ii, 114), or

Harriet Peach the sailor's widow becomes a rather improbable pantomime character not least because of her droll repetition of 'avast, my shipmate!' (ii, 470ff).

Just as language varies from one occupational group to another, it varies from age-group to age-group. This is a type of variation which Hardy can also render with great economy, as when he captures the restricted syntax and unconventional vocabulary of a small child in: '"And my totties be cold, an' I shan't have no bread an' butter no more!"' (ii, 131), or, at the other end of the spectrum, the drooling baby-talk of amorous old age in: '"Bess its deary-eary heart! it is going to speak to me!"' (iii, 27). In such instances the linguistic peculiarities are to some extent dependent on physiological and psychological factors, but when the linguistic differences between generations reflect changes in society and the outside world we can more properly speak of historical dialect. Old Mrs Chundle's 'I woll' (iii, 14) and Mr Day's 'inkhorn' for 'inkstand' (ii, 191) are cases in point. Here we have residual dialect as Hardy must actually have heard it, but when we come to his historical stories proper we shall have to ask what his strategies were in representing still earlier stages of standard language and dialect, of which he can have had no direct experience.

In his historical stories Hardy generally represents dialect impressionistically, as in his more modern stories, using a sprinkling of non-standard forms which are hardly likely to hinder comprehension. Geographical differences are scarcely to be found, but otherwise, except in the children's story 'The Thieves Who Couldn't Help Sneezing', which is linguistically rather uniform, the same types of variation occur that we have observed above: other things being equal, men speak more broadly than women (compare Roger and his sister in 'Master John Horseleigh, Knight', Squire Dornell and his wife in 'Dame the First'), and the upper classes less broadly than their inferiors (compare Lady Baxby with the 'wench' in 'Dame the Seventh'), except that the 'ordinary bucolic county landlords' have a strong proclivity towards the vernacular. Compare for instance in the following the 'shrewd courtier and wise man of the world' Reynard with the rusticated Squire Dornell:

'Upon my honour, your charge is quite baseless, sir,' said his son-in-law. 'You must know by this time – or if you do not, it has been a monstrous cruel injustice to me that I should have been allowed to remain in your mind with such a stain upon my character. . . . That you was really opposed to the marriage was not known to me till afterwards!'

Dornell professed to believe not a word of it. 'You shan't have her till she's dree sixes full – no maid ought to be married till she's dree sixes! – and my daughter shan't be treated out of nater!'   (i, 231)

Perhaps because dialecticisms (e.g. *maid, nater*) frequently have an archaic ring about them, Dornell's speech is not otherwise marked as belonging to the eighteenth century, but Hardy has found it necessary to intersperse Reynard's standard with forms redolent of that period (e.g. *monstrous cruel, you was*) in order to provide temporal colour. Not surprisingly, the farther we go back in time, the more frequent archaisms become. Take for instance the speech of the bystander at the beginning of 'Master John Horseleigh, Knight':

'I liked him not. . . . He seemed of that kind that hath something to conceal, and as he walked with her he ever and anon turned his head and gazed behind him, as if he much feared an unwelcome pursuer. But, faith,' continued he, 'it may have been the man's anxiety only. Yet did I not like him.'
                                                                (ii, 361)

In order to match such an archaistic style, dialect, too, has to be interspersed with archaisms:

'The fond thing! I thought it; 'twas too quick – she was ever amorous. What's to become of her! God wot! How be I going to face her with the news . . .?'   (ii, 366)

Reference was made to Page's remark that in Hardy's novels the easy naturalness of the dialect speeches is all the more striking by contrast with the formal style of the narrative. A similar claim could hardly be made about the short stories, since here the narrative style is generally less formal and, indeed, can on occasion be colloquial, or even dialectal. Some of the stories in *A Group of Noble Dames* are for instance couched in the somewhat conversational style of their alleged narrators, while the 'framework' of 'A Few Crusted Characters' gives an opportunity for dialectal narrative.

However, this reduction in the tension between narrative and dialogue in the shorter stories is only relative, except perhaps in 'A Tradition of Eighteen Hundred and Four', and in any case other types of contrast are possible. Different varieties of English can act as a foil for each other in dialogue, as when the Duke interviews the shepherd boy in 'What the Shepherd Saw' (ii, 339f.), or, more subtly, since dialect as such does not come into play, when the Marchioness visits Milly in 'Dame the Third' (i, 287f.). The effect is underlined when speakers with different linguistic backgrounds 'echo' one another:

> 'Now father, listen . . .!' she sobbed: 'if you taunt me I'll go off and join him . . .!'
> 'I don't taant ye!'   (ii, 234f.)

> 'Hang it, ye look so tired and wisht . . .!'
> 'I am – weary and wisht, David; I am!'   (ii, 401)

In this last example Baptista's uncharacteristic lapse into dialect is indicative of her spiritual and physical exhaustion.

Moreover, the 'framework' technique offers opportunties for surprise and irony, as when, in 'A Few Crusted Characters', a curate is called upon to render village folk's speech, or a master-thatcher acts the contrasting parts of parson and clerk, or reproduces the Squire's words, but partly in dialect. Even in narrative, where we occasionally come across the phenomenon of 'parallel' or 'coloured' indirect speech,[12] a similar effect can be achieved, but with greater subtlety: 'The boy said that she was a widow-woman, who had got no husband, because he was dead' (i, 156). 'A little girl crept in at the summons, and made tea for him. Her name, she said, was Marther Sarer, and she lived out there, nodding towards the road and village generally' (i, 157).

Another way in which dialect can encroach on narrative is when, for the sake of local colour or for want of standard equivalents, dialect expressions are embedded in the text. As often as not, Hardy will provide his own explanation where the context does not help the reader sufficiently: ' "wuzzes and flames" (hoarses and phlegms)' (i, 14); 'a long white pinafore or "wropper"' (i, 56). In dialogue he will sometimes allow a character to explain: '"all this dark – that's what we call the time between moon and moon"'; '"a creeper – that's a grapnel"' (i, 179). However, it is clear that the latter device can be used only sparingly, and for most readers a glossary will be essential. Those appended to the volumes of the New Wessex Edition containing the short stories and to Pinion's *Hardy Companion*[13] obviously aim to provide unobtrusive help for the general reader rather than a linguistic commentary for the specialist. But even if we accept this objective, we shall still find that a number of dialect expressions have fallen through the net, and I include below all that I have lit upon.[14] Even though many of these are explained by their context, or are so similar to their standard counterparts that any commentary may seem superfluous, that there is still room for misunderstanding is demonstrated for instance by a German translator's rendering of *water-carriers* and *waterman* in 'The Waiting Supper' as the equivalent or 'cart' and 'ferryman' respectively.[15] In addition I include a few expressions whose 'official' interpretation seems to me to be open to doubt. My glosses are generally based on those to be found in *EDD*. Nouns are generally given in the singular, and verbs in their uninflected form.

VOLUME ONE

p. 60   *whew* To whistle; to rustle sharply.

p. 97   *fleet* To float.

p. 118   *all's winter* All this winter.

p. 131   *drong* A narrow passage or lane between two walls, hedges, etc.

p. 157   *by now* Just now. Martha Sarah's 'Just by now' is thus tautologous.

p. 179   *a little-ways* A short distance. This use of the plural *ways* for the singular is typical of the SW. See *EDD*, vi, 408 & *Grammar* §384.

p. 184   *brother-law* Brother-in-law.

p. 187   *owl's light* Twilight, dusk.

p. 195   *arm* Axle.

p. 269   *knotting* Hill gives 'knitting'. 'Tatting' seems more likely.

VOLUME TWO

p. 117   *cranky* Full of twists or windings, crooked.

p. 125   *plumness* Solidity.

p. 148   *sack-bag* Sack.

p. 149   *swound* Swoon, fainting-fit.

p. 151   *put, all-fours* Names of two card-games.

p. 164   *spitish* Ready to spit like a cat; spiteful; snappish, out of humour. According to Wright the first syllable is pronounced as *spit*, and he obviously assumes a link with this verb rather than with *spite*.

p. 223   *water-carrier* Ditch, watercourse in water-meadow. Compare *carriers* at p. 434, which Hardy explains as 'narrow artificial brooks for carrying the water over the grass'.

p. 228   *waterman* A man who waters the meadows.

p. 302   *beaufet* A corner cupboard, a recess for holding glass and china, generally with glass doors.

p. 411   *tacker-haired* A *tacker* is a shoemaker's waxed thread.

p. 417   *rithe* 'He's been living too rithe.' *A Hardy Companion* (p. 527) has '*rithe* (or *rathe*), fast'. However, *rathe* could hardly occur as *rithe*, and given the occasional tendency for *f* to become *th* in the SW,[16] equivalence between *rithe* and *rife* suggests itself. Compare the Somerset phrase *rife living*, meaning 'high living' (*EDD* under *rife*).

p. 466   *couch-heap* Heap of coarse grass roots piled up for burning.

p. 471   *'Talian iron* An Italian iron was an iron for crimping cap-frills.

p. 472   *guide my heart* Bless my soul. In exclamations or expletives *guide* can mean 'keep, preserve'. Compare p. 416: '"Guide the girl's heart! What! don't she know?"'

VOLUME THREE

p. 99   *Lord send* An exclamation or expletive. (*EDD* under *lord*)

p. 174   *meanfully* Presumably the meaning is 'deliberately'.

NOTES

1. Among the more wide-ranging studies are: Sabra D. Gilcreast, 'The Dorset Dialect in the Wessex Novels of Thomas Hardy' (Columbia University, unpublished M.A. dissertation, 1956); Patricia Ingham, 'Dialect in the Novels of Hardy and George Eliot', in George Watson, ed., *Literary English since Shakespeare* (London: Oxford University Press, 1970) pp. 347–63; Norman Page, *Speech in the English Novel* (London: Longman, 1973).

2. References are to the hardback issue of the New Wessex Edition: *The Stories of Thomas Hardy*, ed. F. B. Pinion (London: Macmillan, 1977) vols i, ii & iii.

3. Harold Orton, *Survey of English Dialects: Introduction* (Leeds: Arnold, 1962) p. 15.

4. Page, op. cit., pp. 68–9.

5. See Thomas Hardy, *Her Shattered Idol or The Romantic Adventures of a Milk Maid* (Chicago: Stein, 1910).

6. Joseph Wright, ed., *The English Dialect Dictionary* (1898–1905; rpt. London: Oxford University Press, 1970) iii, 403.

7. Randolph Quirk *et al.*, *A Grammar of Contemporary English* (London: Longman, 1972) p. 14.

8. William Barnes, 'The Waggon A-Stooded', *Poems of Rural Life* (London: Kegan Paul, 1898) p. 199.

9. Harold Orton et al., eds, *The Linguistic Atlas of England* (London: Croom Helm, 1978), maps M9, M15 and M27.

10. Yoshinoshin Gotol & Mamoru Osawa, eds, [A Draft of] *A Hardy Grammar*, pp. 156, 162, 164 & 169. (Copy in Dorset County Library, Dorchester.)

11. Ingham, op. cit., p. 354.

12. Page, op. cit., pp. 34–5.

13. F. B. Pinion, *A Hardy Companion* (1968; rpt. with alterations London: Macmillan, 1976) pp. 521–30.

14. I have, however, generally omitted any dialect words explained in the notes to Thomas Hardy, *The Distracted Preacher and Other Tales*, ed. Susan Hill (Harmondsworth: Penguin, 1979) pp. 351–61.

15. I.e., 'Karren' and 'Fährmann'. See Thomas Hardy, *Der angekündigte Gast*, trans. A. W. Freund (Leipzig: Insel, 1928) pp. 23 and 32.

16. See Martyn F. Wakelin, *English Dialects: An Introduction*, rev. ed. (London: Athlone, 1977) p. 98.

(Note: the above essay was in press before the appearance of Ralph W. V. Elliott's *Thomas Hardy's English* [Oxford: Blackwell, 1984], which will be reviewed in the next volume of the *Annual*.—Ed.)

Hardy's Deathbeds

Norman Page

Writing in 1880, John Ruskin found himself troubled by certain tendencies in the contemporary novel and pinned the blame for them on the conditions of urban life: according to his argument, city-dwellers, bored to desperation by the monotony of their existence, had begun to seek a synthetic excitement in the reading of fiction, and novelists had been quick to oblige by supplying a highly sensational variety of product. Nowhere, suggested Ruskin, was this more obvious than in the fictional treatment of death: 'the ultimate power of fiction to entertain [the Londoner]', he wrote, 'is by varying to his fancy the modes, and defining for his dullness the horrors, of Death'. Thus, in *Bleak House*, Dickens had killed off no fewer than ten of his characters; but (Ruskin goes on) it is not so much the number of deaths that is significant as the fact that nearly all these deaths are of 'inoffensive, or at least in the world's estimate, respectable persons; and that they are all grotesquely either violent or miserable'. This, he concludes, constitutes 'the peculiar tone of the modern novel'; and he contrasts Dickens with Walter Scott, whose novels demonstrate that 'In the work of the great masters death is always either heroic, deserved, or quiet and natural.'[1]

Hardy's career as a novelist was well under way by the time Ruskin wrote the essay I have quoted from; in fact *The Trumpet-Major* was appearing in *Good Words* at the same time that Ruskin's essay was being published piecemeal in *The Nineteenth Century*. Neither in that essay nor anywhere else in his voluminous writings does Ruskin mention Hardy; but I think it is worth enquiring how far Hardy was infected by this fictional fashion and how far he was prepared to yield to contemporary taste in this respect. His first published novel was a painstaking exercise in the popular genre of the 'sensation novel'. How far, in his major works, we may ask, does he rely upon death-scenes to stimulate the jaded appetite of the metropolitan or urban reader? What is the mortality rate in his novels? And how, and why, do his characters meet their end? – are their deaths (in Ruskin's phrases) 'heroic, deserved, or quiet and natural' (in the commendable manner of Scott), or 'violent and miserable' (in the regrettable manner of Dickens)?

First, though, two general points need to be made. Death is not just a literary convention but a fact of life, and the Victorian novelist accused of sensation-mongering may, from another point of view, be faithfully and legitimately representing the social realities of his time. Dickens in *Bleak House* fashions pathetic episodes out of the deaths of Jo the crossing-sweeper and the brick-maker's baby; but homeless waifs *did* die young, and the infant mortality rate *was* appallingly high. There is a curious parallel to Ruskin's scornful list of Dickensian deaths in a letter written by George Sturt in the 1890s. Speaking of village life in Surrey, he says:

> I was counting up last night the elemental tragedy stuff that has occurred in the cottages within 100 yards from here, since I came here seven years ago. Here's the bald catalogue:
> 4 deaths of old men
> 2 deaths of young men, leaving families
> 1 death of a mother
> 1 death of an infant
> 1 case of sunstroke, with delirium
> 1 case of haemorrhage: fits (man still lying between life and death)
> 1 girl home 'in trouble'

Sturt adds that 'All these affairs were more or less dramatic',[2] but a novelist who faithfully transcribed this catalogue of village tragedies would no doubt be accused of drawing it a bit strong. Since Dorset in the nineteenth century was something of a byword for rural misery, Hardy's experience may well have resembled that of Sturt, and he would not have needed to resort to imagination, or literary convention, to have a sense that life, especially the life of the poor, could be held on a very precarious tenure.

Again, quite independently of literary fashion, there is the peculiar cast of Hardy's own sensibility. His imagination was richly and readily nourished by the idea of death and its concomitants; his mind brooded congenially and habitually on worms and graves and epitaphs, and he was exceptionally receptive to the voices of things growing in a churchyard. A close brush with death may have accompanied his very entrance into the world. As he related in the autobiography.

At his birth he was thrown aside as dead till rescued by [the monthly nurse] as she exclaimed to the surgeon, 'Dead! Stop a minute: he's alive enough sure.'[3]

He adds in the same place that his mother 'had been near death's door in bringing him forth'. I shall not speculate how far the knowledge of this so nearly tragic – doubly tragic – start in life may have contributed to Hardy's temperamental gloom; and of course it could have had the opposite effect and have led him to regard himself as the favoured child of fortune. But we can be fairly sure that he would have become acquainted with these dramatic pieces of family history (or legend) at a tender age. Throughout Hardy's work there is a sense of the world as a place he might very easily never have entered, of life as a burden he only just failed to escape.

In the poem 'A Necessitarian's Epitaph' he speaks of 'A world I did not wish to enter', and in another very striking little poem, 'A Wish for Unconsciousness', he muses on what it would have been to have existed without being saddled with human consciousness:

If I could but abide
As a tablet on a wall,
Or a hillock daisy-pied,
Or a picture in a hall,
And as nothing else at all . . .

But live he did, and some of the most vivid and memorable images of his recorded experience are connected with mortality. To select a few at random: the silk-gowned murderess wetly dangling from a rope's end and watched by the wide-eyed village boy standing close to the gallows; the Montmartre cemetery incongruously glimpsed by the middle-aged Hardy through a window at the Folies Bergère; the ghastly mass exhumation from St Pancras churchyard under his nocturnal supervision; the Paris Morgue visited during the Hardys' honeymoon; the pets' graveyard he created at Max Gate; and the Roman skeletons he was gratified to discover during the excavation of the foundations of that house. Hardy was fascinated by the idea of bodily dissolution, and the ghosts to which his reason could not grant credence powerfully haunted his imagination. He was 'much possessed by death' and 'saw the skull beneath the skin'; and I suspect that a concordance of Hardy's poetry, for instance, would show such words as *death*, *funeral*, *coffin*, *pall*, as well as *ghost*, *spectre*, *apparition* and *haunt* to be very prominent. Given this sensibility, it would have been surprising if death had not played a large part in his fictional world, even if Victorian novelistic convention and social reality had not conspired to encourage him.

Hardy does not quite attain the Dickensian scale of mortuary lavishness, but there is no shortage of deaths in the Wessex Novels. In the six major novels there are some two dozen important deaths, more than half of which are violent or untimely. They include one judicial hanging, two drownings (of which one is probably a suicide), two other suicides, two deaths in childbirth or pregnancy, and five murders. Even those who die in bed do not necessarily enjoy deaths that (in Ruskin's phrase) are 'quiet and natural': thus Marty South's father dies suddenly and (as Ruskin would no doubt have insisted) grotesquely on learning that the elm-tree has been felled. His death is of the kind that sets in train momentous events; for his passing causes Giles to be turned out of his home, just as Jack Durbeyfield's death leaves his family homeless and the death of Henchard's child inaugurates a far-reaching history of misunderstanding. We can distinguish between those deaths which mark an ending (like those of Tess and Jude) and those which initiate a series of events (Mrs Henchard's passing allows another relationship to develop, and Mrs Yeobright is another character of more use to the novelist dead than alive). To all these we may add other intimations of mortality such as the premonition of death (as when Henchard sees his own 'corpse' floating down the stream) and the narrow escapes (as when Angel Clare nearly perishes of fever in Brazil, Clym Yeobright barely escapes drowning, and Boldwood is prevented from taking his own life).

Before we turn to the major novels in more detail, a glance at *A Pair of Blue Eyes* will serve to illustrate the early appearance of one or two persistent features of Hardy's treatment of death. The arresting image that dominates the final chapter of that novel is the heroine's coffin, and Hardy not only compels the reader's awareness of it as an object of a certain appearance and weight but shows a keen interest in the logistics of transporting a corpse from London to Cornwall. Elfride, it seems, has died of the effects of a miscarriage acting on an already weakened state. But in a sense she has been dying for a large part of the novel: *fragile* is a favourite epithet for her, she has the habit of turning deathly pale easily and often, and in a story containing many references to graves, tombs, vaults and coffins, she is a vulnerable and even a doomed figure. Early in the story she talks to Stephen Smith while they are seated on the tomb of a young man who has died for love of her; a later scene takes place in a family vault, where she is eventually to join the occupants. (Long afterwards Hardy put it on record that he had witnessed a similar scene at the age of fifteen; and it had evidently laid a permanent hold on his adolescent imagination.) For a novel partly based on the author's courtship and set in scenes of great beauty with which he had the happiest associations, *A Pair of Blue Eyes* seems remarkably impregnated with the taste of mortality. One other feature is worth noting: Elfride is last seen alive at the end of chapter 34. She then disappears from the action, to reappear five chapters later as a coffined corpse. As we shall see, this kind of withdrawal and dying at a distance is very characteristic of Hardy's handling of death.

Far From the Madding Crowd offers two contrasting episodes that exemplify quite different modes of presenting death. Pathos and sentiment predominate in the death of Fanny Robin, whereas Troy's murder is highly dramatic, even sensational. Fanny's death and its important aftermath extend through no less than four chapters. In chapter 40 Fanny reaches the Casterbridge Union, having walked from Melchester. In the following chapter Joseph Poorgrass tells Bathsheba that Fanny is 'dead in the Union'; again, Hardy shuns the deathbed itself and bounces the reader from a Fanny still engaged in the struggle for existence to a Fanny who is the subject of epitaphs. When Joseph is asked what she died of, he replies, '"general neshness of constitution . . . she was such a limber maid that 'a could stand no hardship . . . and a' went like a candle-snuff, so 'tis said. She was took bad in the morning, and . . . she died in the evening"'. I quote from the published text; but Simon Gatrell has shown that Hardy's

revisions had the effect of increasing the mystery of the cause of
Fanny's death.[4] (In the original version, Poorgrass says that he
believes 'it was from inflammation of the lungs, though some say
she broke her heart'.) Chapter 42 opens with a reference to a man
writing 'the name and a few other words' in chalk on the coffin-lid,
and ends with Gabriel rubbing out the last two words of the
inscription *Fanny Robin and child*. Again, this represented a change
of intention on Hardy's part, for the manuscript shows that in an
earlier version the existence of Fanny's child was disclosed at the
beginning of the chapter. In chapter 43, which opened a new
instalment in the original serial, Bathsheba hears a rumour from
Liddy, unscrews the coffin-lid, and learns the truth. It was this
chapter that provoked Leslie Stephen's objections to the excessive
emphasis on 'the cause of Fanny's death': Stephen found the
conversation between Bathsheba and Liddy 'a little unpleasant'
and added, 'I have some doubts whether the baby is necessary at
all.' Dr Gatrell has shown that Hardy removed 'almost every
direct reference to the baby' and toned down the drama of Liddy's
communication (her original 'there's *two of 'em* in there!' became
'whispered the remainder of the sentence slowly into Bathsheba's
ear'); in addition, the detailed description of the corpses in the
coffin was drastically cut.

Although Hardy did not describe Fanny's deathbed, then, his
original inclination was to dwell on her corpse and that of her
child at considerable length: there is surely something fascinated
and lingering in the deleted passage. He seems to be less
interested in the dramatic process of dying than in the static,
pictorial aspect of the dead, and his narrative comment under-
lines the effect of death on the girl:

> The one feat alone – that of dying – by which a mean condition
> could be resolved into a grand one, Fanny had achieved.

He adds that Bathsheba's 'humiliation' is Fanny's 'success'.

Nor is he in any hurry to quit the scene, for he now makes Troy
arrive and kiss the corpse, whereupon Bathsheba cries hysteri-
cally, '"I love you better than she did: kiss me too, Frank – kiss me!
You will, Frank, kiss me too!"' For the modern reader the really
startling aspect of the episode, especially in the original version, is
not the disclosure of the baby but the preoccupation with Fanny's
corpse as an object to be gazed on and touched. Hardy's

1a Magritte, 'The Listening Chamber', private collection, USA.

1b Max Ernst, 'Joie de Vivre', private collection, London (© DACS 1984).

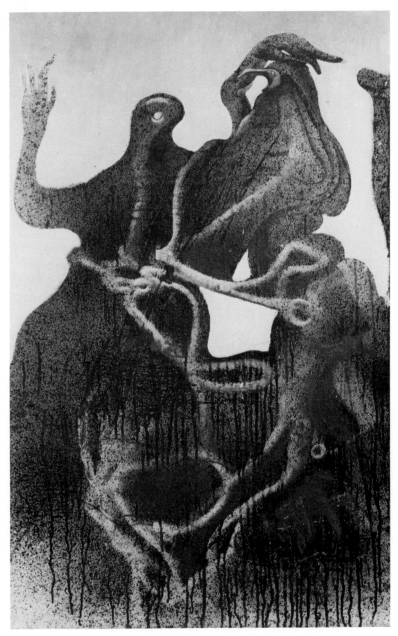

2 Max Ernst, 'Zoomorphic Couple', 1933 (by kind permission of the
Peggy Guggenheim Collection, Venice).

3a Hardy's illustration for 'In a Eweleaze near Weatherbury'
(*Wessex Poems*).

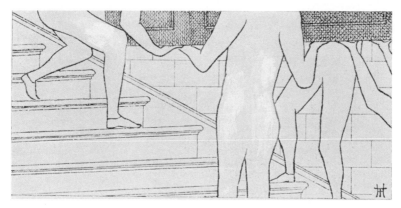

3b Hardy's illustration for 'Heiress and Architect' (*Wessex Poems*).

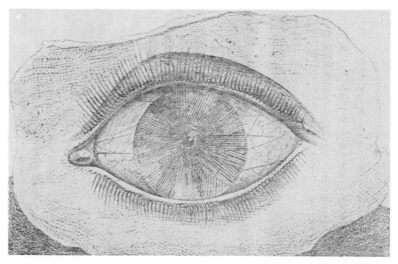

4a   Max Ernst, 'The Wheel of Light' (by kind permission of Thames & Hudson, © DACS 1984).

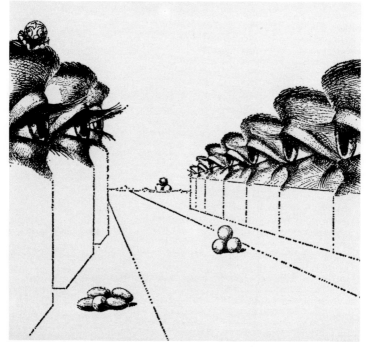

4b   Max Ernst, 'Visible Poem' (by kind permission of Thames & Hudson, © DACS 1984).

fascination – presumably the same fascination that prompted him shortly afterwards, to inspect the drowned bodies in the Paris Morgue during his wedding trip – comes close to that memorably expressed by Charles Wesley:

Ah, lovely appearance of death!
   What sight upon earth is so fair?
Not all the gay pageants that breathe
   Can with a dead body compare.

Fanny dead commands the stage as she has never done in her lifetime.

Troy's demise, in contrast, takes place onstage and is as sudden as it is brief. When Bathsheba refuses to go home with him, he seizes her arm, she gives 'a quick, low scream', and Boldwood shoots Troy at point-blank range. He is despatched to the next world in a single sentence:

He uttered a long guttural sigh – there was a contraction – an extension – then his muscles relaxed, and he lay still.

No dying speech, and this time no lingering over the corpse: Troy has to go to make possible a happy ending, and Hardy does the job without fuss and without any evident enthusiasm, though with competence, since the device effectively removes Boldwood from the scene at the same time.

In *The Return of the Native* Hardy's ambitions were altogether more grandiose, and the three major deaths in that novel have tragic aspirations. The fourth book of the novel ends with the death of Mrs Yeobright, and the final paragraph describes the procession that conveys her body off-stage. She has died, according to the doctor, of exhaustion acting on a weak heart, and in realistic terms the explanation is sufficient. But Hardy in this novel runs with the hares of symbolism as well as hunting with the hounds of realism; and Mrs Yeobright's heart is not only over-strained but broken. She has also been bitten by an adder – an accident in which Hardy sometimes lets his symbolic intentions break the surface, as when he makes Christian Cantle refer to 'the old serpent in God's garden'. Eustacia Vye's diverse literary ancestry surely includes Coleridge's Christabel and Keats's Lamia, and Hardy's scrupulous account of the natural history of Egdon (the whole episode contains many references to non-human life) accommodates a hint that the woman has transformed herself into a snake: Eustacia Vye becomes Eustacia Viper. On the other hand, Hardy the realist makes the doctor deliver the opinion that the snake's bite has not in fact been a cause of death.

Hardy makes a good deal of Mrs Yeobright's dying, and rightly so, for much hangs on it. But although he has not often been admired for narrative or stylistic economy, his account of her end is a model of effective simplicity and total relevance:

> Then there was a weeping of women, then waiting, then hushed exclamations, then a strange gasping sound, then a painful stillness.
> 'It is all over,' said the doctor.

At the same time it is a spectator's account: as so often in Hardy, the narrator is laying no claim to privileged status or inside information.

The final chapter of the fifth book, like the end of the fith act of a Shakespearian tragedy, also contains a funeral procession: this time no fewer than three bodies are placed in a horse-drawn vehicle. Clym is later resuscitated, but Eustacia and Wildeve prove to be beyond recall. Wildeve, it is clear, has been accidentally drowned: with characteristic impetuosity he has gone to rescue Eustacia 'without showing sufficient presence of mind even to throw off his great-coat'.

Eustacia's fate is more ambiguous, but the irresistible inference is that she has committed suicide, and it is hard to see what other fate than death could have awaited her. Like Elfride Swancourt, only with greater potency and insistency, she has almost from the start been associated with the idea of death. From her first appearance in the novel, Eustacia strongly recalls Tennyson's Mariana: Egdon is her moated grange, like Mariana she longs for an ideal lover who never materializes, and she only just fails to utter the cry that Mariana makes explicit: 'I would that I were dead!' Like Emma Bovary she cherishes romantic dreams that are doomed to disappointment and perhaps incapable of fulfilment: she longs to go to Paris like a Chekhov heroine pining for Moscow, but it is hard to imagine how she would actually have passed the time if she had suddenly found herself there. She anticipates

Hedda Gabler in appropriating her grandfather's pistols. All these obvious parallels – to which we may add her striking physical resemblance to the kind of Pre-Raphaelite maiden who winds up playing Ophelia (as in a sense Eustacia does) – suggest that she is a typical specimen of a familiar type of nineteenth-century heroine: not only a *femme fatale* but a fated female.

She leaves her home impulsively, and then realizes that 'she had not money enough for undertaking a long journey'. This realization causes her to droop like the melting effigy that Susan Nunsuch has fashioned in her likeness; the rain drips from her, and the tears stream down her face, as the wax melts and drips. Eventually she 'ceased to stand erect, crouching down under the umbrella as if she were drawn into Barrow by a hand from beneath'. She evinces that sinking tendency that Tennyson evokes in 'Tithonus' as part of the universal human fate:

Man comes and tills the field and lies beneath,
And after many a summer dies the swan.

Eustacia finds herself trapped: pride will allow her neither to ask Wildeve for money so that she can escape alone nor to flee with him as his mistress. After her final soliloquy we see her no more; the narrator's attention shifts to Susan Nunsuch, Clym, Thomasin, Diggory and Wildeve, and it is only fourteen pages later that Clym and Wildeve hear 'the fall of a body into the stream'. Once again, Hardy has withdrawn his narrative presence from the doomed heroine: her death is shown not as a process but as an accomplished fact. The peculiarity of Hardy's method and its curious lack of inwardness – its voyeuristic indifference to the inner life of the character at a moment of supreme crisis – is brought out by comparing Eustacia's end with that of Tolstoi's Anna Karenina a couple of years earlier. We not only see Anna to the very end but are made privy to her thoughts and perceptions. Like the tourists in the Paris Morgue, Hardy seems eager to contemplate Eustacia dead but has no interest at all in Eustacia dying.

Of Susan Henchard's death in *The Mayor of Casterbridge*, Douglas Brown remarks: 'The death itself, what is common to all, Hardy relates admirably, and as a social reality'.[5] Strictly speaking, though, Hardy does not relate Susan's death: he recounts a conversation between Susan and Elizabeth-Jane, and in the next paragraph abruptly informs the reader that 'some time later' Farfrae notices that the blinds are down in Henchard's house and on enquiry is told that Mrs Henchard is 'dead – just dead – that very hour'. As usual, the reader has been whisked out of the sick-chamber; or, to put it another way, Hardy's narrator has contrived not to be a witness of the woman's end. The 'social reality' that Brown rightly praises consists in the communal response to the news of the death. What is conspicuously missing, a gap in the text, is the *individual* reality of the dying woman.

Michael Henchard's death is somewhat more elaborately presented, but the lines of communication between protagonist and reader are cut before Henchard's last moments arrive: having witnessed at first hand so many dramatic incidents in which Henchard is involved, we are denied (or spared) a direct narrative of his end. The penultimate chapter of the novel ends with the words 'she saw him no more', following Michael's farewell to his pseudo-daughter: ' "I'll never trouble 'ee again, Elizabeth-Jane – no, not to my dying day! Good-night. Good-bye!" ' That dying day turns out to be not far off, and neither Elizabeth-Jane nor the reader does see him again directly. But a chance meeting with Joseph Whittle about half an hour after Henchard's death enables her, and us, to learn something of what has happened. Michael has walked, for the last time, along a road, just as he did on the first page of the novel, though he is now walking away from the reader rather than towards him, and his step is no longer 'measured' and 'dogged' – in Whittle's phrase, 'he wambled, and could hardly drag along'. He has been installed in an empty house (in this respect anticipating Tess's withdrawal from the world), has grown steadily weaker, and at last died. The nearest we get to direct contact with the dying man is through his will – the written equivalent of a deathbed soliloquy. The narrator speaks of 'the anguish of his dying', but we have not been permitted to witness the event or to feel that anguish. Hardy has characteristically distanced both event and emotion, leaving the reader to imagine it as best he may. Whittle has played the Fool to Henchard's Lear, and there is a Shakespearean echo in Henchard's reference to him as a 'poor fond fool'; but the parallel is less with the explicitness of Elizabethan or Jacobean drama than with the discreet holding at a distance of the business of dying that we find in the Greek tragic dramatists.

In *The Woodlanders*, not only do several deaths occur in the course of the action but the presence of the dead is quite strongly felt from the outset. The isolation of the major characters in their respective houses is intensified by the bereavements they have suffered: no character is shown with a complete set of parents, nor for that matter does any major character appear to possess any siblings. Some of these dead are explicitly referred to and felt as present: Grace Melbury's relationship with her stepmother is a rather formal one, and her motherless condition contributes to her sense of alienation; the history of Giles's dead father is recounted (and at one point Mr Melbury stands beside his grave); Mrs Charmond's late husband has purchased the remote house that constitutes a kind of prison for her. In this 'sequestered spot', as Hardy calls it, the dead outnumber the living; and this is a fact of life that for Hardy is of central importance. In a highly characteristic passage he defines the conditions under which life in such a spot is 'tolerable' for a thinking man:

> He must know all about those invisible ones of the days gone by, whose feet have traversed the fields which look so grey from his windows; recall whose creaking plough has turned those sods from time to time; whose hands planted the trees that form a crest to the opposite hill; whose horses and hounds have torn through that underwood; what birds affect that particular brake; what bygone domestic dramas of love, jealousy, revenge, or disappointment have been enacted in the cottages, the mansion, the street or on the green. The spot may have beauty, grandeur, salubrity, convenience; but if it lack memories it will ultimately pall . . . (ch. 17)

In other words, what is needful is the companionship of the dead.

At the end of *The Mayor of Casterbridge*, in an almost Shakespearean phrase, Hardy had referred to life as 'a brief transit through a sorry world'. In *The Woodlanders* it is not only the brevity, sadness and transience of life that are stressed but its subordination to the non-human world and the community of the dead. Whereas most novels present human activity against the background of a non-human setting, in *The Woodlanders* the setting is foregrounded and humanity, like its homes, makes only a limited impression upon it. In a novel in which the presence of trees is felt so strongly, we perhaps ought to add to the human casualty list the suffering and death of various trees – the elm that is felled outside old South's window, the oaks that are barked and left naked and wounded in chapter 19. Trees (like men) live and die, struggle and suffer: 'wrestl[e] for existence' is Hardy's phrase in chapter 42. As for the human dead, they seem to have an importance – it might almost be paradoxically described as a solidity of presence – that the living lack; and Marty South recognizes this when, in the novel's closing paragraph, she tells the ghost of Giles: 'Now . . . you are mine, and only mine.'

The death of Marty's father relatively early in the novel is (as I have already suggested) of the kind that initiates events rather than concluding them. Towards the end, chapter 43 contains an almost Elizabethan huddle of corpses, though it is true that the deaths of Mrs Charmond and her American lover are rather perfunctorily reported and are distant in place and time. Mrs Charmond clearly has to go, and Hardy's introduction of the passionate globetrotter from South Carolina is a fairly desperate remedy, the Victorian equivalent of the Shakespearean 'Exit pursued by a bear'. In contrast, Giles's death is in a vein of quiet realism and occurs on stage; still, the narrator's attention is fixed less on the dying man than on the two watchers by his bedside, Grace and Fitzpiers: they may be watching Giles, but they are also very conscious of each other, and the reader watches them rather than him. Giles has shown himself wilfully indifferent to his own welfare, so that there is an element of self-destruction blended with the natural causes of his death. He resembles Henchard in being dogged by ill-luck that is on analysis seen to be largely of his own making, and his end has something in common with Henchard. He exemplifies, too, Hardy's favourite theme of the extinction of the family: he is the last of his line, and Mr Melbury's epitaph on him is that 'now I've seen the end of the family, which we can ill afford to lose . . .'.

Untimely and even gratuitous though it is, the death of Giles Winterbourne, perhaps more closely than that of any other Hardyan hero, fits Ruskin's description of the 'quiet and natural' passing. If not quite natural in the sense of inevitable, it is a merging or reconciliation of the human with the non-human world: in Jean Brooks' expressive phrase, Giles 'dissolves into the wood',[6] and his dissolution has the quality we find in the bodily decline and decay of Wordsworth's peasants. It does in fact strongly recall the fate of the woodman described in Book VIII of *The Prelude*:

> Where the harm,
> If, when the woodman languished with disease
> Induced by sleeping nightly on the ground
> Within his sod-built cabin, Indian-wise,
> I called the pangs of disappointed love,
> And all the sad etcetera of the wrong,
> To help him to his grave.[7]

Tess of the d'Urbervilles also contains several deaths, and the manner of their presentation is by no means uniform. John Durbeyfield's is a necessary death – he has to die so that the family may become 'expellable' from their cottage – and it is quite summarily dealt with. He dies off-stage and suddenly, dropping down dead; the doctor's verdict, as reported by 'Liza-Lu, is that 'his heart was growed in'. Tess's baby dies onstage, if so brief and fragile a presence can be thought of as an actor in the drama; and Hardy dismisses it in a sentence that glances ironically at both orthodox Christianity and the tragic jokes of common life:

> . . . that fragile soldier and servant breathed his last, and when the other children awoke they cried bitterly, and begged Sissy to have another pretty baby.

As so often, however, Hardy shows an interest in the disposal of the mortal remains, and the reader is made vividly aware of the infant's burial and grave.

When we look at the deaths of the major figures, Alec and Tess, we predictably find Hardy faithful to his policy of bouncing the reader from a moment when the character is alive and even well to a later moment when his death already belongs to the past. Alec is seen in chapter 52 and does not appear again until chapter 56, where he is very briefly overheard by the landlady but not actually seen. After the scene at Stonehenge, Tess does not appear in the final chapter of the novel: only the symbolic black flag informs us of her death, as the drawn blinds inform us of Susan Henchard's. In his recent book *Fiction as Repetition*, J. Hillis Miller argues that these reticences are part of a significant pattern in the novel. He notes that, just as earlier Hardy has avoided describing his heroine's violation, later on he avoids describing the murder of Alec and the execution of Tess. Miller also notes that while 'Death and sexuality are two fundamental human realities, events which it seems ought to be present or actual when they happen, if any events are present and actual. In *Tess* they happen only offstage, beyond the margin of the narration, as they do in Greek tragedy.'[8]

Now one can readily think of sufficient reasons for the avoidance of direct description of these particular events: editors and circulating libraries, having strained at so many Hardyan gnats, would hardly have swallowed the camel of a detailed ravishing; to have shown Tess wielding the knife might have forfeited some of the reader's sympathy and would have jarred with the presentation of her as a passive victim; to have shown her mounting the scaffold or dangling from a rope's end like Martha Browne would have been distressingly painful. But such avoidances are in fact part of a wider tendency in Hardy: as we have seen, not only in *Tess* but throughout much of his best work death-scenes are avoided more often than not, and while making considerable fictional use of the *fact* of death Hardy seizes very few opportunities of describing the *act* of dying. There are novelists who firmly escort the reluctant or fascinated reader to the bedsides of their dying characters and spare him none of the details: but Hardy is not one of them. Not for him the stylized emotionalism of Dickens staging the death of Jo the crossing-sweeper, or the appalled realism of Lawrence describing the death of Mrs Morel, or the relentless clinical detail with which Flaubert charts the terrible last hours of Emma Bovary, and still less the harrowing presentation of the dying man's experience that Tolstoi subjects us to in 'The Death of Ivan Ilyich'. Conrad shows Winnie Verloc killing her husband like a butcher slaughtering a pig, but Tess's murder of Alec takes place behind a closed door. Hardy happily practises the kind of fiction deplored by Ruskin that involves a high mortality rate and a remarkable incidence of violent deaths, but he shows no relish for the actual dispatching of his characters to another world, though he shows no reluctance to contemplate a corpse in its coffin or a new-made grave. In the last chapter of his last novel it looks for a moment as if he is about to break his own rule: the reader is, for once, allowed to stand beside Jude's deathbed, and this hero endures a long dying. But at the last moment Hardy reverts to his custom: the instant of death is not described, the account jumping from Jude's bitter quotations from the Book of Job to Arabella entering the room and finding him dead.

After so many fictional deaths, let me conclude with three real ones. The death of Hardy's mother in 1904 is commemorated in a fine poem, 'After the Last Breath'. As the title indicates, the focus is not upon Jemima Hardy's death but upon its aftermath: with a characteristic movement Hardy turns aside from her last hours or moments to reflect on a world in which she has ceased to have a place. The capacity for feeling that she now no longer possesses is transferred to the inanimate objects of the sickroom:

> The lettered vessels of medicaments
> Seem asking wherefore we have set them here; . . .

What seems to be at work here is a strategy comparable to the narrative leaps of the fiction, and the reason is perhaps the same: the dying (which Hardy is too honest to sentimentalize or idealize) is something that he refuses to contemplate – it is so painful as to force him to avert his gaze (as he does quite literally in the Strang portrait in the National Portrait Gallery); and a means is found of implying the death through its antecedents and its consequences rather than presenting it directly. In a less personal poem, 'Her Death and After', the method is very similar: the narrator describes a visit to the deathbed of a woman he has loved and who has married another, but in the poem's most striking lines he turns from the dying woman to the non-human world:

> The rooms within had the piteous shine
> That home-things wear when there's aught amiss; . . .

The death of Emma Hardy is known in greater detail, and biographers have been able to reconstruct both the events leading up to it and her last moments. They are agreed that Hardy was present: the narrator of the Wessex Novels had the knack of slipping quietly away when a death was imminent, but the historical Thomas Hardy was not always so fortunate. We know that he was summoned to the dying woman's room by Emma's maid Dolly Gale. To quote Robert Gittings:

> When he saw how ill Emma was, he was at last shaken. 'Em, Em, don't you know me!' he cried. She was too far gone to answer him; . . . and in five minutes she was dead. The little

maid stood at the end of the bed, and saw Emma die with
Thomas bending over her.[9]

Denys Kay-Robinson's account is more tentative and properly
recognizes that Dolly Gale's recollections sixty years after the
event may have been subject to the fallibility of human memory:

> As soon as he saw Emma . . . his composure vanished, and
> hurrying to the bedside he asked her, 'Em, Em, don't you know
> me? It's Tom', or something similar. . . . it remains obscure
> whether Emma was by this time still conscious; what is certain
> is that she was unable to answer Hardy. Within less than five
> minutes her life flickered to a close; during those minutes the
> servant remained at the foot of the bed, and would have heard if
> Hardy had spoken again.[10]

Michael Millgate's recent account does not refer to the words
Hardy is said to have spoken to his dying wife, but confirms his
presence by her side at the moment of death.

So much for what Kipling calls 'the undoctored incident That
actually occurred'. But when Hardy came to describe Emma's
passing in the first of the 'Poems of 1912–1913' something rather
odd happened. He writes there:

> Never to bid good-bye,
>   Or lip me the softest call,
> Or utter a wish for a word, while I
> Saw morning harden upon the wall,
>   Unmoved, unknowing
>   That your great going
> Had place that moment, and altered all.

We can accept that Emma did not 'bid good-bye' or 'utter a wish
for a word', but Hardy was certainly not 'unknowing' that her
death was taking place. In the poem he has placed himself *outside*
the room in which Emma lay: his actual presence at the moment
of death has been transformed into an ignorant and innocent
absence. In the fiction created by the poem he has done something
very similar to what he had so frequently done as a professional
novelist, shirking the harrowing thought of Emma dying and

moving directly from Emma alive and apparently well to Emma dead, and a subject for elegies.

Of these three deaths, Hardy's own is the most fully and reliably documented. There is a whole series of memorable vignettes of his last days and hours – Florence reading aloud Browning's 'Rabbi Ben Ezra' and a favourite stanza from FitzGerald's *Rubáiyát*; Hardy signing (perhaps his last written words) a cheque for the Society of Authors Pension Fund; and dictating (his last poetic effusions) those startling squibs on Chesterton and Moore; more touchingly, Kate Hardy finding him looking 'just like father', and Hardy sipping 'kettle-broth' and asking for a piece of bacon grilled over the fire as his mother used to cook it. There is, however, a tantalizing obscurity about his last words. Robert Gittings tells us that 'Nellie Titterington heard him call out to Florence's sister, "Eva, Eva, what is this?"', and states that these were Hardy's last words.[11] but Florence Hardy's account in the typescript of the *Life* suggests that this may not be the whole truth. The printed version of the *Life* (p. 446) states baldly that 'Hardy remained unconscious until a few minutes before the end. Shortly after nine he died', with no mention of a last utterance. But the typescript contains twenty-four cancelled words, and the passage as originally written by Florence runs: 'Hardy remained unconscious until a few minutes before the end, when a few broken sentences, one of them heartrending in its poignancy, showed that his mind had reverted to a sorrow of the past. Shortly after nine he died.'[12] Now, 'Eva, Eva, what is this?' is not 'a few broken sentences', and it can hardly be described as 'heartbreaking in its poignancy' or taken as indicating that 'his mind had reverted to a sorrow of the past'. Professor Millgate tells us that Florence seems not to have been in the room when Hardy died; on the other hand it is hard to imagine what motive she could have had for inventing such a detail and then suppressing it. We shall probably never know what that poignant last utterance was, if it was ever spoken. Still, it is surely appropriate that Hardy's last major prose work, the autobiography, even in a portion that Hardy himself did not write and could not have written, should perhaps maintain a familiar pattern by holding back from telling us the full truth about the most interesting deathbed of all.

NOTES

1. John Ruskin, 'Fiction, Fair and Foul', *Nineteenth Century*, VII (1880); the relevant passage is reprinted in Philip Collins (ed.), *Dickens: the Critical Heritage* (London: Routledge & Kegan Paul, 1971) pp. 298–9.
2. George Sturt's journal for 26 June 1898; quoted in Arnold Bennett's introduction to Sturt's *A Small Boy in the Sixties* (Cambridge: University Press, 1932) pp. ix–x.
3. *Life*, p. 14.
4. Simon Gatrell, 'Hardy the Creator: *Far From the Madding Crowd*', in Dale Kramer (ed.), *Critical Approaches to the Fiction of Thomas Hardy* (London: Macmillan, 1979) pp. 86–8.
5. Douglas Brown, *Thomas Hardy: 'The Mayor of Casterbridge'* (London: Edward Arnold, 1962) p. 28.
6. Jean R. Brooks, *Thomas Hardy: The Poetic Structure* (London: Elek, 1971) pp. 228–9.
7. Wordsworth, *The Prelude*, VIII, 437–43 (1850 text).
8. J. Hillis Miller, *Fiction as Repetition* (Cambridge, Mass.: Harvard University Press, 1982) p. 118.
9. Robert Gittings, *The Older Hardy* (London: Heinemann, 1978), p. 149.
10. Denys Kay-Robinson, *The First Mrs. Thomas Hardy* (London: Macmillan, 1979) p. 228.
11. Gittings, op. cit., p. 211.
12. Richard H. Taylor (ed.), *The Personal Notebooks of Thomas Hardy* (London: Macmillan, 1978)). 287.

Hardy's Humour

Bryn Caless

> Withdrawing the stem of his pipe from the dental notch in
> which it habitually rested, he leaned back in the recess
> behind him and smiled into the fire. The smile was neither
> mirthful nor sad, not precisely humorous nor altogether
> thoughtful. We who knew him recognised it in a moment;
> it was his narrative smile.
> (From the description of Solomon Selby in Hardy's 'A
> Tradition of Eighteen Hundred and Four' in *Wessex Tales*.)

Humour is elusive of definition: few will agree on what is amusing
or comic, and even fewer will agree on why it is. Humour is a
subjective thing, requiring some emotional response from those
who experience or regard it. At the same time as calling forth our
happiest feelings, it suggests a threat to those feelings. The general
inadequacy of literary criticism to come to terms with humour in
any work of the imagination, let alone Hardy's, is perhaps a
demonstration of the unease, even the threat, which such humour
poses.

Mark Story perceptively remarked that 'The moralist lurking
within most critics' breasts has always felt rather threatened by
comedy'.[1] We may take humour, for the moment, to be a more
embracing term than comedy, and not synonymous with it, but
the sense of Storey's comment holds good. In Hardy's fiction, that
sense of unease or threat is often acute, and is directly related to
the way in which Hardy saw his world and commented upon it.
Humour in his work is by no means confined to mere quaintness of
rustics or ironic distance. In fact, the more distanced that we, the
readers, are from the source which expresses Hardy's humour, the
less successful it is likely to be. Rather, we respond most when
Hardy's emotional sympathy with a character is fused with his

111

sense of the incongruity inherent in that character's situation. It is within the tension generated by what is, compared with what should be, that Hardy's humour finds its characteristic potency. It is precisely there that the reader may experience the undercurrent of unease. Hazlitt's observation that

> Man is the only animal that laughs and weeps: for he is the only animal that is struck with the difference between what things are and what they ought to be[2]

finds essential correspondence in Hardy's expression. I hope to show that this incongruity between what exists and what is desired is a powerful element in Hardy's writing, and that, further, there was a development in his fiction from humour as an equation with innocence to humour as an artistic device which helped to express his belief in the 'ache of modernism'. I cannot hope to be comprehensive in so brief a discussion, but I will at least try to be specific.

Innocence is the hall-mark of Hardy's early humour. His rustic characters comment on affairs around them, but their ignorance of the world outside their own nooks and their unsophisticated, even fetichistic, reaction to events put them at a remove from the reader. They offer only an incidental gloss on what is happening in the foreground. When the choir discusses Fancy, Dick Dewy or Pa'son Maybold in *Under The Greenwood Tree*, there is much humour in their wry observations, but they are powerless to intervene, even when their occupation is threatened by the arrival of an organ. When the farm workers sing in *Far From The Madding Crowd* at the shearing supper, the irony of the lyrics is appreciated only by the reader, and then only retrospectively. They have no role to play in events. Active participation in the main action is left to Gabriel, Troy, Bathsheba and Boldwood.

Hardy's problem, if he was to make of humour and his 'chorus' more than simply a diversion, was to integrate these light moments with the momentous narrative actions. He had to find some way in which humour could be made to work in presenting a perspective on what was happening, not just a rest from it. In *The Return of The Native*, the rustics comment on the action, but Hardy's 'classical' purpose in the novel still subordinates them. In *The Mayor of Casterbridge*, the two groups who give perspective to the actions of the principals act as well as talk. The skimmington-ride is perhaps the main action that precipitates a crisis. By the time Hardy wrote *Tess of the d'Urbervilles*, the rustic 'chorus' were simultaneously observers and participants. The moment when all four milkmaids, trying to sleep in their bedroom, are racked with love for Angel Clare is on one level amusing, on another satiric of love's folly, and on a third mimetic of Tess's own internal struggle (chapter 23). This integration of the provision of humour with the wellspring of narration gives Hardy an artistic vehicle to express his purpose in a far broader and more complete way.

The role of anecdote can be seen to follow the same kind of development. Those in the early novels are simply funny snippets, often incorporating a wry experience. Mr Penny, shoemaker in *Under The Greenwood Tree*, recalls an instance of his professional acumen:

> I was a-walking down the lane, and lo and behold, there was a man just brought out of the Pool, dead; he had been bathing and gone in flop over his head. Men looked at en; women looked at en; children looked at en: nobody knowed en. He was covered with a cloth; but I catched sight of his foot, just showing out as they carried en along. 'I don't care what name that man went by,' I said in my bold way, 'but he's John Woodward's brother; I can swear to the family foot.' (ch. 3)

The lightness of tone which characterizes Hardy's 'Rural Painting' is not disturbed by the introduction of death. Our concern is with Mr Penny's demonstration of his skill as a recognizer of feet, and his recollection of his part in a grim event. The grimness itself is not insisted on; we are too soon involved in the gentle whimsy of the rest of the story. The purpose of the anecdote is to reveal something of Mr Penny's delightful character and to round out some of the action at the tranter's party. We can readily recall other instances: Joseph Poorgrass and the owl in *Far From the Madding Crowd*, Granfer Cantle's time with the militia during the Napoleonic invasion scare in *The Return of The Native*, and Charl's account of his fight with Joe the gamekeeper in *The Mayor Of Casterbridge*. By this point, the role of anecdote had developed considerably: Melbury's tale of his humiliation at school directly impinges on his preoccupation with Grace's education in *The Woodlanders*. When we get to *Tess of the d'Urbervilles*, Hardy has not only integrated anecdote into narrative substance but makes it serve directly in bringing the main concerns into focus. An example is found when Tess, rallying at Talbothays from the birth and death of her child, finds herself drawn to love Angel Clare. For his part, Clare idealizes her, seeing her as a virginal goddess in the half-lights of dawn when they meet. On one occasion, the butter will not 'come' from the churning, and Dairyman Crick relates this memory of the last time it happened:

> Jack Dollop, a 'hore's-bird of a fellow we had here as a milker at one time . . . courted a young woman over at Mellstock, and deceived her as he had deceived many afore. But he had another sort o' woman to reckon wi' this time and it was not the girl herself . . . we zid the girl's mother coming up to the door, wi' a great brass-mounted umbrella in her hand . . . and saying 'Do Jack Dollop work here? – because I want him! . . .' . . . [Jack] scrambled into the churn through the trapdoor, and shut himself inside, just as the young woman's mother busted into the milkhouse. . . . How the old woman should have the wit to guess it I could never tell, but she found out that he was inside that there churn . . . round she swung him, and Jack began to flop about inside. 'O Lard! stop the churn! Let me out!' says he, popping out his head. . . . 'Not till ye make amends for ravaging her trustful innocence!' says the old woman . . . and on went the churn, and Jack's bones rattled round again. Well, none of us ventured to interfere; and at last 'a promised to make it right wi' her. (ch. 21)

The garrulous old dairyman relishes the taming of the seducer, and the story is told with verve. The reader enjoys it too, but the enjoyment is tempered by knowledge of surrounding factors. Firstly, the tale is told directly to Angel Clare. Clare finds the story funny, but he is of course ignorant of its application to Tess. Tess is listening and feels that the anecdote has a direct bearing on her history. What is a 'humorous narration' to the listeners is depressing to her; 'not one knew how cruelly it touched the tender place in her experience'. The story directly brings Tess's dilemma into sharp focus for her, and for the reader it brings strong overtones of irony. No one will so forcibly take Tess's part as the old woman took her daughter's; no amends can now be made for the event which blighted Tess's life. When we later learn that

Dollop reneged on his promise and instead married an old woman for her money (chapter 24),[3] the thrust of the anecdote is made even more pertinent to Tess's wretchedness and the irony is further strengthened.

In this example, we can see that Hardy has made the anecdote into something much more than mere light relief or local colour. It points up Tess's agonizing internal struggle, and brings into play the fact that what happened to Tess had happened to many others before her and that, while we are concerned with the effect of Alec's violence upon her, the event itself is as old as time. It is the stuff of which the uninvolved make humorous capital, and within that tension between the spectator and the participant the success of the anecdote in furthering Hardy's artistic aim is to be estimated. Gabriel Oak's remark to Bathsheba that 'what is mirth to the neighbours is ruin to the woman' (ch. 29) is apposite here. It is the perspective which the humour provides – both broadly funny in itself and illustrative of the narrative theme – which shows that Hardy's own appreciation of what to do with the comic had deepened.

If we think about the use of language itself, we can detect a similar development in depth and broader application in the overall narrative scheme. Language with humorous intent is generally confined to the rustic characters, and in the early novels is principally located in malapropisms and unintended solecisms which reinforce rather than diminish the distance between reader and the object of the humour. Our sophistication is pandered to, but Hardy's intention is not to belittle his country people.

Let us look at two episodes which demonstrate the development. In 'The Three Strangers', tension is created when two men arrive at a party uninvited, and the news is received that a convict has escaped. Unknown to the partygoers, the first stranger, Timothy Summers, is the convict. A posse of men, led by the elderly parish constable, stumble off into the night in pursuit of Summers' brother, believing him to be the fugitive. The man is chased and cornered in the darkness, under a tree:

The band noiselessly drew up and faced him. 'Your money or your life!' said the constable sternly to the still figure.
'No, no.' whispered John Pitcher. ''Tisn't our side ought to say that. That's the doctrine of vagabonds like him, and we be on the side of the law.'

> 'Well, well,' replied the constable impatiently: 'I must say
> something mustn't I? and if you had all this weight o'
> undertaking upon your mind, perhaps you'd say the wrong
> thing too! – Prisoner at the bar, surrender, in the name of the
> Father – the Crown I mane!'

There is great delight in reading this, and the humour is precisely
located in the constable's self-conscious inadequacy of language.
Allied to the reckless chase across country at night and the posse's
Gilbertian trepidation when it confronts its quarry is the constable's awareness of the importance of his challenge, and the
legal 'weight o' undertaking' in how he does so. Things must be
done with a due fitness, with a ritual for the occasion. The rag-bag
of words is absurd only in context. The lawman is painfully alert
to the fact that he must 'say something' to bring the chase to its
proper conclusion, and the jumble of phrases, juxtaposing the
sacred with the legal, is a commentary upon the whole enterprise
– especially since they've got the wrong man entirely. Even John
Pitcher's comment that 'Your money or your life!' is the 'doctrine
of vagabonds' carries on the consistency of the moment. The root
of the incongruity is the importation of that other ritual in the
rustics' lives, that of the Church, because the moment demands
something dignified and appropriately sonorous. Yet there is also
a sense in which the wedding of Church and State, as the
combination of law-enforcement, is criticised. The constable is
very much a part-time law officer, and there is little radical
difference in moral value between the 'criminal' and the constable. The confrontation is a show, a façade, and is not to be taken
seriously.

  If we now contrast this episode with one from *The Mayor of
Casterbridge*, we can see how Hardy put the same basic comic
formula to greater use. The parish constable, Stubberd, is giving
evidence in the case of a female who committed an indecent
offence in public:

> 'Hearing a' illegal noise I went down the street at twenty-five
> minutes past eleven p.m. on the night of the fifth instinct,
> Hannah Dominy. When I had . . . proceeded to the spot I saw
> defendant at another spot, namely the gutter. . . . Spot
> measuring twelve feet nine inches or thereabouts from where
> I . . .'

'I object to that', spoke up the old woman, '"spot measuring twelve feet nine or thereabouts from where I," is not sound testimony!' The magistrates consulted and the second one said that the bench was of opinion that twelve feet nine inches from a man on his oath was admissible.

Stubberd, with a suppressed gaze of victorious rectitude at the old woman, continued: 'Was standing myself. She was wambl-ing about quite dangerous to the thoroughfare, and when I approached to be near she committed the nuisance, and insulted me.'

'"Insulted me." . . . Yes, what did she say?'

'She said, "Put away that dee lantern," she says.'

'Yes.'

'Says she, "Dost hear, old turmit-head? Put away that dee lantern. I have floored fellows a dee sight finer-looking than a dee fool like thee, you son of a bee, dee me if I haint," she says.'

'I object to that conversation!' interposed the old woman. 'I was not capable enough to hear what I said, and what is said out of my hearing is not evidence.' (ch. 28)

There are a number of elements which combine to produce the humour in this very funny court scene; and under those, again, is a serious artistic purpose on Hardy's part. The constable is well-versed in court procedure, so he can stop at any point in his evidence to allow the clerk to catch up in his note-taking. Stubberd inadvertently parodies the deliberate and ponderous delivery of a police officer, making incidentally a hash of the precision required of a testimony on oath. His malapropisms and over-literal evidence make a mockery of the august formality of the court, and the seriousness with which a trifling misdemeanour is taken adds to the air of pomposity. The old woman punctures these proceedings with her sharp interjections, and we learn that, having appeared in court so often, she is better versed in the legal niceties than those sitting in judgment. Her version of 'hearsay' evidence is delicious. The whole scene forms a coarse and earthy contrast with the tensions of the previous chapter (in which Henchard had browbeaten Lucetta into agreeing to be his wife) and at first we are content to enjoy the contrast for its own sake. Hardy's purpose is deeper. Sitting as one of the magistrates is Henchard, performing one of the few roles as civic dignitary left to him. The old woman is the furmity woman, in whose tent

Henchard had sold his wife twenty-one years before. She suddenly and maliciously reveals the sorry episode, and in the midst of the public court, before the other magistrate and law officers, Henchard is ruthlessly exposed for his past cruelty. The ex-mayor's humiliation is total – he goes on to lose Lucetta to Farfrae, as well as losing his business and his social status. Mrs Goodenough becomes his nemesis, and through the broad comedy there is a massive thrust towards Henchard's decline into oblivion. The mood of humour is inverted with consummate ease, and what Hardy has done is to create an episode in many ways similar to that in 'The Three Strangers', with this difference: instead of carrying on the lightness of tone, the comedy turns acid; the surprise is complete and Hardy has achieved a narrative coup. Hardy uses the same technique a little later in the same novel, when the constables encounter the skimmington-ride crowd and push their 'Gove'ment staves' up a waterpipe rather than face the possible belligerence of the merry-makers. The excuses they offer, and their generally well-developed sense of self-preservation, contrast with the more serious effect of the skimmington-ride for Lucetta and Henchard. The misuse of language, so much a stock-in-trade of the humorist, is developed and extended by Hardy, until it becomes a narrative technique in its own right, and a very effective way of highlighting the main actions in the story.

In common with many who write comedy, Hardy makes use of certain character-stereotypes to create humorous effect. One of these stereotypes is the old man, the ancient who relives his past glories, insists on his continued vitality, and exhibits a toothless irreverence for social forms. The same pattern of development from innocence to serious narrative purpose may be detected when we recall the saintly Grandfather William Dewy in *Under The Greenwood Tree*, the boastful old Maltster in *Far From the Madding Crowd*, the jigging and jocular Granfer Cantle in *The Return of The Native*, the incompetent but loyal Robert Creedle in *The Woodlanders*, the wily rogues Coney and Longways in *The Mayor of Casterbridge* and perhaps the shiftless John Durbeyfield in *Tess of the d'Urbervilles*.

We might suppose that the type can be taken no further, and that Hardy had squeezed all the limited humour from sterile old age and its associated infirmities.[4] However, Hardy did return to it once more, with a purpose of making more of the character than simple comic by-play.

In *The Well-Beloved*, Jocelyn Pierston's pursuit of an elusive ideal woman has dominated his life. Its futility is the object of sharp irony from Hardy, and the focus of some bitter humour. When Jocelyn first meets Avice Caro III, he is sixty but could pass for any age, it being a dark night and he being 'well-preserved, still upright, trimly shaven, agile in movement' (part III, chapter ii); but he confronts himself in a mirror and is forced to admit that he is not young any more. What he sees belies his conviction that he is still spry:

> There was history in his face . . . his brow was not that blank page it once had been. . . . He remembered the coming of this pale wiry hair . . . this wrinkled corner, that drawn bit of skin. . . . Time was against him and love. (III, iii)

The reflection of himself as he is, and not as he believes himself to be, returns at dawn one morning, when he catches sight of 'something ghostly'. It is 'his own shape' which startles him:

> The person he appeared was too grievously far chronologically in advance of the person he felt himself to be. Pierston did not care to regard the figure confronting him so mockingly. Its voice seemed to say 'There's tragedy hanging on to this!'. (III, iv)

The full absurdity of 'a young man of sixty' paying court to a girl still in her teens is only brought home to Pierston when he admits to having been in love with both her mother and her grandmother. The following exchange takes place:

> 'My mother's and my grandmother's,' said she, looking at him no longer as a possible husband, but as a strange fossilized relic in human form. . . .
> 'Your mother's and your grandmother's young man,' he repeated.
> 'And were you my great-grandmother's too?' she asked, with an expectant interest in his case as a drama that overcame her personal considerations for a moment. (III, iv)

There is cruel satire and irony here, but at the same time we are made aware of Pierston's reluctant acceptance of his unsuitability as a lover, and his growing into an old man. There is sadness in his acknowledgement of his lost youth, in his frustrated search for the well-beloved, and in his proximity to impotence, senility and death. Beneath the absurdity and folly of Pierston's pretension, Hardy is showing us something of the pain of old age, and the lack of dignity in one in whom the flame still burns but the wherewithal has gone. We can see that here the humour is being put to use over and above the merely comic. From being a stereotype, wheeled in for a cheap laugh, the old man has become an object of pity and a character with depth and dimension. Hardy achieves through this a synthesis between laughter and tears, exemplifying his own dictum that comedy is tragedy if you look deep enough.

Another stock character in Hardy's comic repertoire is one whom we might term the 'village idiot'. He is invariably sexless, gangling, physically weak and feeble-minded. Thomas Leaf is the first such, in *Under The Greenwood Tree*. He does little but laugh nervously, is treated with kindly severity by other members of the choir, and says that he 'never had no head, never!'. His timidity and inadequacy are the focus for some rather cruel humour – cruel because in many ways it is uncharacteristic of Hardy to invite us to laugh at handicap or misfortune. The recurrence throughout Hardy's fiction of the 'Leaf' type suggests that Hardy saw some possibility of getting comic mileage from such a character. Subsequent characters, Andrew Randle, Laban Tall in *Far From the Madding Crowd*, William Worm in *A Pair of Blue Eyes* and Christian Cantle in *The Return of The Native* advance the stereotype little, and it is not until we reach *The Mayor of Casterbridge* that Hardy finds an effective additional role for the 'idiot' to play.[5]

Abel Whittle is solidly in the 'Leaf' pattern, being a lean

> round-shouldered blinking young man of nineteen or twenty, whose mouth fell ajar at the slightest provocation, seemingly because there was no chin to support it. (ch. 15)

Whittle is the cause of the first breach between Henchard and Farfrae, after the mayor had driven Whittle trouserless from his house to teach him a lesson for being perpetually late to work. When Farfrae sends Whittle back to get dressed, Henchard feels publicly and deliberately thwarted, and he and Farfrae become estranged. However, at the end of the novel, when Henchard is alone, friendless and a 'dark ruin' of his former self, Whittle rises above the merely comic and achieves an elegiac dignity. He describes Henchard's final hours to Elizabeth and Farfrae:

'I zeed that he was low, and I followed on still. Then 'a said, "Whittle, what do ye follow me for when I've told ye to go back all these times?" And I said, "Because, sir, I see things be bad with 'ee, and ye wer kind-like to mother if ye were rough on me, and I would fain be kind-like to you." Then he walked on, and I followed; and he never complained at me no more. We walked on like that all night; and in the blue o' the morning. . . . I zeed that he wambled, and could hardly drag along. By that time we had got past here, but I had seen that this house was empty as I went by, and I got him to come back; and I took down the boards from the windows, and helped him inside. "What, Whittle," he said, "and can ye really be such a poor fond fool as to care for such a wretch as I?" . . . But he didn't gain strength, for you see ma'am, he couldn't eat – no, no appetite at all – and he got weaker; and today he died."' (ch. 45)

Whittle's stature, as he tells the manner of Henchard's passing, far surpasses any comic function he had. It hearks back to Marty South's broken-hearted requiem for Giles Winterborne, but the great difference is that Marty had always had a quiet dignity. Whittle had had none, until now. He had been the fool ('wittol') to Henchard's Lear, and in his simplicity and innocence, he confirms the greatness of the Mayor's fall. It is apposite that one whom Henchard had treated so harshly should befriend him in his hour of despair, and be the only one to offer comfort in his final moments. Farfrae's comment ('Dear me, is that so?') confirms him as a cold character, lacking in breadth of sympathy. For all his skill and ability, it requires a fool to show him how to feel. Hardy gambled much on his transmutation of the character of the idiot into the elegist, but he succeeds triumphantly, demonstrating the proximity again of laughter to tears.

I want to complete this short foray into the world of Hardy's humour by examining two different aspects of his genius. Both are from short stories.

'Absent-Mindedness in a Parish Choir', from 'A Few Crusted Characters',[6] is a story which expands the anecdote and demonstrates the affectionate comedy that Hardy could find in his fellow country dwellers. The choir had been playing vigorously in its secular role at jigs and dances in Christmas week up and down the parish. They were so cold in the church gallery on the Sunday after Christmas that they imported some warm drink for the afternoon service. The effects of the alcohol and an inordinately long sermon sent them all to sleep, so that they did not hear the vicar announce the final hymn. A boy nudged the leader awake and said 'Begin!' The leader of the choir is fuddled and bemused:

> . . . The church being so dark . . . he thought he was at the party they had played at all the night before, and away he went, bow and fiddle at 'The Devil among the Tailors', the favourite jig of the neighbourhood at that time. The rest of the band, being in the same state of mind and nothing doubting, followed their leader with all their strength, according to custom . . . then Nicholas, seeing nobody moved, shouted out as he scraped. . . . 'Top couples cross hands! And when I make the fiddle squeak at the end every man kiss his pardner under the mistletoe!'

The glorious incongruity of the choir's action, the frenzied activities of the players, the yells of the leader and the stunned incredulity of the congregation make this a comic *tour-de-force*. The juxtaposition of the sacred and secular creates a superb moment of comedy, capped only by the Squire's apoplectic response:

> 'Not if the Angels of Heaven,' says the Squire (he was a wickedish man, the Squire was, though now for once he happened to be on the Lord's side) – 'not if the Angels of Heaven come down,' he says, 'shall one of you villainous players ever sound a note in this church again; for the insult to me, and my family, and my visitors, and the pa'son, and God Almighty, that you've aperpetrated this afternoon!'

The public embarrassment is complete and the choir is routed. The order of the Squire's priority of recipients of insult adds to the amusement, though there is a touch of ironic sadness in that the good-natured musicians are expelled by a 'wickedish' man from their church activities. The story has affinities with *Under The Greenwood Tree*, though in the short story the choir themselves are responsible for their expulsion. In both cases, the choir is replaced by an organ. In the short story, the result is that 'however sinful inclined you was, you could play nothing but psalm-tunes whatsomever'.

The innocence of the humour, the parochiality of the setting, and Hardy's obvious delight in the local peccadilloes find their most complete engagement in this story, and in others from 'A Few Crusted Characters'.[7] The fact that they are grounded in a tiny part of Wessex long familiar to Hardy, concern the local people, demonstrate his dictum that a story must contain something unusual to merit the telling, and have the quality of fireside yarns (with all the characteristic qualities of extraneous detail, affectionate recall and irrelevance) help to base the humour in something Hardy genuinely loved, and about which he clearly enjoyed writing. The stories are at once exaggerated and authentic, funny and gentle, mocking and sympathetic. We do not look for great truths or profound insights from them, but we can find a revelation of the country character in the humour and incongruity, and they are refreshing pleasures, especially when seen in the context of Hardy's serious work.[8] Yet that very innocence limits the stories; they are not fully integrated within Hardy's artistic vision. They do not offer insights into 'the heart of a thing' except tangentially. We must take them as they are: glimpses into a long-vanished, innocent, unworldly world of the Wessex peasant.

Where 'Absent-Mindedness in a Parish Choir' offered a picture of a world in which things were ordered and defined, the second story to concern us offers a completely different perspective. I will try to show that Hardy's skill as a humorist is fused with his ability as a 'seer' to create an artistic whole. 'Old Mrs Chundle',[9] concerns the efforts of a zealous young curate to 'save the soul' of old Mrs Chundle, and the lengths he goes to in order to secure her attendance at church. At first, he tries to remedy her deafness with an ear-tumpet, but this is unsuccessful. He then fixes up a tube direct from the pulpit to her seat in church, and on the following Sunday the arrangement is put to the test for the first time:

As soon as he came in from the vestry the curate perceived to his satisfaction Mrs Chundle in the seat beneath, erect and at attention, her head close to the lower orifice of the sound-pipe, and a look of great complacency that her soul required a special machinery to save it, while other people's could be saved in a commonplace way.

Unfortunately for the enterprising curate, drawbacks in the machinery soon develop, and he realises that steam is rising from the bell-mouth of the tube-end in the pulpit, and he can smell onion stew from Mrs Chundle's breath. Failing to block out the smell with his handkerchief, he soldiers gamely on with his sermon:

> 'If you carefully analyze the passage I have quoted,' he continued in somewhat uncomfortable accents, 'you will perceive that it naturally suggests three points for considera-tion –'
> ('It's not onion: it's peppermint,' he said to himself.)
> 'Namely, mankind in its unregenerate state –'
> ('And cider.')
> 'The incidence of the law, and loving-kindness or grace, which we will now severally consider –'
> ('And pickled cabbage. What a terrible supper she must have made!')
> 'Under the twofold aspect of external and internal conscious-ness.'

We might pause here for a moment, and consider what is happening. Not only is Mrs Chundle's activity with the tube a source of amusement for the reader (and of hilarity for the choirboys in the stalls), but we also find humour in the curate's increasing desperation. The identification of peppermint, cider and pickled cabbage picks up, and echoes mockingly, his three points for 'several' consideration in his sermon, including, ironically, the state of 'loving-kindness or grace'. His lofty discourse, pitched in academic language far above his flock's understanding and dealing in abstractions, is undermined by the very real and prosaic smells wafting up to him through the tube. It is also a 'coming irony' when he talks so airily about loving-kindness, because his lack of common understanding (and kindness in the sense of fellowship with one's kind) is exposed both in his inappropriate sermon and in his treatment subse-quently of Mrs Chundle. His addressing of his congregation as 'brethren' and his 'discernment' of actions as 'morally good and indifferent', not only act as an ironic commentary on his present actions and feelings towards Mrs Chundle, but directly anticipate what he will do. Finally, the mention of the 'twofold aspect of external and internal consciousness' parodies his own thought-processes while the episode unfolds. He is externally concerned with the elaboration of his sermon text, but internally agonized by the miasma from the tube. The 'layers' of humour interact, each commenting on the others.

Mrs Chundle is delighted with the new machinery, for she can hear every word; but the curate's patience is wearing thin. He withstands another Sunday, but finally decides to have the tube removed before going through it all again. A message comes from the old woman asking him to visit her, but he does not go – partly out of irritation with her and partly from fear of a tirade about taking the tube away. He eventually trudges out to her house in a 'vexed mood' determined to stick to his resolution, only to find that she is dead. A neighbour explains that she was too anxious to get to church, and strained her heart running up the hill.

> 'Two or three times she said she hoped you would come soon, as you'd promised to, and you were so staunch and faithful in wishing her good, that she knew 'twas not by your own wish you didn't arrive . . .'

The broad satire and comedy has now developed into a sharp irony, and the curate feels suitably humbled. The old woman's faith in him, her eagerness to attend the service, her faith that he would come and her death are all inversions of the mood of Rabelaisian humour which went before. We are no longer enjoying burlesque or fun, but a confrontation of the gap between intention and action. Mrs Chundle's simplicity, which before was amusing, is now dignified by her death, but her gestures of love and faith are not yet finished:

> It was a small folded piece of paper, directed to him and sealed with a thimble. On opening it he found it to be what she called her will, in which she had left him her bureau, case-clock, four-poster bedstead and framed sampler – in fact all the furniture of any account she possessed.

This is the final twist of the knife in the curate's wound of shame. The reader has very probably followed with the curate through the story, seeing Mrs Chundle as a funny but exasperating person; and with the curate's humbling comes ours also. From seeing Mrs

Chundle as a figure of fun, with a wheezy wit and a crusty temper, we realize that she was capable of love and self-sacrifice. It is a story whose ending makes one gasp, so unexpected and complete is the inversion. Nothing I know by Hardy so clearly and aboslutely expresses his belief that laughter is close to tears. In the pathos of Mrs Chundle's death, we have one of the most moving moments in Hardy's fiction.

I have deliberately avoided the temptation in this article to catalogue all the varieties of humour in Hardy's fiction. Such a listing would make Hardy appear more deliberate and more programmatic in his use of humour than is the case. We have become so familiar with the character of the gloomy Hardy, fostered alike by recent biographers and by his later, darker work, that it is easy to forget or ignore that he had a lighter nature. Even if we acknowledge that lighter side, we are apt to relegate it to his early writing and prefer to think that *Jude the Obscure* or 'In Tenebris' is the 'real' Hardy. There is no doubt that Hardy was constitutionally melancholic, and as time went on, the darkness obtruded more and more into his interpretation of the world; yet there is plenty of evidence to suggest that he retained his robust and finely-tuned sense of humour. The humour can be savage (as with some of the waspish asides in *The Life*) or flat-footed and contrived (as in *The Hand of Ethelberta*). When concerned with articulate, educated people, his humour is laboured and often self-defeating, but when fully engaged with the 'Wessex Folk' whom he exasperatedly loved he finds his surest touch.

He was aware, as perhaps few writers have been, of the pervasive effects of incongruity. He remarked in the General Preface to the Novels and Poems, written for the Wessex Edition of 1912, that

> Some natures become vocal at tragedy, some are made vocal by comedy, and it seems to me that whichever of these aspects of life a writer's instinct for expression the more readily responds, to that he should allow it to respond. That before a contrasting side of things he remain undemonstrative need not be assumed to mean that he remains unperceiving.

In other words, Hardy is telling us that just because he isn't always funny doesn't mean he is blind to the humorous, or that conversely, he is unaware of sadness lurking beneath the most joyous of his humorous interludes. If he was a person who responded, as his life went on, to the more tragic aspects of existence, then at least he could make humour serve his turn by elaborating it, and giving it a broader role in his canon. In 'Old Mrs Chundle' he comes closest to synthesizing comedy and tragedy without detriment to either. His ability to perceive the inter-relationship between the two is matched by his capacity to express it. Within his presentation of humour, we find perceptions of the difference between what might be and what is – a mode which Hardy found perfect for his particular vision. The incongruity expresses both itself and his world-view. His humour is not to be dismissed lightly, or explained away as a recreation between bouts of deep gloom, but ought to be regarded as an integral part of his artist's perception. Baffling though it may sometimes be, we must see it as a component of his personality that informs and enlivens his fiction and poetry.

NOTES

1. Mark Storey, *Poetry and Humour from Cowper to Clough* (London: Macmillan, 1979) p. 3.
2. *The Complete Works of William Hazlitt*, ed. P. P. Howe (London: Dent, 1930) IV, p. 5.
3. Dollop is himself served by discovering that the woman's money is lost by her marriage.
4. One might include also Lord Mountclere in *The Hand of Ethelberta*, Squire Derriman in *The Trumpet-Major*, and Farmer Lovill in 'Destiny and a Blue Cloak'.
5. However, Cantle does take part in the action of *The Return of the Native*, particularly when he loses the money entrusted to him by Mrs Yeobright for Clym, while gambling with Wildeve.
6. R. C. Carpenter's 'How to read "A Few Crusted Characters"', in *Critical Approaches to the Fiction of Thomas Hardy*, ed. Dale Kramer (London: Macmillan, 1979), offers a stout defence of these stories. Kristin Brady describes the collection as one in which 'ostensibly farcical situations' are turned into 'Tragedies of Circumstance' (*The Short Stories of Thomas Hardy* [London: Macmillan, 1982] pp. 152, 98).
7. Specifically, 'Tony Kytes, the Arch-Deceiver'; 'Old Andrey as a Musician'; 'Andrey Satchel and the Parson and the Clerk'; and 'An Incident in the Life of George Crookhill'.
8. While Hardy was writing 'A Few Crusted Characters' he was also engaged in completing *Tess of the d'Urbervilles*, and the short sketches seem very much like a holiday from the great novel.
9. The story was written, according to Hardy, 'about 1888–1890' but remained

unpublished until 1929, when Florence Hardy arranged its appearance in a Philadelphia journal. It is included in *Old Mrs Chundle and Other Stories*, ed. F. B. Pinion (London: Macmillan, 1977). Pinion suggests that Hardy did not publish the story because he was reluctant to be accused of irreverent intentions.

A Survey of Recent Hardy Studies

Richard H. Taylor

The review-essay is a seductive medium in which the writer may exercise his idiosyncrasies, prejudices or enthusiasms under the banner of scholarly objectivity. It is instructive to compare the attitudes and practice of three distinguished recent exponents of the form. Graham Hough, in 'Embarrassed' (1982), starts from the even proposition that 'there has been an abundance of good critical writing about Thomas Hardy, from Lionel Johnson in 1894 to our own day', and goes on to give an urbane yet searching account of several recent studies. John Bayley, in 'His Eye for the Ladies' (1982), reminding us that 'Hardy's imagination was always in the intellectual forefront of his age', observes that 'Hardy's popularity still increases and his status has never been higher, even in the avant-garde circles which at one time extended to him a friendly but evident condescension.'

The odd man out is Donald Davie, in 'Raining' (1983), whose essay is fuelled by just such reactionary condescension, and a querulous cynicism towards, apparently, both Hardy and those who are attracted to his work. The latter, we learn, tend to have 'second-class minds'. I understand that a response to Davie's concern about 'the academic growth-industry' in Hardy studies is to be found in the Editor's introduction to the present volume, but a deprecatory word should be said about Davie's gratuitous pot-shots at the admirable Hardy Society and its publications (edited by Dr Frank Pinion and Dr James Gibson, who could scarcely be convicted of possessing second-class minds!). Davie's old-fashioned attitudes are expounded in an essay which may be commended as entertaining knockabout stuff, though his fairly arrogant assumption that most Hardy critics are either complacent hagiographers or practitioners of 'bare-faced book-making', or both, is to be deplored.

The reasons for the Hardy 'growth-industry' are simpler and more positive than Davie predicates. As John Bayley tells us, Hardy 'wrote about class and sex – the great topics of public interest – in his own inimitable way', and he responded 'self-consciously to changes in feeling about God and social justice and the New Woman' and 'absorbed these things into his own peculiar creative process'. Bayley claims that 'it is to this that the English common reader has always effortlessly if uncomprehendingly responded, and highbrow critics are now getting around to a methodical analysis of how it works'. This is both a more generous and a more accurate explanation of, and justification for, current Hardy criticism.

EDITIONS AND TEXTUAL STUDIES

This year has seen something of a recession in the Hardy 'growth-industry'. Only one book-length critical study has appeared, and among new editions of Hardy's work only one is textually significant. It is not Walford Davies's *Selected Poems* (1982) for the Everyman Library, which has a sound introduction and some useful analyses, but also an arrangement of the poems in thematic groupings which compare unfavourably with those in T. R. M. Creighton's 1974 selection, *Poems of Thomas Hardy*. Nor is it Carl J. Weber's *Hardy's Love Poems* (1983), a museum piece from 1963 ungraciously revived without revision after two decades of scholarship have exposed the factual errors in Weber's editorial introduction to 'Hardy's Cornish Romance' (itself a pastiche of passages from *Hardy of Wessex*, published 1940, and *'Dearest Emmie'*, published 1963). Only poems relating to Emma are published (not 'all his love poetry' as the blurb promises) and Weber alters their sequence, including that of the '1912–13' poems, to one of his own devising. Weber's introduction is laced with bio-critical assumptions and surmise, and the reprinting of his original bibliography is inexcusably misleading to those who seek enlightenment about the love poetry which probably constituted Hardy's finest poetic achievement. Weber's unremitting and pioneering contributions to Hardy studies are ungratefully served by this revival.

    A substantial contribution to textual appreciation of Hardy is, however, made by the fine new Clarendon Edition of *Tess of the d'Urbervilles*, edited by the late Juliet Grindle and Simon Gatrell (1983). In a 1979 essay on 'Hardy, House-Style, and the Aesthetics of Punctuation', Simon Gatrell demonstrated the degree to which Hardy's punctuation was vandalized by compositors. Because of this, Hardy's manuscript of *Tess* is here used as the copy-text: in the *Graphic* serialization of the novel over 3000 such punctuation changes were made by the printers, and many were transmitted into the Wessex Edition text. Every substantive variant through the manuscript and succeeding editions is recorded in this impeccable editorial enterprise. Like Dale Kramer's 1981 Clarendon Edition of *The Woodlanders*, this is a rich yet austere production, justified not on pedantic grounds but because it authoritatively restores the precision of Hardy's intentions.

The second revised impression of *Tess* in 1892 is the subject of one of L. E. W. Smith's 'Bibliographical Notes' (1983), a brief but helpful amplification of some points in Richard Purdy's *Thomas Hardy: a Bibliographical Study*.

TOPOGRAPHICAL STUDIES

'Could you, whenever advertising my books, use the words "Wessex novels" at the head of the list?' Hardy asked his publisher, 'I find that the name *Wessex*, wh. I was the first to use in fiction, is getting to be taken up everywhere: and it would be a pity for us to lose the right to it for want of asserting it.' Hardy's revival of the word 'Wessex' has not only reestablished the geographical identity of an entire region, but it has done so in such a way that the real life appellation is now invariably associated with the author whose 'partly real, partly dream-country' (as he described it) has become such a vivid psychological entity.

Hardy was so consciously concerned to establish the exact topographical dimensions of his fictive world that he drew maps of Wessex which are discussed in Alan L. Manford's interesting essay, 'The "Texts" of Thomas Hardy's Map of Wessex' (1982). The first of two versions drawn by Hardy was used in the Wessex Edition, though revisions later suggested by him were never incorporated by Macmillan. The inclusion of the map in editions of the novel was always important to Hardy.

Two especially pleasing celebrations of Wessex, respectively invoking the pictorial media of water-colours and photography, appeared in 1983: Gordon Beningfield's *Hardy Country*, with text by Anthea Zeman, and Desmond Hawkins's *Hardy's Wessex*, with photographs by Anthony Kersting. Gordon Beningfield is a countryside artist of delicate skill and amiable texture, whose concern is to show present-day Dorset in the context of Hardy's writing. The sketches and paintings are born of a visual and emotional response to Hardy's country evocations and, like Hardy, Beningfield is inspired by the later Turner. Beningfield's personal feelings for Dorset are explored and his strong environ-mental concern for its vanishing features is a counterpoint theme of the book. His captions to the paintings are a delight: crisp and personal, recording the circumstances of each painting and often relating its subject to his own life and experiences and home. Anthea Zeman's accompanying text is a model of straightforward narrative, combining a brief biography of Hardy with an account of the places and people of Wessex by reference to Hardy's writings. 'Hardy's Wessex', she says, 'gave him what every novelist has to find in one way or another: a space where he can both record meticulously and invent freely.' In the *Life* Hardy admits to his 'wilful purpose in his early novels until *Far From the Madding Crowd* appeared, if not later, having been to mystify the reader as to their locality, origin and authorship by various interchanges and inventions'. *Hardy Country* does not emulate Hermann Lea in seeking precise identifications, though it does this too where appropriate, but aims to reflect the atmosphere and feeling of the region. This is successfully achieved in a handsome, evocative and original book.

Desmond Hawkins is one of the best-loved frequenters of the Hardy scene, and he is well placed by virtue of expertise and domicile to explore those mystifications of locality in Hardy's fiction which 'gave elasticity to the constraints of literal topogra-phy'. Like Beningfield, but with more direct reference to Hardy's texts and to wider cultural issues, Hawkins seeks 'the interplay between the past and the present' and sees Wessex in an organic historical perspective, 'unfolding and developing, living and dying . . . not something frozen rigid'. It is 'those areas of Wessex which most dynamically vitalized Hardy's imagination' that are his principal subject. These include Mellstock, Egdon Heath, Lyonnesse and the Valley of the Great Dairies, as well as various Wessex Heights. Hawkins does not turn away from the reality of an era in which an atomic energy establishment disfigures part of Egdon Heath, but his detailed celebration of the natural life and general character of the region, supplemented by Anthony Kersting's fine colour and black-and-white photography, is sometimes moving. This too is a distinctive book, with a direct prose narrative of compulsive interest, and each of these excellent books is faithful to Hardy and to the region.

BIOGRAPHY

Following Michael Millgate's major biography of 1982 it is unlikely that any further comprehensive attempt to tell Hardy's story will be made in the foreseeable future, but documents and researches continue to turn up to confirm, supplement or modify, with varying degrees of accuracy, the picture. Michael Rabiger, producer of the 'oral history' television series 'Yesterday's Witness', which records the recollections of the elderly, has explored in 'The Hoffman Papers: An Assessment and Some Interpretations' (1982–83) a cache of documents left by Professor Harold Hoffman (1893–1941) of Miami University. Hoffman intended to write a bio-critical study of Hardy and interviewed people who had been associated with him, including Tryphena Sparks's daughter, Eleanor Bromell, whose recollections two decades later notoriously fuelled Deacon's and Coleman's *Providence and Mr Hardy*. Rabiger's presentation of the material is competent and unsensational, and all the more interesting for this restraint. But the lengthily drawn allegation that Hardy suffered (or feared that he suffered) from syphilis seems a wild hare to chase, not least since it derives from the notably unreliable Marie Stopes, with whom Florence, however, had clearly discussed sexual matters: thanking her on 14 September 1923 for 'kind advice with regard to the alkaline douche', Florence writes of Hardy that 'he said he would have welcomed a child when we married first, ten years ago, but now it would kill him with anxiety to have to father one'.

Rabiger also casts some further light on the ambiguous sexuality of Hardy's mentor, Horace Moule, whose relationship with Hardy is also discussed in William E. Buckler's 'The Hardy-Moule Affair with a Reading of Four Hardy Poems' (1982). Most of the Rabiger-Hoffman disclosures, however, relate to young women in Hardy's early life: Louisa Harding, Cassie Pole (whom Hardy is said to have jilted and who is thought to be the inspiration for the poem 'At Mayfair Lodgings'; she was a lady's maid who later associated herself with Hardy's Ethelberta), Rachel Keats (the model for Arabella Donn?) and the unidentified 'H. A.'. Harold Hoffman's interviw with Kate Hardy is also included, and further details of the life and career of Tryphena Sparks are given.

G. F. Bartle also presents 'Some Fresh Information about Tryphena Sparks – Thomas Hardy's Cousin' (1983), drawing upon the records of Tryphena's training as a teacher at Stockwell College, which were released on the college's closure in 1980, and including some letters from Tryphena as she embarked on her teaching career. Another early sweetheart, Eliza Nicholls, whose 1863–67 engagement to Hardy was revealed by Michael Millgate, is the subject of Nicholas Hillyard's 'Eliza Nicholls and Hardy Poems of 1865–7' (1983). Hillyard challenges Millgate's interpretation of evidence and his association of Eliza with such poems as 'The Musing Maiden' or the 'She, to Him' sonnets, and suggests that the association with Eliza ended as it began in 1863.

The prevalence of unflatteringly bovine pictorial representations of that longer-term, spiritually lost and posthumously rediscovered sweetheart of Hardy's, his first wife Emma, is deplored in Donald J. Winslow's 'Some Images of Emma Hardy' (1982–83). Winslow describes the one extant painting and the various extant photographs of Emma and shows how those depicting her wearing an expression of oppressive severity have regularly been used by writers to support an unsympathetic or hostile attitude towards her. He makes a reasonable plea for fairer play and a wider exposure in future of the kinder photographs of Emma. Charles Sparrow of Dorchester Post Office, quoted by W. G. L. Parsons in 'Recollections of Hardy' (1983), would not agree: 'She looked what she was, a dour dominant woman.' Parsons, one of the Christmas singers at Max Gate in 1920, is author of one of the year's retrospective snapshot recollections of the elderly Hardy, remembering both the author's encouraging words and quoting Sparrow's account of a charabanc breaking down outside Max Gate: Sparrow believed that, when he told Hardy that it was an outing of the Agricultural Workers Union, Hardy mumbled, 'You mean the peasants.' A less grumpy Hardy emerges from Margaret Windeatt Roberts's revival of a 1913 record of 'A Visit to Blandford by John Lane of the Bodley Head and Thomas Hardy' (1983).

Yet it is Hardy as 'A Miserable Old Man' (1982–83) that insidiously, and rather comically, has tended to persist in local tradition. The latest pedlar of this image, under the succinct quotation above, is Mrs Cynthia Burt, who recalls: 'We girls did not like Hardy; we always thought him a miserable old man, as that is how he always looked when we saw him. I remember seeing Hardy accompanied on his walks by a snappy little dog. Actually, we took very little notice of him, as we had all taken a strong dislike to the man. Apart from this feeling of strong dislike he made very little impact on us. Even after having read some of his books I find it extraordinary even today that people make so much fuss of him.'

CRITICAL STUDIES

The longevity of Hardy's appeal to readers is self-evident and it is largely independent of readers' responses to Hardy as a man, miserable or otherwise. In the 1980s we are sufficiently removed from the facts of Hardy's life that his work may more readily be appreciated as a detached corpus or, as Peter Widdowson would call it, an 'artificial construct'. In 'Hardy in History: a Case Study in the Sociology of Literature' (1983), Widdowson examines the case of Hardy, unarguably a major cultural presence, in the context of a plea for a literary analogy for historiography. This he calls a 'critiography': 'a study of texts *in history*; not merely as productions of their 'period', nor, then, as receptacles of historical messages from that period which criticism decants, but as cultural productions of the 1980s'.

Widdowson makes a strong case, though often in a neologistic or contrived style ('iterability', 'improbablism', 'the politics of the critiographical project', 'the variable facticity of the fact', 'the alienating fictiveness of the fiction') that is not very engaging. Once this terminological screen is penetrated, and once it is accepted that Hardy's fiction is now 'present as the concept "Hardy": as a cultural phenomenon defined by its place, function and parameters of intelligibility within the contemporary social formation', a worthwhile thesis emerges, consonant with some of the trends in recent critical theory. Widdowson describes the constricting social and critical determinants that have shaped our conception of Hardy. The social determinants are those of the media (the availability of film and television adaptations) and education: in the school syllabus 'Hardy' is said to have been exclusively constructed around *Far From the Madding Crowd*, *The Mayor of Casterbridge* and *The Return of the Native*; *Tess* was not set as an Advanced Level text until 1961, nor *Jude* until the 1970s, and the appearances of both have been limited.

The predilections of earlier ciriticism are perpetuated through the syllabus: the late nineteenth-century 'character and environment' conception of Hardy still prevails, with its preference for realism and tendency to disparage melodrama, plot contrivance or social didacticism as faults. The other fictions, including the 'minor' novels, which would challenge the organic coherence of this view, Widdowson argues, are excised from the canon. *The Hand of Ethelberta* is persuasively given as the novel which, if properly attended to, could be 'the one most uncompromisingly to demystify that social and literary ideology' created by the prevailing canon.

There is a particular lack of criticism of Hardy as a social novelist, Widdowson reminds us, and 'bourgeois criticism', in its perpetuation of the 'major' Hardy, tends to devalue the honourable exceptions of Merryn Williams, Raymond Williams and Terry Eagleton. Widdowson makes a stimulating plea for the 'suppressed discourses' in Hardy (the minor novels, social ideology) to be released and to 'take their place as constituent discourses of a different "Hardy"'.

A more diversified 'Hardy' than Widdowson's analysis allows for has, however, surely emerged in recent years, though the fundamental direction of his argument is sound. Beyond Roger Ebbatson's passing concern with social evolution (harvesting at Marlott as feudal labour, threshing at Flintcomb-Ash as capitalist mechanization) in *The Evolutionary Self: Hardy, Forster, Lawrence* (1982), there has been strikingly little concern with Hardy's social ideology this year. (Ebbatson's book, incidentally, is a distinguished contribution to the subject of Hardy as a Darwinian, and repays close reading for its textual support of the theory that evolution stimulated the fictional imagination of the writers concerned. Tess Coslett's *The 'Scientific Movement' and Victorian Literature* (1983) sets Hardy in the context of Victorian scientific writers such as Huxley and Spencer, and sees Hardy as ready to accept the findings of scientific theory while reserving his right to question.)

Only a few of the 'minor' novels have received sustained attention. Annie Escuret eloquently challenges the 'minor' status of *The Trumpet-Major* in 'Le Trompette-Major ou l'Histoire de Perroquet et de l'Agami' (1983), exposing the violence beneath its even surface and identifying the novel as 'une farce qui serait grotesque par son tragique'. Pearl Hochstadt considers two neglected novels in 'Hardy's Romantic Diptych: A Reading of *A Laodicean* and *Two on a Tower*' (1983), and Charles Pettit's contribution to the rehabilitation of the novel regarded as Hardy's worst, in 'A Reassessment of *A Laodicean*' (1983), is equally to be welcomed. Pettit validates through illustration the 'subtle and complex integration' achieved by Hardy in the earlier part of the novel, before it degenerated, because of Hardy's illness, into little more than a fast-moving thriller.

In *A Laodicean* Hardy offers a pre-Freudian insight into the psychology of the *voyeur*, and instances in Hardy's fiction of '"the voyeuristic moment", the moment in which the seeing subject and the seen object intersect in a diegetic node that both explicitly and implicitly suggests the way in which the world is constituted in and through the scopic drive' in other early fictions are the subject of Judith Bryant Wittenberg's 'Early Hardy Novels and the Fictional Eye' (1983). Psychoanalytic theories of seeing are enumerated: the voyeuristic impulse may be either normative or perverted, and once the writer has created his text he becomes an exhibitionist, transforming the voyeuristic process into an exhibitionist defence. The aural correlative of peeping is eaves-dropping, and this too runs through Hardy's fiction. *Desperate Remedies* and *A Pair of Blue Eyes* are particularly explored in this respect: in these novels, and in *Under the Greenwood Tree* and *Far From the Madding Crowd*, 'Hardy depicts again and again versions of the crucial and disturbing voyeuristic moment in which so many of his psychological and epistemological concerns are expressed.' Hardy is shown in these works making fictional use of visual trauma and peeping and eavesdropping compulsions, encouraged by the influences of his early architectural training and the time he spent in art galleries. All this is seen in the raw at this early stage in his career; but Wittenberg's topic is an important one because, as she says, virtually all his more mature novels 'would contain significant versions of the voyeuristic moment'.

There have been only three 'full-length'.publications devoted to Hardy, apart from the *Annual* itself, and the slimmer two of these are familiar serial publications: the *Thomas Hardy Year Book* (1982–83) and the *Thomas Hardy Society Review* (1983). The *Year Book* continues to appear at irregular intervals and might more accurately be described as biennial, or even triennial, but its editors, James and Gregory Stevens Cox, sensibly exploit the flexibility of its format to include varying combinations of long and short contributions. The Stevens Cox publications, from earlier monograph series to the present *Year Book* format, have proved a valuable repository for Hardy ephemera, and the *Year Book* still shows a bias towards biographical interest, the present issue devoting 44 pages to Michael Rabiger's account of the Hoffman papers (already discussed) and another eight to the sketch-book of James Sparks, Tryphena's nephew. There are also two academic essays. The *Thomas Hardy Society Review* contains a similar but quite differently proportioned mixture, bearing a heavier cargo of critical essays, selected discriminately by the editor, Frank Pinion. In the present issue there is also a touching poem, 'Pentargan' by M. R. Skilling, recording one couple's grateful response to Hardy for the joys and the places his work has brought them. Both the *Year Book* and *Review* are short collections, comprising 92 (including some advertisements) and 32 pages respectively, but both are worthwhile. The cumulative achievement of the *Review*, now approaching the end of Frank Pinion's editorship and so far totalling 298 pages, is impressive. The inclusion of *Society* in its title, though accurate, perhaps gives an unduly parochial impression of its constitution and content, and the word might profitably be discarded to enable the *Review* to gain a more widespread bibliographical recognition and library distribution.

Hardy collections in libraries will be enhanced by Marlene Springer's *Hardy's Use of Allusion* (1983), which is the first extended study of a vital constituent of Hardy's creative practice. The abundant use of literary allusions was, as Springer reminds us, a stylistic trait of the period, but Hardy developed it as a deliberate tonal and narrative device: 'Ultimately his allusions become intricately polyvalent within his fictional world as they afford comic relief, endow his rustics with universal significance and allow Hardy to comment ironically on his characters.' Springer analyses the increasing sophistication in Hardy's use of allusion, from *Desperate Remedies*, with its allusive clues to the unfolding of mysterious events, to *Jude*, and shows that the ways in which he employs allusive references are 'as various as the fictional modes he attempts'. In *Under the Greenwood Tree* the allusions inform the reader of the light tone of the novel; *A Pair of Blue Eyes* is overloaded with allusions, yet the emotional climax is 'allusively fortified' so as to 'inject the biting irony so prevalent in Hardy's world', and Springer shows how Hardy earlier gives Knight 'the allusive trouncing he deserves'; by *Far From the Madding Crowd* Hardy has lost much of his 'allusive artlessness' and can use the technique at a new psychological level. He is still too keen to impress his audience – Fanny Robin's use of a crutch becomes 'oddly exercising the faculty of invention upon the specialty of the clever Jacquet Droz, the designer of automatic substitutes for human limbs' – yet his skilful underscoring of Bathsheba's pride and caprice by allusion is shown to have been followed by equally effective support of her struggle for maturity.

Allusions play a major part in Hardy's creation of character, both major figures and rustics: allusions 'spoken by the narrator tend primarily to elevate and enlarge, while those spoken by the rustics themselves branch out into the even more multifarious functions which their complex serio-comic position and outlook require'. By *The Return of the Native* Hardy has reached allusive maturity, an achievement evident in the way in which he uses 'at least twenty evocative allusions to embellish, solidify, and particularise the subtle dimensions of [Egdon] Heath's personality', and the formidable allusive structure supporting the anti-Hebraic spirit of Eustacia Vye. The allusions have by now achieved a powerful ironic edge that is only intensified in *Tess* and *Jude*. Though allusions also sharpen the settings and particular scenes in *Tess*, it is those allusions surrounding Alec, Angel and Tess which show the technique of allusive patterning at full stretch. In *Jude* Hardy returns to a device abandoned in *Tess* and applies the standard Victorian epigraph to each section of the book. Here, more than in any previous novel, Hardy 'creates referential place-names that are ironic touchstones of the events they witness'; and there is almost no allusive comic relief. His allusive pattern for Sue is 'intricate, ironic, and an indictment of

Christianity as Victorians interpreted it', and that for Jude follows a similar pattern.

Marlene Springer's book is well conceived and executed, closely and subtly exploring Hardy's allusive strategies. At times there is too much contextualizing of novels discussed: this needs to be done but sometimes slackens the pace of the critical analysis. This is an important study which shows how 'Hardy drew from many worlds to enlarge his own novelistic universe, making allusions serve his audience as avenues into his fiction. Once inside his world, the reader is manipulated into the desired responses as Hardy undermines or ennobles his characters, foreshadows events, injects his humour, and projects his irony – all through his masterful choice of what Coleridge calls "sovereign fragments".'

Analysis of Hardy's allusions to other writers is less usual than comparison between his work and the writings of others, and some valuable work has again been done in this latter area. A thoughtful note on 'Joyce's "The Dead" and Hardy's *The Woodlanders*' by Patrick Diskin has appeared in 1983; George Wing compares 'The Confessions of Tess Durbeyfield and Esther Waters' (1981); in 'Henchard and Falstaff' (1983), T. J. Diffey compares the tonal and stylistic presentations of the death of each character; Diane Bonds makes a thematic comparison in 'Fleshly Temptation in Robert Penn Warren's *A Place to Come To* and Hardy's *Jude the Obscure*' (1981), while in 'Death as Option: the Heroine in Nineteenth-Century Fiction' (1981) Katharine Hanley makes a more expected comparison in considering together *The Mill on the Floss* and *The Return of the Native*. Lawrence Jones also draws George Eliot into the picture in 'George Eliot and Pastoral Tragi-Comedy in Hardy's *Far From the Madding Crowd*' (1980).

Among a number of essays which enliven our reading of other individual novels, a few may be briefly mentioned. Kevin Moore (1982) and Glen Wickens (1982) contribute to the continuing revaluation of *Desperate Remedies*, which Moore defines as a 'hybrid detective-Gothic narrative'. R. P. Draper, in an essay unambiguously entitled '*The Mayor of Casterbridge*' (1983), which is written with engaging clarity, says that *The Mayor* 'seems to become a novel reflectng a Schopenhauerian rather than an Aristotelian view of tragedy. In fact, however, it reflects both': Hardy 'allows the two to co-exist in a tension which is both heroic and disenchanted. The result is a novel which is all the greater for being so oddly at variance with itself'. As usual, *Tess of the d'Urbervilles* has attracted more critical attention than any other single novel, and the last three pages of the first 'phase' are chosen as a telling case study in Peter Grundy's 'Linguistics and Literary Criticism: A Marriage of Convenience' (1981). Jeffrey Sommers, in 'Hardy's Other Bildungsroman' (1982), argues that, unlike that of a ballad heroine, Tess's character does change, and that she matures only when reality succeeds dream and she murders Alec.

In his review-essay discussed earlier, Donald Davie quotes R. S. Thomas's 1970 quatrain about Hardy:

Then Hardy, for many a major
Poet, is for me just an old stager,
Shuffling about a bogus heath,
Cob-webbed with his Victorian breath.

This witty, though ungenerous, estimate prompts Davie to observe that 'inside twenty years, with astonishing velocity, Hardy has been lifted from "old stager" status, briefly elevated as the great modern poet that independent witnesses like Yvor Winters and John Crowe Ransom had always considered him, and in many quarters is now being just as promptly and precipitately returned to the Victorian cobwebs'. The latter assertion is questionable. In the aftermath of Leavis's famous denigratory judgement, which after all was discharged in *New Bearings in English Poetry* a full half-century ago, it was certainly hard for the average critical reader unselfconsciously to recognize, or at least salute, the range and variety of Hardy's production as a poet, but this kind of inhibition has long passed. It has been succeeded by recognition of Hardy as a poet who may be traditional in pattern (though even within formal constraints he was astonishingly inventive and experimental) but whose aesthetic and feeling are modern.

Davie himself, acknowledging the pleasurable virtues of Hardy as an 'imperious verbal engineer' and the conjunction of this ability with what Hardy called his 'cunning irregularity', identified a modern Hardy tradition more than a decade ago; and in 1980 Samuel Hynes, in 'The Hardy Tradition in Modern English Poetry', showed with exemplary clarity the continuity of modern poetry with that of the past, and identified Hardy's role in the modern tradition. R. S. Thomas, a poet who usually abjures formal pattern, may well find Hardy's exploitation of it to be cob-webbed and therefore miss the vision within, and it is left to Hynes to observe that 'the apocalyptic uniqueness of modern experience has been exaggerated'. Hardy's outlook remains convincingly modern and he addresses interior problems common to our own age.

I cannot locate the 'many quarters', to which Donald Davie alludes, in which there is a new disposition to reassign Hardy to the Victorian cobwebs, and have found little evidence of this in recent critical practice. On the contrary, a tendency to celebrate the greatness of Hardy's poetry prevails. H. A. Mason, for example, in 'Wounded Surgeons' (1982), explores the basis of Leavis's claim for 'The Self-Unseeing' as a major poem. Leavis praises it as a 'record of poignant and particular memories', but Mason claims that Leavis thus misses a central truth, that 'great poetry is always general', and that this greatness is what Hardy achieves. Mara Maciejowski, in 'The Idea of Time in Thomas Hardy's Poetry' (1982), associates Hardy's poetic greatness with his unflinching recognition, despite occasional 'moments of intuitional release from temporality', of the illusion of permanence, and suggests that the sculpted effect of Hardy's poetry as recognized by Donald Davie is 'a manifestation of Hardy's desire for rigidity, permanence in a world of flux'. This is, however, too simplistic an explanation of Hardy's veneration for form. Peter Coxon, in '"The Voice" and Horace: Odes ii, xiv' (1983), suggests, with particular reference to one poem, the classical basis of Hardy's concern with metrical scansion. (Comparisons with other poets this year include Pauline Fletcher on Hardy and Rossetti (1982) and Bruce Bawer on Hardy and Yeats (1982), while W. J. Keith's 1980 book, not previously noticed, contains material on Hardy and Barnes, and Ian Ousby, on 'The Convergence of the Twain' (1982), shows how Hardy's poem adapts Plato.) Jean Vaché, in *'Paroles d'Hiver*: Hardy et Britten' (1983), elegantly celebrates the 'rich symbiose avec le texte poétique' of Benjamin Britten's *Winter Words* song-cycle. If comparatively little has been written about Hardy's poetry during the period under review, this is at least partly because its very accessibility frees it from some of the explicatory pressures exerted by the work of poets who are apparently more complex.

'One smart paragraphist', Hardy recalled of the reception of one of his volumes of poems, 'said that he was nearly deluded into a belief in Hardy's verses after reading them one night; but he saved his critical credit by getting up on a cold wet morning and reading them again on an empty stomach. It happily cured his weakness.' Now there is a genuinely cob-webbed Victorian view! The uncompromising message implicit in modern critical writing on Hardy's poetry is that, for most readers in the 1980s, the smart paragraphist's cure simply does not work.

REVIEWS

Samuel Hynes (ed.), *The Complete Poetical Works of Thomas Hardy*, vol. I (Oxford University Press, 1982) pp. xxviii + 403.

Reviewed by Simon Gatrell

The first volume of Samuel Hynes's edition of Hardy's poetry is published in the Oxford English Texts series, and is thus designed for a reader who wants a carefully edited text; who is interested in the way that Hardy revised his poems; who wants sufficient but not over-detailed information about the writing and publication of the poems, and the editorial procedures; and who also expects well-researched and germane explanatory annotation. Such a reader, who will certainly be representative of the majority of this volume's readership, should be well satisfied; especially when added to these qualities is a pleasant page with an uncluttered impression despite the presence of line numbers and exhaustive foot-of-the-page annotation, and the appearance of Hardy's illustrations to *Wessex Poems* (including one that he omitted).

But there will inevitably be another readership with slightly different requirements, which will discover that one of the virtues of this edition as a reading text becomes for it a limitation. For those who are famliar with the complexity of the development of Hardy's texts and their transmission and who are interested in the problems of editing them, the conciseness of the introductory and explanatory material will seem excessive, forcing Hynes into assertion without adequate justification and occasionally into omission of less important but relevant detail. Since I count myself among this readership I should like to draw attention to some of the points where the brevity Hynes gladly or unwillingly adopts leaves open important questions, though before I do so I must stress that there is no doubt of the fineness of Hynes's scholarship here, nor of the accuracy of his editing.

The transmission of Hardy's poems is more complicated than

147

that of most of his novels, rendered particularly so by the fact that Hardy at different times gave authority to different versions, both in print at the same time, and never managed completely to reconcile the two despite an evident desire to do so. The two main strands are readings based upon the Wessex Edition (1912–13 for this volume) and upon the *Collected Poems* Edition (1919); where these editions, or derivatives from them, have different readings, the editor has to make a choice between them. Hynes is quite clear about his approach; in his 'Note on the Present Edition' under *Substantives*, he writes:

> I have considered substantive revisions that reached print to be expressions of Hardy's fixed intention, and have incorporated these revisions into the established text. Where there is more than one revised version of a line or a word, I have taken the latest one where chronology can be determined with certainty (as is usually the case); in those instances where the chronology is uncertain, I have relied on my critical judgement and my sense of what is characteristic of Hardy's mature style. (xxiv)

This is brief and assured; but it is all that we have on the matter. The principle enunciated in Hynes's first sentence means that in places where Collected Poems follows the first edition text, and the Wessex Edition has a variant, the Wessex reading is preferred despite the fact that it was published six or seven years earlier. As Hynes shows on pp. xiv–xv of his Introduction, this preference is appropriate for *Wessex Poems* and *Poems of the Past and the Present*; the *Collected Poems* text of these volumes was set in type by the printers in 1909, though not printed until ten years later. With *Time's Laughingstocks*, the other collection of Hardy's verse in this volume of Hynes's edition, the case is rather different. In his note on its composition and publication, Hynes writes (p. 380) that in its *Collected Poems* form it was 'substantially revised, but not identical with the Wessex Edition, and probably an earlier revision'. We are not told why this is a probability, and indeed what Hynes has to say in his introduction rather suggests the reverse. His outline of the early history of *Collected Poems* makes it seem unlikely that *Time's Laughingstocks* was included in the project before it collapsed towards the end of 1910; and 'the next two years were given over to the preparation of the Wessex Edition' (p. xvi). A footnote to p. xxi seems further to imply that this collection was first set in type in 1919 (along with *Satires of Circumstance* and *Moments of Vision*) for its appearance in *Collected Poems*.

If Hardy did revise *Time's Laughingstocks* in 1919, then it is quite possible to argue that he consciously rejected the seven Wessex Edition variants that do not find their way into the *Collected Poems* text of the collection. Three-quarters of the substantive differences between the first edition and later versions of *Time's Laughingstocks* are common to both Wessex Edition and Collected Poems, which makes it almost certain that if the *Collected Poems* text *was* prepared in 1919 it was either set from the Wessex Edition, or else made with the copy for it or a list of its revisions to hand. In this situation the only justification for allowing unique Wessex Edition readings into the established text would be to suggest that Hardy had indeed a list of the changes made for the Wessex Edition, but one that did not include the changes made for that edition in proof; the seven readings not in *Collected Poems* thus represent these proof-changes and should be accorded authority.

Both Wessex Edition and *Collected Poems* were reprinted in 1920 with minor changes; it is a further possible indication of the superiority of the *Collected Poems* that in places where the two texts revise the first edition differently, twice the reprint of the Wessex Edition has the *Collected Poems* reading of 1919 – the reverse never happens.

This discussion of an important question is speculative and uninformed, and may quite possibly be shown to be irrelevant by information at the editor's disposal; if so, I wish he had shared it with his readers. It would also be good, taking into account the statement on the incorporation of revisions as evidence of Hardy's fixed intention, to have some explanation of why two revisions found uniquely in the *Selected Poems* text of *Time's Laughingstocks* poems (1915) are not admitted to the established text. One of them, in 'The Dear', is quite substantial. In all other texts the third verse reads:

> The busy breeze came up the hill
>   And smartened her cheek to red,
> And frizzled her hair to a haze. With a will
>   'Good-morning, my Dear!' I said. (p. 330)

In *Selected Poems* the third line became 'And hazed her hair.

Commiserate still', but Hynes ignores it, as he does the other *Selected Poems* variant to line 3 of 'Shut out that Moon' (p. 265). These excluded changes might be compared with one from a more esoteric source which *is* included: the alteration of 'made' to 'wring' in the publication of 'News for her Mother' in the *Dorset Year Book* for 1922. Perhaps the fact that *Selected Poems* antedates *Collected Poems* is sufficient to account for the distinction; but if so, *Collected Poems* is afforded an authority it is not held to possess with regard to the earlier Wessex Edition. The *Dorset Year Book* change is given an explanatory note, but there is nothing on the two *Selected Poems* revisions. Another eccentric variant witness that might have merited an explanatory note is the American periodical publication of 'One We Knew'; it is not clear whether the unique readings it contains represent an early version subsequently revised for the English magazine publication ten days earlier, or later alterations that became stranded, but were evidence of some sort of early 'fixed intention'. It is quite likely that Hynes himself doesn't know the answer, and hence there is no note; The imposition of brevity upon the edition has a lot of unexplored detail to answer for.

Another such is the fact that occasionally revisions that reached print nowhere are granted authority – as for instance in line 218 of 'Panthera' (343), where a reading found only written in Hardy's study-copy of the 1923 impression of *Collected Poems* is accepted into the established text. Hynes says nothing in his Introduction about the status of these late holograph changes. Nor do we discover why a unique reading in the 1920 impression of the Wessex edition is included in the edited text of line 3 of 'Shut out that Moon' (p. 265), but excluded from the text of line 30 of 'A Trampwoman's Tragedy' (p. 244). Reasons suggest themselves, but it would have been better to have them in print before us, and it would have been helpful to be able to consult a list of places where the standard editorial procedure has not been followed.

Hynes has chosen the first edition as copy-text for each of Hardy's collections of verse except the last, *Winter Words*; his justification of this choice is as concise and confident as his statement on substantive revision:

Hardy was not careful about punctuation in the holographs that he prepared as printer's copies: clearly he was one of those writers who expected his copy to be corrected by the printer, and who would alter in proofs any corrections that displeased him. That he was a meticulous proof-reader the existing proofs make clear . . . (pp. xxiv–xxv)

Several distinct points are compressed here into a sentence and a half, each of which deserves separate consideration.

The quality of Hardy's manuscript punctuation has been discussed at some length by Dale Kramer in his edition of *The Woodlanders* (Clarendon Press, 1981), by Juliet Grindle and myself in our edition of *Tess* (Clarendon Press, 1983), by Robert Schweik and Michael Piret with regard to *Far From the Madding Crowd*, in their 1981 *Browning Institute Studies* essay 'Editing Hardy', and by myself, for *Under the Greenwood Tree*, in an essay in *The Novels of Thomas Hardy*, edited by Anne Smith (Vision Press, 1979); of these, only Schweik and Piret suggest that Hardy's own punctuation is too fragmentary to serve as the basis for an edited text of the novel they discuss. I disagree with their judgment, but at least they present an amount of convincing evidence to support it; Hynes presents none to support his assertion (perhaps was prevented by the available space from presenting any). This is not the place to present counter-evidence of the value of Hardy's holograph punctuation in *Far From the Madding Crowd*, and it might in any case be argued that poetry is sufficiently different in kind from prose in this respect to merit a different approach, even in a writer who shows such consistency in other aspects of his writing, from the beginning of his creative life to the end. It is, however, possible to make out a brief prima-facie case for using Hardy's poetic manuscripts as copy-texts, even though his verse punctuation does have some idiosyncratic features.

There is one piece of external evidence which Hynes himself quotes on page 367 of this volume:

Hardy prepared [the manuscript of *Poems of the Past and the Present*] as printer's copy, and his instructions to the printer, written in pencil at the head of the first poem and later erased, can be made out. They read:
- Words in IZE to be spelt as in MS.
- Punctuation to be as in MS.
- Poems copied here in double columns to be in single columns only.

These demands would seem to establish that Hardy felt sufficient confidence in his manuscript punctuation to wish to preserve it. We have no proofs of the first edition of this collection, but there is no reason to expect that the compositors paid much attention to Hardy's instructions. As he said in another context, 'no human printer, or even one sent from Heaven direct, can be trusted with verse . . .'. Another detail that seems to suggest that Hardy gave care and thought to his manuscript punctuation is that there are some twenty-five places where Hynes annotates a revision of punctuation in the manuscript of *Time's Laughingstocks*. One of these revisions highlights a chief source of possible dissatisfaction with Hardy's punctuation; at line 41 of 'A Sunday Morning Tragedy' Hardy has cancelled in the manuscript a comma that seems obligatory by all the conventions:

> 'To-morrow I will walk your way[,]'
> He hinted low, alas for me. –

A cursory study of the differences between manuscript and the first edition of *Time's Laughingstocks* shows that Hardy has a strong sense of the pause-value of the end of a line; it happens sufficiently frequently that the first edition adds a comma at the end of a line that one might suggest that Hardy saw the line-ending as representing a pause lighter than a comma which conventional punctuation supplies. One example from 'After the Club-Dance':

> At dawn my heart grew heavy
>   I could not sip the wine,
> I left the jocund bevy
>   And that young man o' mine. (p. 292)

The first edition has a comma after 'heavy'. In addition to these specific matters it is also clear that in poetry as in fiction, Hardy's punctuation is lighter than that of any printed version, and there are plenty of examples which are comparable with his practice in the novels. Again one example, from 'The Two Rosalinds':

> in their travail, teen[,] or joy,

Were I anxious to make a case in detail I should present many more quotations and some statistics; in so doing I should also have to concede that some of the manuscript punctuation is eccentric, and is occasionally unworkable; on the other hand Hynes in this edition accepts that the manuscript punctuation is superior at some points – line 98 of 'A Sunday Morning Tragedy' is a good example. The verse reads in the manuscript:

> 'But you are pale – you did not know?'
> They archly asked, alas for me.
> I stammered, 'Yes – some days – ago,'
> While coffined clay I wished to be.

In every printed version the full point after 'me' becomes a comma; in the Introduction such returns to the manuscript are justified by the phrase 'where the sense clearly requires it'. Personally I find it sad that the comma that appears in the next line of the poem is included in Hynes's text:

> ''Twas done to please her, we surmise?'

Its non-appearance in manuscript versions is quite characteristic of Hardy's punctuation elsewhere.

I suppose by the time Hardy began to publish collections of verse he must have been used to the fact that his manuscript punctuation was altered wholesale by compositors, and it is possible that he may consciously have accepted the situation and made the most of it; but it is much less sure that if he had been confronted at each individual case with a choice between his manuscript punctuation and that of the first printing, he would have preferred the latter.

As far as proof-reading is concerned, Hunes is surely right about Hardy's attention to detail, but is it certain that such attention was maintained throughout a volume at an equal pitch? I am not familiar with the proof for *Human Shows*, which is an important witness in this context, but in the two proofs for the appearance of 'A Trampwoman's Tragedy' in the *North American Review* there are three changes to punctuation in a total of 208 lines.

It has been argued by a number of writers that the survival of Hardy's copy for the Wessex Edition of *The Woodlanders* with its more than 400 punctuation revisions provides a good argument for using the Wessex Edition as copy-text for critical editions of

Hardy's fiction. Can the same suggestion not be made for the verse? I don't know, but I feel sure Professor Hynes does; the more puzzling then that the edition gets no mention as a candidate for copy-text in the Introduction.

It seems to me that the question of the proper copy-text for an edition of the poems cannot be settled by a statement of a sentence and a half and a paragraph of subsequent adjustments and exceptions; there should be some discussion, some acknowledgement of alternative possibilities which certainly exist. Once again we come back to the problem of imposed brevity, under which imposition it is irritating for the textual critic that this edition should lie.

This is even true with regard to Hardy's illustrations for *Wessex Poems*; though there is a separate appendix devoted to them, a number of relevant details are not clarified. They are printed here in dimensions differing from those in the early published forms of the collection: are they now presented in the size that Hardy drew them? What media did Hardy use to produce them? Why did he leave one out, and what is the justification for now printing it? What is the source of the manuscript inscription beneath the illustration on the half-title page (p. 1)? There is an uncancelled note on p. 361 of this edition that shows that Hynes at one time intended the illustrations to be collected together in an appendix at the back of the volume; it is good that this decision was reversed, and I could only wish that he had had second thoughts about Hardy's own explanatory notes to poems. They seem to me to be as much an integral part of the text as the illustrations, and yet they find themselves mingled with Hynes's own explanatory notes at the end of the book. Are they not part of the edited material?

It is testimony to Hynes's meticulous accuracy that in a fairly detailed analysis of the variant readings in *Time's Laughingstocks* I noted only three places where he has missed an error – in each case trivial. The note to line 90 on p. 246 should presumably begin:

90 weak,]

Line 8 of 'Autumn in King's Hintock Park' (p. 264) should read

Raking up leaves,

In the note to line 1 on p. 290, cap. should be *cap*.

Now that Hynes has taken James Gibson's work on the texts of Hardy's poems the final step into a critical edition, it is unlikely that there will in the near future be a third comparable piece of work; it does seem, however, that there is scope for further detailed discussion of the development and transmission of the poetry. For the moment the proper thing to do is to salute the achievement of Samuel Hynes, and to hope that future selections of Hardy's verse will use this careful and intelligent edition. Of course his inclusion of unfamiliar readings, mostly from the Wessex Edition, occasionally causes a jolt in the reading of a favourite poem: the one that particular struck me was in the twelfth line of 'The Ruined Maid'. When one knows by heart

'Some polish is gained with one's ruin,' said she.

with its heavy stress on the first syllable, expressive of the girl's elevated sarcasm, it comes as quite a shock to have to readjust that emphasis and throw it onto the second syllable of

'A polish is gained . . .'

However, as every editor is aware, the reader is always at liberty to prefer his own reading, and here I think I shall stick to mine.

Juliet Grindle and Simon Gatrell (eds) *Thomas Hardy: 'Tess of the d'Urbervilles'* (Clarendon Press, 1983) pp. xiv + 637.

Reviewed by J. T. Laird

Following closely on the heels of the Clarendon edition of *The Woodlanders* (1981) and the 'Oxford English Text' edition of volume 1 of *The Complete Poetical Works of Thomas Hardy* (1982) comes the Clarendon *Tess of the d'Urbervilles*, a scholarly critical edition based on an edition of Hardy's novel prepared as a doctoral dissertation at Oxford by the late Juliet Grindle. The published edition incorporates the fruits of not only Dr Grindle's original research over the period 1966–74 but also the re-checking and notes for revision that she was able to complete before her death in August 1980, together with the revisions made to the introductions, text, and textual apparatus by Dr Simon Gatrell after he took over the editorial responsibility of preparing the work for publication in Easter of that year.

Although the Clarendon *Tess* is a joint editorial enterprise, it rests firmly on the solid scholarly basis of the Grindle dissertation, which has become well known to Hardy textual scholars since it was deposited in the Bodleian Library in July 1975. The 54-page 'General Introduction' is an updated and improved version of the original account given by Grindle of the history of the writing and publication of the novel and of Hardy's revisions at each stage in the development of the text. The 49-page 'Editorial Introduction' closely follows Grindle's account in its discussion of substantive readings in the edited text, the choice of manuscript as copy-text, and some features of the manuscript's punctuation, but also incorporates (with some modifications) two topics dealt with under separate headings in the dissertation, namely 'Description of the Principal Texts' and 'Editorial Conventions'. In both critical editions, the edited text is supported by an apparatus of substantive variants printed at the foot of each page and by a number of appendices (including one devoted to variants in punctuation and styling). Appendices 3, 4, 5, and 6 of the Clarendon *Tess* correspond to Appendices 1, 2, 3, and 5 of the dissertation and deal with part-division (in the manuscript, serial, and editions), variation in personal names, variation in place-names, and punctuation and styling variants. Appendices 1, 2, and 7 contain entirely new material: a critical text of the sketch 'Saturday Night in Arcady'; the text of the sketch 'The Midnight Baptism', as published in *The Fornightly Review*; and a list of end-of-line hyphens appearing in the Clarendon text that should not be quoted.

There are several important changes made by Simon Gatrell to the original dissertation which affect the text and the textual apparatus. The original Grindle text did not take account of the serial versions of *Tess* published in the *Nottinghamshire Guardian* and the *Sydney Mail*, but Gatrell's collation of these versions, both unrevised serial printings (and thus closer to the serial manus-cript than either the *Graphic* or *Harper's Bazaar* versions), has enabled him to remove some 70 compositorial errors over and above the 50 whose removal first occurred in the dissertation. These errors entered the novel when it was first put into type by the *Graphic*'s compositors. Some fourteen readings hitherto found only in the little-known Harper Paperback Edition of 1900 have also been included by Gatrell. In addition, he has broadened the scope of the critical apparatus by recording the variant readings of the American First Edition of 1892 and the Harper Autograph Edition of 1915 and by identifying the manuscript amendments marked by Hardy in blue ink or crayon. These manuscript readings, it should be remembered, were originally intended to be for 'serial publication only', but many of them were retained in the text of the novel (either through oversight or by design), when Hardy prepared the printers' copy for the English First Edition in 'August and the autumn' of 1891.

Two examples may be cited of the compositorial errors removed by Gatrell. In the scene where the heroine wipes Alec's 'kiss of mastery' from her cheek during her ride with him in the dog-cart to begin her employment at 'The Slopes' (ch. 8), we are now able to learn, for the first time in print, that the words Hardy wrote were '*unweeting of* the snub she had administered by her instinctive rub upon her cheek' (NOT '*unheeding* . . .', which has appeared hitherto in all printed versions). Similarly, we learn that

Tess's loss of her walking boots at Emminster (ch. 44) occurred when one of Angel's brothers 'probed the hedge *carelessly* with his umbrella, and dragged something to light' (NOT *carefully*). The restorations (which are the manuscript readings) are clearly more consistent with Hardy's usual portrayal of both Tess and the operations of chance than are the readings mistakenly introduced by the *Graphic* printers.

The fourteen hitherto disregarded variants in the Harper Paperback Edition that Gatrell accepts into the edited text constitute only a small proportion of the 175 substantive changes made by Hardy for that edition in 1900. As Gatrell fully explains in the Editorial Introduction (pp. 71–73) and the General Introduction (pp. 50–1), Hardy, himself, incorporated 60 of these changes without alteration, and 31 in modified form, into other eidtions of his novel – mainly the 1902 and 1912 editions. Gatrell's choice of fourteen additional variants, which he admits is based partly on 'editorial judgement', affects chapters 45, 46, 51, and 54, and most of the variants clearly have the effect of lessening the sincerity of Alec d'Urberville's religious phase. Decreased religiosity is apparent, for example, in the chosen 1900 reading 'think small of', which now replaces the Wessex Edition reading 'despise', in Alec's remark to Tess in chapter 46: 'Why I did not think small of you was on account of your being unsmirched in spite of all.'

Of the alterations made by Gatrell in the 'Editorial Introduction' one of the most important is the additional bibliographic information provided in the 'Description of the Principal Texts' about the so-called 'Second Impression Revised'. Gatrell's description of this first reprint of the three-volume English First Edition indicates that far from being a revised 'impression' (as Purdy and Grindle term it) it is really a Second Edition, a 'hybrid text' in which the amount of reset material so far revealed by collation of an admittedly small number of copies is 'just over half the whole' (p. 65). The same section of the 'Editorial Introduction' also contains some new useful (and not widely known) information about some of the less important, but not irrelevant, early editions of *Tess*, such as the three first American editions, the Harper's Autograph Edition of 1915, and the Colonial editions published by George Bell and Sons and Macmillan in 1894 and 1895, respectively.

Gatrell also introduces some interesting speculations in the

'General Introduction', for example, about Hardy's real motives in sending his manuscript of *Tess* to Edward Arnold and Mowbray Morris (pp. 9–10) and Hardy's leaving out two leaves now in the B. L. manuscript (describing Angel's carrying of the four dairymaids across the flooded road) *before*, rather than *after*, he sent his novel to Locker (which seems highly likely in the light of the evidence provided by manuscript foliation) (p. 12). He also speculates – as Grindle had done – about such things as the nature of the printers' copy provided by Hardy for the English First Edition. A mixture of revised *Graphic* proofs and manuscript material seems most likely (pp. 14–15).

Compared with the recent Clarendon edition of *The Woodlanders*, edited by Dale Kramer, the Clarendon *Tess* more than holds its own as a work of definitive textual scholarship. Like Kramer, the editors of *Tess* have chosen to go back to the author's manuscript for their copy-text, their reasons for so doing being based on not only the Kramer (and Fredson Bowers) argument of the superior authority of the author's own accidentals, but also the more personal (and perhaps, also, more British) conviction that Hardy's own accidentals can be justified on purely critical grounds. Despite the strong arguments against the need to go back to the manuscript for the copy-text of a Hardy novel, as put forward by Philip Gaskell in his discussion of *The Woodlanders* in *From Writer to Reader* (1978), the editorial decision taken by Kramer, Grindle and Gatrell seems to me to be justified by the results.

While there are many other similarities between the two editions, such as an acceptance of the general authority of the Wessex Edition for substantive readings, the placing of the list of substantive variants at the foot of each page of text, the presence of lengthy, authoritative, introductions devoted to textual criticism, bibliography, and editorial procedures (totalling 71 pages in the case of *The Woodlanders*), and the inclusion of useful Appendices, there are also some significant differences. Perhaps the most important difference lies in the degree of completeness of the historical record they offer of both substantive and accidental variants. Whereas *The Woodlanders* offers only a 'Selective List of Revisions within the Manuscript' (Appendix 6), *Tess* includes every substantive variant within the manuscript in the critical apparatus at the foot of each page of text. And whereas *The Woodlanders* limits its historical record of variants in accidentals to two chapters of the novel (given in Appendix 5), *Tess* gives a virtually complete record for the whole novel (in Appendix 6). These relative advantages in *Tess* are only partly counterbalanced in *The Woodlanders* by the appendices which illustrate certain editorial decisions more precisely – a summary of departures from the substantive readings of the Wessex Edition (in Appendix 1) and of departures from the accidentals of the manuscript and the 1912 printers' copy (in Appendix 2), together with ten pages of brief textual notes (in Appendix 4). The method of recording variants in the critical apparatus is, I believe, also superior in *Tess*. However, I found Kramer's convention of using superior numerals in the text (to cue the variants below) to be helpful, in that it draws the reader's attention to the presence of the variants.

Two mildly critical observations may, perhaps, be offered on this edition of *Tess*, by way of conclusion. One concerns the joint editorial decision to adhere throughout to the principle *not* 'to restore to the text manuscript readings which may have been bowdlerized specifically for the *Graphic* but were never restored in the volume editions by Hardy'. In my view there are a few occasions when the restoration of such original (i.e. pre-bowdlerization) readings would have been justified on the grounds of authorial intention. One such example occurs in chapter 55, during Tess's conversation with Angel after he has found her living with Alec at the Sandbourne boarding-house. Here (514:12), the Clarendon edition retains the bowdlerized reading found in all printed texts and which goes back to the blue-ink amendment in the manuscript, 'He – '. What Tess originally said in the manuscript on this occasion was 'He [i.e. Alec] bought me.' That Hardy continued to prefer the original (i.e. black-ink) reading is shown by the fact that he inserted it in the revised *Graphic* proofs which he prepared as printers' copy for the American serial version and the American First Edition. Although the *Harper's Bazaar* reading shows evidence of subsequent editorial interference ('He – brought me'), the American First Edition printed Hardy's amendment without change. Thus, it can be argued that Hardy's failure to include the clearly preferred reading 'He bought me' in the English First Edition most probably occurred as the result of an oversight and that restoration is desirable. Any other similar editorial decisions

would require specific evidence, supplied by the normal processes of textual criticism.

Finally there are a few misprints that need correcting. Some
which I noted (in the introductory section) are 'perparation' for
'preparation' (p. 26), 'p. 00' for 'p. 8' (p. 27), 'p. 00' for 'p. 51'
(p. 72), 'living' for 'luring' (p. 73), 'weakness' for 'weaknesses'
(p. 73), and 'delted' for 'deleted' (p. 80).

Richard Little Purdy and Michael Millgate (eds), *The Collected Letters of Thomas Hardy*, vol. 3, 1902–08 (Clarendon Press, 1982) pp. x + 367.

Reviewed by Norman Page

This volume maintains the high editorial standards set by its predecessors. Volume 2 of the *Collected Letters*, reviewed in *Thomas Hardy Annual No. 1*, covered nine years of Hardy's life; the present volume, which is about one-fifth as long again, covers seven years; and we can no doubt expect the letters to come in even greater abundance in the subsequent volumes of this projected seven-volume edition.

The writer of these letters was a man in his sixties who was conscious of his age and a good deal preoccupied with his health. Minor ailments make frequent appearances: he tells Florence Henniker in 1904 that he has had 'face-ache, ear-ache, & aches of other sorts' (p. 114), and in the following year he describes himself as 'a martyr to influenza' (p. 161). His solicitude for the health of others, paricularly his young female friends, irresistibly recalls Jane Austen's Mr Woodhouse: he reproaches Florence Dugdale ('Why were you so careless as not to change when damp?', p. 249), and confides to Dorothy Allhusen that the best safeguard against rheumatism is 'to make as little change in underclothing all the year round' (p. 265). Understandably enough, he is troubled by the deaths of friends of his own generation ('those I used to find in houses I find in the churchyard', p. 40), and could scarcely have ventured to hope that in the event he himself would survive for another quarter of a century.

But Hardy, of course, was not just an elderly party sitting by the fire with a woollen comforter wrapped around his head (a picture, it is only fair to say, that he himself is capable of finding comical). He was a professional author; and a large proportion of these

letters relate to the profession of authorship. Many of them deal
with matters of copyright, permissions, and other business
details, and will be of scant interest to most readers. But a number
concern his great literary enterprise of these early Edwardian
years, *The Dynasts*, and reveal what a heavy burden its composition was to Hardy. At first he is optimistic, expressing to one
correspondent the belief that 'you & others will find the drama as
readable as a novel' (p. 91); but the critical reception of the First
Part deeply disappoints him, neither age nor success having
lessened his extreme sensitiveness to criticism, and he soon
declares it 'most unlikely that I shall carry the drama any further'
(p. 99). Most of his reviewers, he observes, have been women –
the notes in this volume do not tell us whether this rather
unlikely-sounding claim is true – and 'Surely Editors ought to
know that such a subject could hardly be expected to appeal to
women' (p. 112). Nineteen months later he puts the Second Part
in the post, exclaiming 'Would it were the Third!' (p. 182), and
confesses himself 'pumped dry' (p. 183). But he soldiers on – the
metaphor is not an idle one, for he later declares that he has
immersed himself so thoroughly in Wellington's campaigns that
'I am almost positive that I took part in the battle of Waterloo, &
have written of it from memory' (p. 287). Two years later Part
Three is dispatched with the wry comment that it brings to an end
'what I believe to be the longest English drama in existence'
(p. 277).

The Dynasts is greedy of his creative energies and leaves little
time for anything else, though he continues to write and publish
poems, and edits a selection of William Barnes's verse. He tells a
correspondent at the end of 1902, 'As to my adding to my already
long list of novels I don't know at all' (p. 43) – which at least seems
to leave the door half-open for a belated successor to *Jude*; but a
couple of years later he states that 'for years past I have not
written a line of fiction or thought of the subject' (p. 132), and
even claims rather implausibly that he has 'almost forgotten the
prose effusions for the time' (p. 133). To an editor's request for a
poem he replies that he is 'unable to write to order'; more bluntly,
he tells Clodd 'I am not going to write for money at my time of life'
(p. 20). It looks as though, probably quite consciously, Hardy
steered his career in a different direction after publishing his last
novel: he who had 'written to order' for so long was now no longer
a journeyman but a gentleman of letters.

His fame is assured (Asquith's offer of a knighthood is responded to near the end of this volume), and he suffers the gratifying annoyance of being a celebrity: in 1904 he recounts the 'unpleasant experience' of being 'Kodaked by some young men who were on the watch' while he, all unsuspecting, was out for a walk (p. 146). It is during this period, too, that 'Wessex' is transformed from a fictional landscape to a tourist attraction, partly thanks to the photographs of the indefatigable Hermann Lea, who is one of the five most frequent recipients in this volume (the others are Edmund Gosse, Mrs Henniker, Frederick Macmillan and Clement Shorter, with Edward Clodd and Emma Hardy running them close). Not without good reason, Hardy repeatedly insists that the fictional sites were '*suggested* by such & such real places' (p. 172) and are not to be taken as accurate transcriptions from life.

My impression is that there is considerably more sprightliness, more candour, wit and humour, with an occasional refreshing touch of tartness, in these letters than in those collected in the previous volume, and that these qualities are particularly manifest in the letters to such male friends as Clodd, Douglas, and Gosse, and in those to Mrs Henniker. To the latter, for instance, he writes of a lady-novelist who has dropped dead:

> I fear she broke down through attempting too much. To keep three plates spinning, literature, fashion, & the Holy Catholic religion, is more than ordinary strength can stand. (p. 225)

Some observations of Hardy's that have previously been quoted out of context, such as the admission that on omnibuses his attention is 'distracted by the young women in fluffy blouses' (p. 270), read differently now that they can be seen as jocular in intent. Even the declaration to Gosse that he has been 'mentally travelling in regions of inspissated gloom' is quickly qualified: 'not that I am habitually gloomy, as you can testify' (p. 282). And he corrects the assumptions of those who suppose that a pessimist is necessarily a misery and a kill-joy:

> Why people make the mistake of supposing pessimists, or what are called such, incurably melancholy, I do not know. The very fact of their having touched bottom gives them a

substantial cheerfulness in the consciousness that they have nothing to lose. (p. 187)

Or, as he tells another correspondent, pessimism 'leads to a mental quietude that tends rather upwards than downwards' (p. 308).

On the other hand, there are some striking passages on man's cruelty to animals, Hardy's attitude to which embodies a sense of *lacrimae rerum* and a universe sadly out of joint. Yet he is no fanatic: he accepts a gift of game, and when the cat catches a leveret on the lawn it is cooked and eaten.

As in the preceding volume, the letters to Emma contain no hint of estrangement and not a trace of bitterness, but are (it seems to me) very nearly exactly the kind of letters – detailed, relaxed, gossipy and concerned – that one would expect an elderly husband to write to a wife of thirty or thirty-five years' standing. Occasionally he finds it necessary to instruct her how to behave, but he does so with unobtrusive tact: she ought not to be 'too friendly with strangers' when abroad alone (p. 334). Even if we feel like reading Emma's eccentricity between the lines, her husband shows no impatience or intolerance. When she plans to join him in London, he tells her he will try to book a double-bedded room (p. 321).

But the most touching moment in the volume occurs in a letter written from London to Bessie Churchill, the Max Gate parlour-maid, instructing her to tell the gardener to 'chimp' the potatoes in the cellar (that is, to pick off the shoots). As the editors point out, the word is to be found in Barnes's *Glossary of the Dorset Dialect*, and it is pleasant to think of Hardy sitting in the Athenaeum and quite naturally – though only to a servant, of course – using a word, 'precise but not pedantic', learned in his childhood. The vignette thus evoked enshrines a good deal of the essential Hardy.

Peter J. Casagrande, *Unity in Hardy's Novels: 'Repetitive Symmetries'* (Macmillan Press Ltd., 1982) pp. xi + 249.

Reviewed by Michael Collie

In this well-written, lucid study of Hardy's novels, supported as it is by useful subsidiary critiques of some of the poems, Peter Casagrande sets out to demonstrate the benefits of regarding Hardy's fiction as a totality, which is possible, he says, because the author's overall vision never really alters but consists of variations on a theme. He puts forward his thesis with characteristic clarity:

> Hardy's novelistic art took the form of variations on the twin stories of return and restoration [which results in] several interpretations of the same phenomenon, that is, of the defect in nature that inexorably drives men and women from their early felicity, or makes them nearly helpless victims of their characters and circumstances. The result of this play of intellect and imagination is an aesthetic and multiple rather than a metaphysical and integrated rendering of nature's defects. Hardy saw in nature's misworkings a beauty that he wished to convey to his readers. Perception of this beauty-in-ugliness was what for him could ultimately redeem defective nature in the eyes of suffering humanity.

This is from the introduction. A few pages earlier Casagrande had identified the two major variations he sees in the fiction and which he examines in detail in his book.

> There are the major novels of return (*Under the Greenwood Tree*, *The Return of the Native*, *The Woodlanders*) and the major novels of restoration (*Far from the Madding Crowd*, *The Mayor of Caster-bridge*, *Tess of the d'Urbervilles*, and *Jude the Obscure*), and all

have their antecedents or rehearsals in early or in minor novels: e.g. *Madding Crowd* and *Tess* in *A Pair of Blue Eyes*; *The Return* in *A Laodicean*; *The Mayor* in the three novels that immediately preceded it. In the novels of return Hardy depicted the attempt – always painful – to return to one's native place after long absence. In the novels of restoration he exhibited the struggle – always futile – to atone for error or mend defect. The theme in both is the same – there is no return, no restoration.

The claim is essentially that Hardy's novels can best be understood in terms which they themselves establish; that to read *Tess* or *Jude* alone, for example, is the 'deeply moral or emotional experience of great art' while to see *Jude* as the complement to *Tess* is 'to read with a sense of other, magnificently realized, possibilities'; that the *corpus* as a whole makes sense, the difficulties of one novel being clarified by the formulations of another; and that in the case of Hardy, at least, it is useful for the reader to search out his 'unity' because the novels are the 'story of his experience of his own temperament at work on his surroundings and its people'. Peter Casagrande refers to his work with students; to say that his book will be particularly helpful to readers who, having enjoyed a number of Hardy's novels, are beginning to search out connections between them, as they read more, is not to damn it with faint praise. He establishes the basis for a sensible discussion of the similarities and differences between Hardy's novels in a clear-headed and helpful fashion.

Peter Casagrande's old-fashioned, descriptive, exegetical method will be a disappointment to anyone interested in either the problems of Hardy's text or in the theory of fiction. Just as he takes his own critical vocabulary for granted, assuming the currency of words like 'art', 'nature', 'imagination' and 'intellect', or 'rehearsal' and 'theme' in the passage quoted above, so he is uncritical in his reading of Hardy's words, preferring visits to the text from which a chart of the imaginative territory can be constructed rather than engagements with the text that might have threatened or at least modified his sense of 'unity'. The chart is a good one, but what is it a chart of? Unity is not necessarily a virtue, nor is it self-evident that to demonstrate unity in an author's work will be helpful. Unity may be a monster, but Peter Casagrande is not familiar with this possibility. For example, he says on p. 170 (in a paragraph that is characteristic of his method throughout) that 'Elfride, Bathsheba, Henchard, Tess and Jude all have this in common – they are incurably flawed', and he then spends two or three paragraphs substantiating this general idea of a recurring theme on the principle that, if it can be substantiated, something useful will have been said about the individual characters as well as about the group. What the characters have in common relates, of course, to the 'twin stories of return and restoration', so the book has a compactness of its own consistent with the thoroughness with which Casagrande examines Hardy's thematic material. It is simply of this that he makes his chart.

Perhaps, however, there are readers of Hardy who do not bring to his books a presupposition about unflawed human beings, readers for whom the implications of the moral term 'flaw' would have only a dated meaning; perhaps (given the extent to which the late nineteenth-century writer, in his assignations with determinism, justified his liaisons with necessity, or the liaisons of his characters, on medical or pseudo-medical grounds) there exist readers who think that, in a later period, the predicament or the mind-set of characters like Henchard or Jude might be, if not distinctly curable, at least viewable more generously in a context in which human fallibility is normal not tragic; and perhaps there are also readers who, while agreeing with Casagrande that certain motifs recur, and that it is useful to notice them, think that of interest would be not so much an exegesis of the canon, but an analysis of Hardy's compulsions as a writer in biographical, psychiatric, linguistic, or at least historical terms. Casagrande's *Unity in Hardy's Novels* is consistently exegetical, consistently unanalytic, and it is merely the opinion of the reviewer that further exposition of texts as familiar as Hardy's novels is hardly necessary, whereas further scrutiny of the words might be interesting. When, for instance, Casagrande discusses Hardy's habit of locating a character's sense of reality in the distant past, all present events being types of dislocation that prevent the character being true to his real self, he compares this retrospective structuring strategy to the 'nostalgic wish' of Hardy himself, as expressed in poems like 'The Voice', which may be all right for preliminary discussion but which does not take one very far; he does not analyse critically the range of problem implicit in Hardy's conjunction of 'character as fate' with his sense of events as irredeemable; he does not explain why Hardy's characters so rarely benefit from sequences of experience, and he does not come to terms with the linguistic and metaphorical turbulence of the Hardy text, that is, words strained to accommodate the author's compulsions. One has to say, therefore, that Casagrande has written exactly that type of efficient book that made a modern theorist argue for a different type of criticism whose target would be 'to reveal the existence of hidden articulations and fragmentations within assumedly monadic totalities'.[1] Casagrande has given us a good chart but his only explanation of why Hardy visited the places marked on it is that Hardy was the kind of person who would visit those places. In other words he begs the whole question of what Hardy thought he was doing when he wrote a book and therefore misses the chance to say anything new about the type of fiction Hardy produced.

It would be wrong to end this discussion of the type of criticism most appropriate nowadays without emphasizing that Peter Casagrande's book is full of good things, not least his glance at Turner and Hardy's interest in Turner's late work. Indeed it is a good book that can be unambiguously recommended to anyone who accepts the limits it sets for itself in the Introduction. The author describes himself as a 'practical critic seeking to explore and illuminate what the novels in their kinships invite'. This he has done and done well.

NOTE

1. Paul de Man, *Allegories of Reading* (New Haven: Yale University Press, 1979) p. 249.

Richard H. Taylor, *The Neglected Hardy: Thomas Hardy's Lesser Novels* (London: The Macmillan Press, 1982), pp. xi + 202.

Reviewed by George Wing

'It is surely wrong', Richard H. Taylor writes in his introduction, 'to isolate the lesser novels as separate and distinct, as aberrations and failures' (p. 3). Having offered in 1963 a full-length MS on Hardy's minor novels to a number of publishers and having been informed that there was no market for such a study, I can do nothing but warmly endorse Taylor's comment and welcome, as long overdue, his book of almost resurrection, *The Neglected Hardy*, an ironically apposite title. I find myself endorsing much of what Taylor writes, especially on his major theme that until recently the minor novels have been deplorably disregarded – as he so ably puts it: 'It is one of the most unfortunate legends, that Hardy's lesser novels are such failures that they are scarcely worth reading . . .' (p. 4).

So much of literary criticism throughout history has been a matter of discipleship to fashionably established critics, a misplaced veneration for attitudes hardened into unchallengable verities, and we may witness the long heedlessness towards Donne as just one example. I suggest that in his creations of Elfride Swancourt, in *A Pair of Blue Eyes*, and of Viviette, in *Two on a Tower*, Hardy has presented two of his intrinsically recognizable heroines whose charm of body and spirit, basic loyalties and fluctuation of emotions, whose dilemma and anguish, exposure to vicious and often unaccountable ironies, can all, on certain occasions, move us to tears for Hardy's vexed and disturbing things with much the same intensity as Tess and Sue do. And in such experiences lie the strength and appeal of the minor novels, although the frequency and duration of such fictional mounting is variable and generally what is obvious in the minor novels is the absence of the latent and controlled stamina of the more

170

acclaimed works and the fact that they are in generic composition to varying degrees different kinds of novels. Even so there is no unanimity about the major works and there are contradictory voices who would claim, say, that *The Woodlanders* is deficient in this, *The Return of the Native* in that. It is totally acceptable that Hardy 'is consistent in his art, that *The Hand of Ethelberta*, whatever its rank as a novel, can be recognized as the work of a great writer' (p. 2); but it is more than this. 'Berta's' genuine daughterly concern – 'O, this false position! – it is ruining your nature, my too thoughtful mother!' – when she reads Mrs Chickerel's letter of earthy advice on marrying Mountclere (so like Mrs Durbeyfield's to Tess), goes as much to the heart of a classically familiar relationship as Clym Yeobright's guilty pity for his mother does. As Taylor judiciously writes, again in general terms, 'In view of the obvious homology of all of his novels it is a typical oddity of Hardy's experience that he should be seen as notoriously uneven.' Although Taylor may at times keep his enthusiasm too much under control, as we all tend to do when faced with the temptation of going out on a critical limb, he has done a praiseworthy job of re-establishment (the word is used advisedly since most of the minor novels were well received on publication) and answers in a survey of the novels, which comprises the bulk of his study, his questions: 'What value can we set upon each of these lesser novels? What do they contribute to the Hardy canon as a whole and what is their relationship to the better-known novels? What themes or other characteristics do they have in common and what can we learn from them about Hardy and the development of his art?' (p. 4).

Let us get one point of disagreement out of the way. Taylor recognizes a received division of excellence in Hardy's fourteen novels, separating them into two precise halves, and he places *Under the Greenwood Tree* in what he sees as the accepted superior category, in other words not only alongside *Tess* and *Jude* but also *The Woodlanders*, *The Mayor* and the rest. I think we are all reluctant to make these sorts of placings of worth, as though we were compiling some baseball or cricket averages, and this assignment of the *Greenwood Tree* to the senior league merely illustrates the peril of this kind of value charting. *Under the Greenwood Tree* is a charming piece, what Hardy calls 'a little rural story', nostalgic for what he perceives to be the old idyllic days before the brutalities of chance and incompatibility and the most profound anguish intrude into his fiction. There are but the mildest hints of these latter in *Under the Greenwood Tree* in Fancy's toying with the idea of Maybold and in Dick's perplexity at his parents' apparent insusceptibility to romance; but generally its weather is what the cuckoo likes. And so do I, because it is indeed 'modest in scope, careful in execution . . . as nearly faultless a novel as Hardy ever produced' (p. 32), but it contains nothing of Hardy's imaginative essence of the tragedy of romance, in all its biting ironies and realism, some of which we can find in other minor novels, even in the most disregarded, *The Well-Beloved*.

It is astonishing to me that a novel so different as *A Pair of Blue Eyes* was written so soon after *Under the Greenwood Tree* and under pressure, also, from Tinsley to meet his deadlines for its serial form in *Tinsley's Magazine*. Among those whom it instantly moved and impressed were Coventry Patmore and Tennyson. As Taylor records, Patmore's widow wrote to Hardy in 1899 to inform him that for over twenty years 'her husband had had the novel read aloud to him: "Each time he felt the same shock of surprise and pleasure at its consummate art and pathos"' (p. 32). Taylor believes that it is because it was 'so highly regarded by the Victorians' that it has so little appeal today: 'It is Victorian in the sense that it is concerned with time and class and men and women whose sexual feelings are deeply constrained by convention' (p. 33). There is much in Knight's ideas of maidenly purity, in his fury and disgust that Elfride has even been kissed by another man, that calls for a magnanimous suspension of scepticism on the part of the modern reader. There are, too, occasions of ironic absurdity, as there are in many of the poems and novels, where the menacing and the jocular are not totally congruent. Elfride's naive confession, while sitting with Knight on Jethway's tomb, of having kissed Jethway once and Smith also once when he was sitting where Knight now is, and the concluding train journey when Smith and Knight travel from London not knowing that Elfride in her coffin is also on the train, are two incidents which depending on the reader's response can be either hilarious or very puzzling. Taylor writes perceptively on this aspect – 'our uncertainty about whether the ironies are comic or tragic weakens the effectiveness of either possibility' (p. 35) – as he does also in analysing the seminal position of *A Pair of Blue Eyes* in the matter of both time and influence. With a rare understanding he records, without damning, the consequences of Hardy's inexperience, his predilection for ironic mischief and equivocation, which in fact he never loses; and yet Taylor hesitates or is unwilling to acknowledge the depth of Elfride's anguish as Knight rejects her, first at The Crags, and shortly afterwards when she comes rushing, distraught and wretched, to his chambers in Bede's Inn. The true Hardyan pity lies in such occasions.

There is a danger in demanding attention for the minor works of any author, or for any minor author, of overchampioning the cause. Whilst there is no doubting Taylor's genuine enthusiasm for the 'lesser' novels, he skilfully avoids such a charge by means of his scholarly and controlled presentation. His study is lucid, eminently readable, and thoughtfully organized and may yet open some eyes to the many sensitivities, in these novels, to the pain of human pairing, to 'the intolerable antilogy/Of making figments feel!'

Kristin Brady, *The Short Stories of Thomas Hardy* (Macmillan, 1982) pp. xii + 235.

Reviewed by Simon Gatrell

It is inevitable that, as the major thoroughfares of Hardy's novels of character and environment become heavy with critical traffic, the minor roads should be explored by the more adventurous or hurried practitioners. Kristin Brady's is the first book-length study of Hardy's shorter fiction, and her courageous navigation makes a good case for reclassifying this particular side-road. The best thing about this book is the confidence with which she assumes that her material is of equal value with Hardy's best work, and deserves similar attention and analysis; the assumption is infectious, and the reader who perhaps begins with thoughts of dismissing the work as of secondary interest continues by accepting her valuation of the stories. This, to my mind, is a great achievement; and though one's assent wavers from time to time, Brady's frank admission of the weakness in the less good stories disarms disagreement, and Hardy emerges as a serious and self-consciously aware short story writer – if one who seems to have worked off the main routes of the genre's development during the last hundred years.

Brady's work is important – essential reading for anyone interested in Hardy as a writer of fiction; but a pioneering work is bound to leave an impression of incompleteness, of paths not taken, of views extolled at the expense of others that subsequent travellers may estimate at a higher rate. She has decided to handle the stories in their first collected forms – *Wessex Tales* (1888), *A Group of Noble Dames* (1891), *Life's Little Ironies* (1894), and *A Changed Man* (1913). It is her contention that Hardy designed each of the first three volumes with an underlying and unifying theme, and she considers this quite as important as the merits of the individual stories. The danger that attends the identification

174

and analysis of such a matrix is that it may become too narrowly or complexly defined for all the stories to fit comfortably within it; and this I think happens with Brady's interpretation of *Wessex Tales*. She subtitles the chapter on this collection 'Pastoral Histories'; one can find nothing to quarrel with in this, for she is evidently correct in suggesting that Hardy had some such thematic relationship in mind when bringing the stories together. The constriction comes when she defines more and more closely what she means by 'pastoral', and what its intentions and effects are; and then implies that these were also Hardy's ideas. In the end it becomes quite hard to fit 'Fellow Townsmen' or 'The Distracted Preacher' into a matrix which has been built with some success around 'The Three Strangers'.

Brady sees two particularly important elements in pastoral: the conflict between rural and urban values, and the author's conscious intention to instruct the urban reader in rural values, which he subsequently perceives to be similar to his own, and thus universal. Though this works for the most part in 'The Three Strangers', even here there is a slight problem: she lays some stress on the distinction 'between the rural man's sense of justice and the urban man's sense of law'. The hangman – or the magistrate – do duty in this respect for urban man; how then do these characters relate to the urban reader that Brady insists Hardy has in mind? With such occasional hiccups the subsequent stories are fitted to the pattern, until we reach 'Fellow-Townsmen'; in a paragraph on pp. 32–3 Brady tries to accommodate the story to her established matrix, but the tone is that of one who protests too much: the story is 'a pastoral history in a special but legitimate sense'. Since she has been making the laws this need not surprise us, but her preceding discussion of the story makes it clear that this 'special sense' breaks rather than stretches the established mould. With the last story, 'The Distracted Preacher', the matrix lies in pieces; she begins her analysis by saying that it is a structural repetition of 'The Three Strangers' (attempting to place the story firmly inside the pattern), but then her critical honesty forces her to point out how different it is in effect. In this case I think Brady is the victim of her own ingenuity; her special definitions of pastoralism are unnecessary, for her accounts of the individual stories are refined and acute.

The stories in *A Group of Noble Dames* are almost all inferior to those in *Wessex Tales* or *Life's Little Ironies*, but Brady does what she can for them; indeed her positive attitude to her material leads her perhaps to ignore the woodenness of much of the writing. She illuminates particularly clearly the interrelationship of the stories, and is also revealing about the function of the narratorial group; but the impression remains of a second-rate collection.

With *Life's Little Ironies*, Brady's subtitle, 'Tragedies of Circumstance', immediately announces possible problems with her view of the collection's underlying theme: there is a tension between Hardy's ironic understatement and her slightly portentous adaptation of another Hardyan title. It is perhaps an open question whether Cornelius Halborough's situation is tragic, or whether Sophy Twycott or Edith Harnham and Charles Raye have tragic stature – it depends on how you define tragedy. The hint too of a comparison with *Satires of Circumstance* serves to highlight the difference between the individual follies and character-deficiencies that the poems reveal, and the sustained attack on social and moral conditions in parts of Victorian society that most of these stories make, and which Brady reveals with keen insight.

It is hard, also, as she finds, to fit 'A Few Crusted Characters' into the shape announced in her subtitle; and her cool but satisfying exploration of 'The Fiddler of the Reels' ends with another of her efforts to fit intractable material into an established pattern.

At this point the book changes direction with some violence, and before turning the hairpin to the final chapter I should like to make a few general comments about the first three. One feature of Brady's writing sometimes limits the reader's assent to her accounts of the individual stories: on occasions she subordinates emotional and sensual response too thoroughly to intellectual control, leaving a sense that the narrative has been netted and pinned and placed in an exhibition case. On the other hand an integral element of her approach that is telling every time is her use of manuscript and periodical versions of the stories; it is remarkable how often the information that a certain phrase or sentence was added or altered at a specific moment draws attention to a central episode or theme of the story.

It is part of Brady's general strategy to consider the stories as separate from the rest of Hardy's fiction (though suggesting on p. 1 that Hardy himself made no theoretical distinction between novel and story), and this on the whole pays dividends in maintaining the status of the stories; but there are times when comparisons with the novels force themselves on the reader, particularly during her discussion of pastoral, and in the conclusion of the chapter on *Life's Little Ironies*. On the whole Brady avoids these detailed comparisons, and then the maintenance of the integrity of the stories seems at the expense of a larger, more interesting perspective. It would be interesting, for instance, to pursue the relationship between the underlying theme she identifies in *Life's Little Ironies* with a very similar theme in *Tess*; but this is perhaps to expect two different books in one.

And when we come to Brady's final chapter, that is what we seem to be presented with. She can find no factor to unify the stories collected together in purely utilitarian fashion by Hardy in *A Changed Man*; so she has to change course, and use this fourth volume as the basis for a chronological study of Hardy as a short story writer. It seems quite possible that a decision to construct the whole book along these lines might have been at least as successful as the one taken; but here she is really trying to have it both ways at the same time, and in the end it is only partially effective – forty-five pages are not enough to give the reader a sense of Hardy's development as a writer of stories. It would have required extensive quotations and reference to stories already discussed at some length; but despite this limitation there is much interesting and essential material in the chapter, and discussion of some important stories, among them 'Destiny and a Blue Cloak', and 'The Romantic Adventures of a Milkmaid'.

With this book we have the first large-scale map of this unfrequented area of Hardy's work; signposts have been erected, roads laid out. Future surveyors and cartographers and tourists will be grateful for the quality of Kristin Brady's mapping.

Marlene Springer, *Hardy's Use of Allusion* (London: Macmillan, 1983) pp. ix + 207.

Reviewed by Timothy Hands

Hardy's use of allusion is amongst the least appreciated aspects of his writing, one of the more slighted features of what Henry James famously identified as a style 'ingeniously verbose and redundant'. Early reviewers generally found Hardy's literary references unhelpful; friends of the author, such as Edmund Blunden, regretted the excess of their use; and many critics have shared Timothy O'Sullivan's suspicion of 'a certain parrotry of allusions and references' in Hardy's work. Even such a champion of Hardy's achievement as Michael Millgate has appeared reluctant to defend Hardy's referential technique. 'No reader can fail to notice – and few critics have failed to deplore – ', he remarks in his study of Hardy's fiction, 'the ponderous allusions to literature and art which strew with their initial capitals the pages of Hardy's early novels'.

Within the last five years, however, critical feeling has begun to alter. Michael D. Wheeler in *The Art of Allusion in Victorian Fiction*, published by Macmillan in 1979, examined representative works of seven Victorian novelists from Charlotte Brontë to Mary Augusta Ward, arguing from an examination of *The Return of the Native* and *Tess* not only that Hardy was more *recherché* in his use of allusion than his mid-Victorian predecessors, but also that his novels contained allusive parallel texts (Keats' *Endymion* for *The Return* and Ovid's *Metamorphoses* for *Tess*) whose appreciation is of fundamental importance for an understanding of the author's intentions. Now Marlene Springer in *Hardy's Use of Allusion* presents a more specialized and equally thought-provoking study. Briefly placing Hardy in the context of his contemporaries she maintains in her opening paragraph that he 'out-alluded virtually every allusionist – not only in substance, but in skill as well'. The rest of her book consists of an examination of the evidence for this claim, achieved by an analysis of eight Hardy novels. Both *Desperate Remedies* and *A Pair of Blue Eyes* are prolific in their use of allusion, and display a mixture of sophistication and crudity in their allusive technique. *Under the Greenwood Tree* contrasts these two works not only in the scarcity of its allusions but also in their predominantly humorous intention. By the time of *Far From the Madding Crowd* Hardy has confidence in his allusive technique, using it to control the reader's response to character and environment. Though *The Hand of Ethelberta* represents a temporary lapse, *The Return of the Native* is seen as a novel of technical maturity, Professor Springer omits discussion of the intervening novels, and ends with a detailed examination of the allusively triumphant *Tess* and *Jude*.

This is an important book. Professor Springer has made a thorough study of the textual history of the novels, has indefatigably traced the sources of Hardy's allusions, and intelligently elucidates their significance. No reader of the book will be able to view a Hardy allusion in quite the same way again. Despite the lack of critical precedent Professor Springer argues persuasively for a high degree of sophisticated purpose in Hardy's deployment of allusion, identifying what appear to be carefully prepared allusive strategies. Whereas Dick in *Under the Greenwood Tree* is associated with non-Biblical references, the rustic chorus is generally associated with Biblical, thus helping, in Professor Springer's words, 'to contrast his position as a main character with their choral function'. Although the characterization of Thomasin in *The Return* makes use of only one allusion, Eustacia receives over thirty-three in a mere twenty pages, secular reference used to describe her by the narrator contrasting with the Biblical images she uses herself, in such a way as to exhibit her rustic ties and her reluctance to follow the dictates of Arnoldian Hellenism. The differences between Alec and Angel in *Tess* are also elucidated by the contrasting allusions associated with them. All the early Shakespearean allusions surrounding Alec are from the comedies, whereas those attached to Angel, with two exceptions, are taken from the tragedies and one sonnet.

Fascinating though the book is in this incidental detail, its general argument cannot command a comparable degree of assent. Professor Springer speaks of a 'steady progression' towards Hardy's late masterpieces, claiming that as Hardy 'constructed his allusive technique he gradually became a master craftsman', and implying that the crudity and showiness of many of the references in Hardy's early novels are satisfactorily purged by the time of the later. This is altogether too pat, and clearly depends on the selectiveness of the fiction examined. *The Hand of Ethelberta*, which Professor Springer briefly mentions, clearly represents the reverse of an allusive improvement on *Far From the Madding Crowd*; whilst *A Laodicean* and *Two on a Tower*, which remain undiscussed in this study, have a showiness and lack of sophistication fortunately lacking in an early novel such as *Under the Greenwood Tree*. Indeed the impression the reader – albeit without the author's intention – takes away from this book is not so much of a development in Hardy's career as of a persistently strong individuality, of an eccentric mixture in Hardy of an author at some times almost wilfully blind to the embarrassingly gratuitous qualities of some of his references, and yet at others, even as early as his first published novel, *Desperate Remedies*, remarkably confident of the sophisticated effects he can gain by their deployment. Professor Springer has to admit to finding references in *Tess* 'that seem to be included primarily to give a veneer of culture' and she surely speaks for many readers when she terms the persistent Samson allusion in *Jude* 'simplistic'. She could, had she chosen, have supported such suspicions of a continuing parrotry in Hardy's references by details of the textual history of the later novels, with which she is admirably conversant. Robert Gittings points out that when Hardy in later editions of *The Return of the Native* wished to alter an allusion to the mediocrity of mind of Bishop Sumner (an attribute of which he had learnt in *The Saturday Review*), he simply substituted the name of the previous Bishop of Winchester, Tomline, rather than searching for a prelate of comparably indifferent intellectual capacities. Such details do not encourage confidence in Professor Springer's verdict that *The Return* represents Hardy's 'coming of artistic age', or her underlying implication that allusion for the purposes of mere show becomes progressively less common in Hardy's fiction. The reader acquires the feeling that this book has made its evidence fit its conclusions rather than allowing its conclusions to be shaped by its evidence.

Hardy's Use of Allusion is a book which adds to our appreciation of Hardy, but it is not one which changes our understanding of him in any significant way. If its readers hope for new information they will not be disappointed, but if they seek new interpretations they will. Wheeler's study of Hardy's allusions offered individual readings of *The Return* and *Tess*, one as a novel of post-Romanticism, the other as a novel of metamorphoses, whereas by contrast some of Professor Springer's interpretative conclusions tend to be disappointingly mainstream. One can hardly be excited at the revelation that 'Troy is not an honourable man' or that *The Hand of Ethelberta* and *The Return of the Native* 'illustrate that even a talent as strong as Hardy's can be limited to a particular environment, and that certain locales and classes proved closed to him', whilst it is somewhat surprising to be told a little blandly of *Tess* that in this novel 'the President of the Immortals is in control'.

Professor Springer has discovered a subject of such major importance for an understanding of Hardy that it is unfortunate that she does not proceed to examine its varied implications. The issues she glances at are more important than those she debates: she seems so confident of the nature and extent of Hardy's achievement as a writer that the issues which have perplexed previous commentators not only on Hardy's allusions but on his whole *oeuvre* enter her work only implicitly. Despite his popularity, despite his critical champions, Hardy remains a writer who is contentiously enigmatic. The most fundamental questions about his fiction, for whom he wrote it, how well he wrote it, and why he came to write it at all, remain provokingly unanswered. To a study of these issues a consideration of Hardy's use of allusion would appear, on Professor Springer's evidence, highly complementary. Unfortunately they are issues which she never deeply considers.

The first issue of the *Thomas Hardy Annual* contained a re-assessment by John Lucas of one of the most controversial studies of Hardy of recent years, Donald Davie's *Thomas Hardy and British Poetry*. Davie's argument, simplified, is that Hardy was too unambitious to be a great writer: his modesty restricted his artistic achievement. Hardy's use of allusion can possibly be seen as supporting this argument. Ruskin held that accumulation of ornament was one of the signs of the humility of the Gothic artists; and John Bayley, commenting in his *Essay on Hardy* on Hardy's use of literary reference, considers it indicative of Hardy's 'modesty' that he is 'never afraid to invoke the grandest of literary parallels'. But the evidence can as easily be made to support the

reverse of this proposition, for many of Hardy's allusions une-
quivocally demonstrate his tendency towards the pomposity of
rhetoric and the daring nature of his literary ambition. The writer
who can compare one of his heroes with Christ, John the Baptist
and Oedipus, and the climax of his narrative with three of the
most turbulent events in Biblical history, is making no uncertain
implications about the significance of his literary material.
Chaucer, modestly unassuming in his earlier works in his
admiration for his Classical predecessors, saw himself as their
equal in the conclusion to *Troilus and Criseyde*. In *The Return of the
Native* both the heightened rhetoric and Hardy's multiple literary
forms announce an author eager to suggest that his work is worthy
of a place in a great literary tradition. The 'litel bok' is intended to
follow in some eminently notable footsteps. Although, ironically,
Hardy's use of allusion may serve to make the reader aware of the
novel's shortcomings, where *The Return of the Native* falls short of its
celebrated literary paradigms it does not do so by its author's
intention. Professor Bayley talks of Hardy's narratives as indifferent to their audience, and Professor Davie notes 'how little
Hardy imposes himself on his reader'. But the references can show
not only Hardy's modesty but also his ambition. They claim the
reader's attention rather than provoking his indifference.

   Hardy's use of allusion likewise raises important questions
about the nature of the audiences for which he was writing. There
has been a critical tendency, encouraged by Hardy himself, to
regard the author's fiction as mere journey-work, aimed at a large
audience and a large financial return, as writing which was in
many ways entertainment rather than art. Though this is not an
issue which Professor Springer discusses explicitly, her study
clearly contains material of much importance for any consideration of this issue. Professor Springer believes Hardy's allusive
technique to be so subtle that he could have intended or expected
it to be understood by only a fraction of his audience: 'he directs
his allusions to the gourmets', she writes in her concluding
sentence. In *Desperate Remedies* the bells of the village church play
Psalm 113 as the fire which has spread from Springrove's
smouldering couch-grass begins to destroy the neighbouring
cottages. Professor Springer has no doubt about the deliberate
ironic relevance of the text of this psalm, 'O Praise ye the Lord . . .
/He raiseth up the poor out of the dunghill', even though the text
itself is not given in the novel. If Professor Springer is correct,

Hardy would appear even as early as *Desperate Remedies* to have nurtured artistic designs rising far above the requirements of mere entertainment. Contrary to popular misconception there was perhaps always something elitist, perhaps even completely private, in Hardy's novelistic art.

Professor Springer's assessment of Hardy as a novelist with a highly sophisticated control of his medium conflicts noticeably with the views of those previous critics whom we have seen to be disturbed by that parrotry of allusive reference which Professor Springer largely ignores. In the words of Browning, 'Truth lies between'. Hardy's allusions impose a dual burden on the reader. Not only must he compute and assess the significance of those allusions – often abstruse – which are intended to add to the meaning and action of the novel, but he must also sort and dissociate these from the succession of allusions whose purpose appears gratuitously orotund. To return to the somewhat unusual comparison with Chaucer, the problem in interpreting Hardy's allusions may be instructively compared with the interpretation of those in the 'Nun's Priest's Tale'. When at the end of the Tale the narrator enjoins us 'Taketh the fruyt and lat the chaf be stille', his advice is deliberately teasing. The many allusions employed in the Tale bewilder the listener as to the poem's tone and intention. The information that Chauntecleer was taken on a Friday may, as some critics have suggested, be intended to represent the redemptive suffering of Christ, but its significance might just as probably be daringly profane or consciously anti-heroic. 'Ernest' and 'game' are far from easily dissociated, and the author as well as listener enjoys their humorous mixture. With the far more inscrutable Hardy one can far less frequently be sure that the combination of 'fruyt' and 'chaf' is either so deliberate or so controlled, and the purpose of the references is therefore all the more difficult to establish. As T. S. Eliot remarked, at times Hardy's style touches sublimity without ever having passed through the stage of being good.

Professor Springer has written a stimulating and informative survey of Hardy's fiction. If sometimes she has not examined the implications of her findings as deeply as she might have done, the newness of much of what she has discovered provides ample mitigation. *Hardy's Use of Allusion* is a study which can be warmly recommended to the novelist's more curious enthusiasts.

A Hardy Bibliography, 1982–83

Richard H. Taylor

Note: Place of publication is London unless otherwise stated. 1982 publications listed in the last number of the *Thomas Hardy Annual* are not listed here again since the successive bibliographies are designed as a serial. A few publications missed in 1980 or 1981 are, however, now listed.

1. EDITIONS AND TEXTUAL STUDIES

(a) *Editions*

Hardy's Love Poems, ed. Carl J. Weber (Papermac, 1983) [first published 1963].
Thomas Hardy: Selected Poems, ed. Walford Davies (Dent, 1983).
Tess of the d'Urbervilles, ed. Juliet Grindle and Simon Gatrell (OUP: Clarendon Press, 1983). [Textual edition.]

(b) *Textual Studies*

Schweik, Robert, and M. Piret, 'Editing Hardy', *Browning Institute Studies*, IX (1981) 15–41.

2. BIBLIOGRAPHIES AND TOPOGRAPHICAL STUDIES

(a) *Bibliographies*

Smith, L. E. W., 'Bibliographical Notes', *Thomas Hardy Society Newsletter*, no. 55 (June 1983) 8.
Taylor, Richard H., 'A Hardy Bibliography, 1981–82' in *Thomas Hardy Annual*, no. 2, pp. 255–61.

(b) *Topographical Studies*

Beningfield, Gordon, *Hardy Country*, with text by Anthea Zeman (Allen Lane, 1983).
Hawkins, Desmond, *Hardy's Wessex*, with photographs by Anthony Kersting (Macmillan, 1983).
Manford, Alan L., 'The "Texts" of Thomas Hardy's Map of Wessex', *Library*, IV (1982) 297–306.

3. BIOGRAPHICAL DOCUMENTS

(a) *Relevant Biography and Autobiography*

Bartle, G. F., 'Some Fresh Information about Tryphena Sparks – Thomas Hardy's Cousin', *Notes and Queries*, n.s. xxx, 4 (1983) 320–2.

Buckler, William E., 'The Hardy-Moule Affair with a Reading of Four Hardy Poems', *Biography*, v (1982) 136–42.

Childers, Mary, 'Thomas Hardy: the Man who "Liked" Women', *Criticism*, xxiii (1982) 317–34.

Gittings, Robert, 'Specific Roots: New Light on Hardy', *Encounter* (November 1982) 42–6. [Review article.]

Gregor, Ian and Michael Irwin, 'Your Story or Your Life?: Reflections on Thomas Hardy's Autobiography' in *Thomas Hardy Annual*, no. 2, pp. 157–70.

Hands, Timothy, 'Arthur Shirley (Vicar of Stinsford, 1837–91)' in *Thomas Hardy Annual*, no. 2, pp. 171–86.

Hillyard, Nicholas, 'Eliza Nicholls and Hardy Poems of 1865–7', *Thomas Hardy Society Review*, i, 9 (1983) 271–3.

Rabiger, Michael, 'The Hoffman Papers', *Thomas Hardy Year Book*, no. 10 (1981, publ. 1982–3) 6–50.

Winslow, Donald, 'Images of Emma Hardy', *Thomas Hardy Year Book*, no. 10 (1981, publ. 1982–3) 55–9.

(b) *Short Accounts and Recollections*

Cox, J. Stevens, 'A Short Memory of Hardy' and 'A Miserable Old Man', *Thomas Hardy Year Book*, no. 10 (1981, publ. 1982–3) 78–9.

Orr, Ed, 'Thomas Hardy' [poem], *Thomas Hardy Year Book*, no. 10 (1981, publ. 1982–3) 79.

Parsons, W. G. L., 'Recollections of Hardy', *Thomas Hardy Society Review*, i, 9 (1983) 269–70.

Redman, S., 'Arnold Bennett and Thomas Hardy's Funeral Service', *Thomas Hardy Society Newsletter*, no. 56 (1983) 7.

Roberts, Margaret Windeatt, 'A Visit to Blandford by John Lane of The Bodley Head and Thomas Hardy', *Thomas Hardy Society Review*, i, 9 (1983) 267–9.

(c) *Letters and Notebooks*

Jones, Bernard, 'Some Observations on Hardy's Letters', *The Powys Review*, iii, 3 (1982–3) 74–8.

Siemens, Lloyd, 'Hardy Among the Critics: the Annotated Scrap Books' in *Thomas Hardy Annual*, no. 2, pp. 187–90.

4. CRITICAL STUDIES OF HARDY'S FICTION, AND GENERAL ESSAYS AND ARTICLES

(a) *Book-Length Studies and Collections of Essays*

Cox, J. S. and G. S. (eds), *Thomas Hardy Year Book*, no. 10 (1981) (St Peter Port, Guernsey: Toucan Press, 1982–3). Individual essays listed.

Page, Norman (ed.), *Thomas Hardy Annual*, no. 2 (Macmillan, 1983–4; New Jersey: Humanities Press, 1984). Individual essays listed.

Pinion, F. B. (ed.), *Thomas Hardy Society Review*, I, no. 9 (Dorchester: Thomas Hardy Society, 1983). Individual essays listed.

Springer, Marlene, *Hardy's Use of Allusion* (Macmillan, 1983; New York: University Press of Kansas).

(b) *Articles, Essays and Parts of Books*

Asker, D. B. D., 'The Birds *Shall* Have Some Dinner: Animals in Hardy's Fiction', *Dutch Quarterly Review of Anglo-American Letters*, x, 3 (1980) 215–29.

Bayley, John, 'His Eye for the Ladies', *Guardian* (10 June 1982) and *Guardian Weekly*, CXXVI (20 June 1982) 22. [Review article.]

Childers, Mary, 'Thomas Hardy: the Man Who "Liked" Women', *Criticism*, XXIII (1982) 317–34.

In Coslett, Tess, *The 'Scientific' Movement and Victorian Literature* (Brighton: Harvester Press, 1983).

Davie, Donald, 'Raining', *London Review of Books* (5 May 1983) 13–14. [Review article.]

In Ebbatson, Roger, *The Evolutionary Self: Hardy, Foster, Lawrence* (Brighton: Harvester Press, 1982).

Escuret, Annie, 'Hardy's Reputation in France' in *Thomas Hardy Annual*, no. 2, pp. 191–5.

Gatrell, Simon, 'The Early Stages of Hardy's Fiction' in *Thomas Hardy Annual*, no. 2, pp. 3–29.

Hough, Graham, 'Embarrassed', *London Review of Books* (7 October 1982) 19–20. [Review article.]

Jackson, Arlene M., 'Photography as Style and Metaphor in the Art of Thomas Hardy' in *Thomas Hardy Annual*, no. 2, pp. 91–109.

Jacobus, Mary, 'Hardy's Magian Retrospect', *Essays in Criticism*, XXXII (1982) 258–79.

Jones, Lawrence, 'Hardy's Unwritten Second Sensation Novel' in *Thomas Hardy Annual*, no. 2, pp. 30–40.

Laird, J. T., 'Approaches to Fiction: Hardy and Henry James' in *Thomas Hardy Annual*, no. 2, pp. 41–60.

Page, Norman, 'Hardy and Brazil', *Notes and Queries*, n.s. xxx, 4 (1983) 319–20.

In Stubbs, H. W. (ed.), *Pegasus: Classical Essays from the University of Exeter* (Exeter: University of Exeter, 1981). [Essays on Arnold, Hopkins, Hardy and Victorian scholarship.]

Taylor, Richard H., 'A Survey of Recent Hardy Studies' in *Thomas Hardy Annual*, no. 2, pp. 196–214.

Widdowson, Peter, 'Hardy in History: A Case Study in the Sociology of Literature', *Literature and History*, IX (1983) 3–16.

In Winner, Anthony, *Characters in the Twilight: Hardy, Zola and Chekhov* (Charlottesville: University Press of Virginia, 1981).

Wittenberg, Judith Bryant, 'Early Hardy Novels and the Fictional Eye', *Novel*, XVI (1983) 151–64.

5. CRITICAL STUDIES OF THE POETRY

Arkans, Norman, 'Hardy's Narrative Muse and the Ballad Connection' in *Thomas Hardy Annual*, no. 2, pp. 131–56.

Bawer, Bruce, 'Two on a Tower: Hardy and Yeats', *YER*, VII (1982) 91–105.

Buckler, William E., 'The Hardy-Moule Affair with a Reading of Four Hardy Poems', *Biography*, V (1982) 136–42.

Casagrande, Peter J., 'The Fourteenth Line of "In Tenebris, II"' in *Thomas Hardy Annual*, no. 2, pp. 110–30.

Coxon, Peter W., 'Thomas Hardy: "The Voice" and Horace: Odes II, xiv', *Thomas Hardy Society Review*, I, 9 (1983) 291–3.

Fain, John Tyree, 'Hardy's "The Convergence of the Twain"', *Explicator*, XLI (1983) 34–5.

Fletcher, Pauline, 'Rossetti, Hardy, and the "hour which might have been"', *Victorian Poetry*, XX, 3 and 4 (1982) 1–13.

In Keith, W. J., *The Poetry of Nature: Rural Perspectives in Poetry from Wordsworth to the Present* (Toronto: University of Toronto Press, 1980).

Langbaum, Robert, 'Hardy as Late Victorian Poet', *Victorian Studies Association of Western Canada Newsletter*, VII (1981) 21.

Maciejowski, Mara, 'The Idea of Time in Thomas Hardy's Poetry', *Thomas Hardy Year Book*, no. 10 (1981, publ. 1982–3) 60–72.

In Mason, H. A., 'Wounded Surgeons', *Cambridge Quarterly*, XI (1982) [189–223] 219–23.

Ousby, Ian, '"The Convergence of the Twain": Hardy's Alteration of Plato's Parable', *Modern Language Review*, LXXVII (1982) 780–96.

Swann, Furse, 'Thomas Hardy and the "Appetite for Joy"', *The Powys Review*, III, 4 (1983) 39–48.

Vaché, Jean, *'Paroles d'Hiver*: Hardy et Britten', *Cahiers Victoriens & Edouardiens*, no. 17 (1983) 21–40.

6. STUDIES OF SPECIFIC WORKS

Desperate Remedies

Moore, Kevin Z., 'The Poet Within the Architect's Ring: *Desperate Remedies*, Hardy's Hybrid Detective-Gothic Narrative', *Studies in the Novel* (North Texas State), XIV (1982) 31–42.

Wickens, G. Glen, 'Romantic Myth and Victorian Nature in *Desperate Remedies*', *English Studies in Canada*, VIII (1982) 154–73.

The Dynasts

Cornick, Martyn C., 'Larbaud's 1908 Review of *The Dynasts*', *Thomas Hardy Society Review*, I, 9 (1983) 287–91.

Far From the Madding Crowd

Jones, Lawrence, 'George Eliot and Pastoral Tragi-Comedy in Hardy's *Far From the Madding Crowd*', *Studies in Philology*, LXXVII (1980) 402–25.

Windram, William J., 'A Discrepancy in *Far From the Madding Crowd*', *Notes and Queries*, n.s. XXIX (1982) 326.

Jude the Obscure
Bonds, Diane S., 'Fleshly Temptation in Robert Penn Warren's *A Place to Come To* and Hardy's *Jude the Obscure*', *American Notes and Queries*, xix (1981) 144–6.
Saldivar, Ramon, '*Jude the Obscure*: Reading and the Spirit of the Law', *Journal of English Literary History*, L (1983) 607–25.
Springer, Marlene, 'Aftercourses: *Tess of the d'Urbervilles* and *Jude the Obscure*' in *Hardy's Use of Allusion*, pp. 121–74.

A Laodicean
Hochstadt, Pearl R., 'Hardy's Romantic Diptych: A Reading of *A Laodicean* and *Two on a Tower*', *English Literature in Transition 1880—1920*, xxvi, 1 (1983) 23–34.
Pettit, Charles P. C., 'A Reassessment of *A Laodicean*', *Thomas Hardy Society Review*, I, 9 (1983) 276–82.

The Mayor of Casterbridge
Diffey, T. J., 'Henchard and Falstaff', *Thomas Hardy Society Review*, I, 9 (1983) 282–4.
Draper, R. P., '*The Mayor of Casterbridge*', *Critical Quarterly*, xxv (1983) 57–70.

The Poor Man and the Lady
Coleman, Terry, 'The Lady Beyond the Hero's Grasp', *Guardian Weekly* (18 April 1982) 19.

The Return of the Native
Hanley, Katharine, 'Death as Option: The Heroine in Nineteenth-Century Fiction', *College Language Association Journal*, xv (1981) 197–202.
Hopkins, V. T., 'Clym the Obscure', *Thomas Hardy Society Review*, I, 9 (1983) 273–5.

Tess of the d'Urbervilles
Bonica, Charlotte, 'Nature and Paganism in Hardy's *Tess*', *Journal of English Literary History*, xlix, 4 (1982) 849–62.
Brown, Suzanne Hunter, '"Tess" and *Tess*: An Experiment in Genre', *Modern Fiction Studies*, xxviii (1982) 25–44.
Freeman, Janet, 'Ways of Looking at *Tess*', *Studies in Philology*, lxxix (1982) 311–23.
Grindle, Juliet, and Simon Gatrell (eds), *Tess of the d'Urbervilles* (OUP: Clarendon Press, 1983). [Textual edition.]
Grundy, Peter, 'Linguistics and Literary Criticism: A Marriage of Convenience', *English*, xxx (1981) 151–69.
Lemos, Brunilda Reichmann, 'Angel Clare in Curitiba', *Notes and Queries*, n.s. xxix (1982) 326–7.
Sommers, Jeffrey, 'Hardy's Other *Bildungsroman*: *Tess*', *English Literature in Transition 1880–1920*, xxv (1982) 159–68.
Springer, Marlene, 'Aftercourses: *Tess of the d'Urbervilles* and *Jude the Obscure*' in *Hardy's Use of Allusion*, pp. 121–74.
Wing, George, 'The Confessions of Tess Durbeyfield and Esther Waters', *Victorian Studies Association of Western Canada Newsletter*, vii (1981) 5–9.

The Trumpet-Major
Escuret, Annie, '*Le Trompette-Major* ou l'Histoire du Perroquet et de l'Agami', *Cahiers Victoriens & Edouardiens*, no. 17 (1983) 1–20.

Two on a Tower

Hochstadt, Pearl R., 'Hardy's Romantic Diptych: A Reading of *A Laodicean* and *Two on a Tower*', *English Literature in Translation 1880–1920*, xxvi, 1 (1983) 23–34.

The Woodlanders

Diskin, Patrick, 'Joyce's "The Dead" and Hardy's *The Woodlanders*', *Notes and Queries*, n.s. xxx, 4 (1983) 330–1.

Essex, Ruth, 'A New Sentimental Journey' [on Felice Charmond], *Thomas Hardy Society Review*, i 9 (1983) 285–7.

Giordano, Frank R., jr., 'The Martyrdom of Giles Winterbourne' in *Thomas Hardy Annual*, no. 2, pp. 61–78.

Hannaford, Richard, '"A Forlorn Hope?"': Grace Melbury and *The Woodlanders*, *Thomas Hardy Year Book*, no. 10 (1981), publ. 1982–3) 72–9.

Irvin, Glenn, 'Structure and Tone in *The Woodlanders*' in *Thomas Hardy Annual*, no. 2, pp. 79–90.

935

GP

JP

crit Hardy